Researching Otherwise

Nitin Bathla, ed.

Researching Otherwise

Pluriversal Methodologies for Landscape
and Urban Studies

gta Verlag

Foreword by Catalina Ortiz 6
A Methodological Pluriverse: An Introduction 11
    Nitin Bathla

Transdisciplinary Methods

The Dirt on Drawing: A Method for Relational Thinking 47
    Luke Harris, Cara Turett, and Bonnie Kate Walker
Recovering Evidence of Existence through Collaborative
Visual Ethnography 73
    Andreea-Florentina Midvighi
Who Owns the Land? On Research Poetics and
Performance as Ways of Knowing 97
    Metaxia Markaki

Sensory Methods

Knowing a Place by Ear: Approaches to the
Sonic Research of Landscapes 133
    Ludwig Berger
Sensing Ocean Space 151
    Nancy Couling
Mirror Images: Cinematic and Sensory Ethnography
for Landscape and Urban Studies 171
    Klearjos Eduardo Papanicolaou

Restitutive Methods

Investigating Subterranean Swiss Banking with
Open-Source Intelligence Tools 199
    Ludo Groen
Mapping Architectural Traces of the Swiss–
South African Gold Trade in Johannesburg:
Film as Investigative Spatial Research 215
    Denise Bertschi
Multispecies Walking: Ways of Knowing and
Researching Landscapes with Experts 241
    Johanna Just

Afterword by Nitin Bathla 262
Acknowledgments 263

Foreword

Our world order is shattering. As I write, the violence of colonial regimes is relentlessly ruining vast landscapes and imposing ideologies of death. That is why now, more than ever, we need to create a world *otherwise*, even when the search for spatial and epistemic justice seems elusive. To transcend canonical Western approaches, *Researching Otherwise* offers alternative onto-epistemological orientations for landscape and urban researchers and practitioners through a collection of contributions that explore formats, vocabularies, and protocols for reimagining urban landscapes. Nitin Bathla, the editor, invites us to stretch disciplinary boundaries for building collectives and spaces of solidarity as a crucial ethos for researching in new ways.

The inquiry on methodological approaches and experimentations is timely. While debates around new ways to frame urban worlds are blooming, methodological repertoires are still nascent. This reveals the disjuncture between discourses and practices of landscape and urban studies. The book contributes to bridging the intent to engage with the urban implications of the colonial matrix of power and the practices that seek to dismantle it. In doing so, *Researching Otherwise* nurtures our impetus to challenge the status quo of current practices of doing, sensing, and being.

Researching Otherwise affirms critiques of universality. It calls for a pluriversal approach to unearth the politics of the possible through the lens of political practice embedded in methodological explorations to unlearn and relearn the urban. Embracing pluriversality invites us to unsettle the synthesis of multiple world visions and how the urban can be reimagined. This approach points to diverse existential projects that challenge the dominant frameworks coming from the project of Eurocentric modernism. That is why the book, instead of formulating a generalized series of steps, tools, and methodologies, formulates a myriad collection of situated provocations and orientations to recalibrate landscape and urban studies.

By conjuring the anthropocentric gaze, this volume presents strategies to think with more-than-human worlds as an essential dimension to reframing how spatial practitioners conceive their work and the focus of the practice itself. The book expands the horizons of how to bring diverse perceptual abilities and engage with landscapes and waterscapes to decenter the epistemological weight from human superiority as the focus of analysis and intervention. It gives us repertoires for focusing on the multifarious relationships between the living and material world as a restitutive strategy for current extractivist modes of city-making.

Catalina Ortiz

Researching Otherwise harnesses the potential of embodied knowledge production. The book provides sharp reflections on the drawbacks of masking objectivity and epistemic privileging in research. The methodological experimentation explored in the book brings about different stances to pursue creative embodiments. These moves assert the weight of fluid epistemologies and reflexive practices that also claim the body as the first territory we inhabit. In this case, the curated contributions presented here push us to think and act with the politics of the sensorium. Yet, the call for embodied research also foregrounds the violence of the spatial processes of racialization and dispossession while embracing the body of collective struggles where research embeds itself. Usually, methodological accounts tend to be ahistorical. However, this book helps us to locate the conjunction of different lineages of myriad ways of knowing. For instance, it invokes the Latin American origin of participatory action research in the 1970s or the use of *flânerie* in France in the 1930s. It invites us to root the power of expanding methodologies in historical and political affairs. In this way, the collection of contributions brings new insights into the domains of landscape and urban research by critically and historically grounding methodological strategies such as ethnographic filmmaking, sonic research, radical counter-cartography, and beyond.

In my trajectory as an engaged scholar, I explore the production of empathic knowledge and links to the poetics of everyday life. I always look for sources of inspiration. This book provides a provocative account of possibilities for framing knowledge-seeking endeavors *otherwise* through transdisciplinary, multi-sensory and restitutive methods.

I celebrate the imperative posed towards the restitution of knowledge and critical fabulation as a kernel of researching otherwise. In my methodological exploration, I have become aware of the relevance of engaging with relational ontologies, reparative justice, and embedding a collective affective dimension as part and parcel of embodying an emancipatory ethos. I believe that knowledge cannot be separated from life, and knowledge creation cannot be separated from poetics and narratives. Above all, this book urges us to deploy the insurgent imagination and disobedience required not only to research otherwise but also to disrupt the unbearable violence of the hegemonic world order manifested in urban environments.

Catalina Ortiz
London, February 1, 2024

Nitin Bathla

A Methodological Pluriverse: An Introduction

Over the last few decades there has been a gradual rise of landscape and urban studies from relatively minor scientific disciplines into major ones in their own right. These disciplines have opened spaces of convergence to think intersectionally about a multitude of complex societal, environmental, and economic challenges that manifest in the form of the Anthropocene, climate change, and social and financial crises. Moreover, there has been an increasing crossover of practitioners from landscape architecture, urban design, and urban planning into academic research, driven largely by an intention and desire to retool these disciplines to reflect societal realities. There is an eagerness among urban and landscape practitioners and the students who have trained in these disciplines to unmask and unearth the problematic histories and presents of landscape and the urban, and to open new and hopeful directions for practices that transcend the current impasse. Contrary to this rise of landscape and urban studies as specialized research disciplines and the radical orientations of researchers engaging with them, there is a relative paucity of books and papers that can provide methodological, pedagogic, and epistemic orientations that researchers in these fields can draw upon. Of the very few books that do exist, such as the edited volume by Adri van den Brink and colleagues on landscape architecture,[1] most tend to concentrate on established and conventional research methods, such as the case study or landscape biography for exploring the histories and ways of knowing landscapes. Similarly in urban studies there has been a (re)turn to comparative and actor-network approaches as a means of knowing pluriversal lifeworlds.[2] While these methods prove to be of continued relevance and versatility, as a teacher and researcher in the fields of landscape and urban studies I observe a few important gaps that this publication aims to bridge:

Neutrality of the field and researcher: Researchers in landscape and urban studies are not merely confronted with power hierarchies in the field but also with the complex colonial and imperial histories of the urban and landscape palimpsests that they study.[3]

[1] van den Brink et al., *Research in Landscape Architecture*.
[2] See, for instance, Robinson, "Comparative Urbanism"; Farías and Bender, *Urban Assemblages*.
[3] See Corboz, "Land as Palimpsest"; Bertschi, Lafontaine Carboni, and Bathla, *Unearthing Traces*.

Nitin Bathla

Privileging of verbal-textual methods: The ultimately textual form of scholarship inevitably privileges verbal and text-based methods of research, such as interviews and observation. The landscape and urban environments that researchers study are poly-sensorial, however, and are imbued with modalities that are visual, aural, and tactile.[4]

Anthropocentricism: While the social focus of landscape and urban research often rightly centers its attention on the disruption of human lifeworlds, such anthropocentricism often unintentionally ends up relegating non-humans—both vital and non-vital, and both integral to these lifeworlds—to the margins.

Disembodiment and secular ontologies: A constructed sense of scientific objectivity forces researchers to operate in defiance of the pluriversal ontoepistemologies that have been geopolitically conditioned.[5]

Participation and restitution of knowledge: Researchers often engage with social groups and communities over extended periods of time. This prolonged engagement is not only a transformative experience for the researchers themselves but also for the social groups and communities they engage with. This requires researchers to be attendant to the ways in which they can incorporate participation into their research methodology and restitute the knowledge back to the communities with whom they are researching.

Disowning of creative and imaginative possibilities of research: The false construction of objectivity has an additional consequence of discouraging creative and imaginative fabulations in the form of design-based research methods that can offer possibilities for *researching otherwise*.[6]

These gaps have compelled researchers in landscape and urban studies to generatively borrow from the fertile methodological experimentations and innovations in the proximate fields of humanities and social sciences. Researchers have consequently deployed pluriversal methodologies for examining multisensory and more-than-human worlds through imaginative, creative, and sensory methods. In addition to

4   See Dicks, Soyinka, and Coffey, "Multimodal Ethnography"; Brar, "Blackness, Radicalism, Sound."
5   See Mignolo, "Epistemic Disobedience."
6   See Rosner, *Critical Fabulations*; Nijhuis and de Vries, "Design as Research."

identifying ontoepistemically disobedient and methodologically anarchic imaginative and creative research practices from the allied disciplines of ethnography, geography, sociology, digital, and environmental humanities that break away from the bounds of conventional research, this book identifies novel and incipient methods developed by various practitioners from landscape and urban disciplines. The book *A Different Kind of Ethnography* by Dara Culhane and Denielle Elliott has provided particularly crucial inspiration for this publication.[7] The call for researching otherwise espoused in this book is a call to deploy sensory, collaborative, and restitutive methodological tools, such as drawing, photography, sounding and listening, filmmaking, walking, and cartography to not only unearth and unmask systems of power and domination but also to research possible other worlds and to counter the disembodiment of research and the researcher.[8] Following Fred Moten and Stefano Harney, it is a call to transcend enlightenment-type critique through engaging in the fugitive methods of researching otherwise.[9]

Rather than being a closed guidebook, this book aims to provide its readers with methodological orientations that are open to continual revision and inclusion. The following section of this introduction will frame some important boundaries and borders that have haunted research in landscape and urban studies.

Breaking boundaries

Research in landscape and urban studies, as in other disciplines, has been subject to the act of border and boundary-making that mediates, conditions, and limits its horizons while determining its outcomes. Some of these borders and boundaries are more familiar than others. In terms of geographical boundaries, for instance, the Global North–South boundary has haunted landscape and urban research, shrouding it under the narratives of developmentalism.[10] In this section I discuss three such borders that condition methods of researching and knowing, and in the subsequent section I discuss the ways in which this book proposes to transcend these borders. Importantly,

[7] Culhane and Elliott, *A Different Kind of Ethnography*.
[8] On this, see further Tilley, "Resisting Piratic Method"; de los Reyes and Lundström, "Researching Otherwise?"
[9] See Moten and Harney, "University and the Undercommons"; see also Khensani de Klerk, "Public aGender."
[10] See Roy and Crane, *Territories of Poverty*.

Nitin Bathla

those that I elucidate here seldom act in isolation but rather shape and define research outcomes in tandem with each other.

The first border imposed on research in landscape and urban studies is a disciplinary one, which attempts to separate it as a specialized domain from other similarly specialized disciplines. This, according to Paul Feyerabend, is due to the tendency of modernity, whereby scientific education "simplifies 'science' by simplifying its participants." First, he claims, a domain of research is defined and separated from the rest of history and given a logic of its own. Then, those working in the domain are thoroughly trained in this logic, making their actions more uniform. An essential part of such training attempts to inhibit intuitions that might lead to a blurring of boundaries. Feyerabend illustrates this using the example of physics, whereby it "is separated from metaphysics and from theology. Thus, the domain of research "is separated from the rest of history … and given a 'logic' of its own":

> A thorough training in such a "logic" then conditions those working in the domain; it makes *their actions* more uniform, and it freezes large parts of the *historical process* as well. Stable "facts" arise and persevere despite the vicissitudes of history. An essential part of the training that makes such facts appear consists in the attempt to inhibit intuitions that might lead to a blurring of boundaries. A person's religion, for example, or his metaphysics, or his sense of humour (his *natural* sense of humour and not the inbred and always rather nasty kind of jocularity one finds in specialized professions) must not have the slightest connection with his scientific activity. His imagination is restrained, and even his language ceases to be his own. This is again reflected in the nature of scientific "facts" which are experienced as being independent of opinion, belief, and cultural background.[11]

Analyzing the methodology of epoch-defining scientists who worked against the grain, Feyerabend finds that rather than being constrained by disciplinary boundaries, most successful scientists were in fact *against method*, or in other words were

[11] Feyerabend, *Against Method*, 11 (emphasis in original).

transgressive and disobedient in that they adopted an anarchic attitude towards science. While anarchism may be disputed as a political philosophy, it is certainly a medicine for epistemology as it deviates from being consistent with accepted theories.[12] Therefore to be against method is to undo the myth that successful science follows a standard procedure, and instead to inculcate anarchic and disobedient methodologies, an endeavor that is finding more and more proponents. Thus in the recent edited volume *Against and for Method*, Jan Silberberger interprets Feyerabend's prophetic call as a prompt to rethink the method of studio teaching in architectural education and its disciplinary siloing.[13] Another successful and hopeful example of such de-siloing has been the unbordering of the disciplines of urban and rural sociology and urban and agrarian studies beyond the city, which several scholars, myself included, have been a part of.[14]

Even though both landscape and urban studies are expansively interdisciplinary fields with a whole spectrum of sub-fields ranging from social sciences to data sciences, practitioners often struggle against the logics internal to the field, having to constantly work and train in a language that not only disembodies the researcher but also feels very alien to the topics they are studying. Moreover, attempts to push methodological boundaries in landscape and urban research often tend to encounter resistance from hegemonic and established pedagogies in the field that operate around a second important border, namely that of "Cartesian dualism." This dualism, introduced with the seventeenth-century invention of the scientific method through the works of proponents such as René Descartes, argues for a radical separation between the mind and body—reason is located in human minds, distinct from human bodies where passion and irrationality lurk. Although attempts have been made to undo Cartesian dualism in landscape and urban research, it often creeps back in the ways in which sensory and imaginative research approaches, as well as other ways of knowing and researching, are relegated to the margins. In the practice and training of becoming "objective," researchers are often taught to be content with studying the products of

12 Feyerabend, *Against Method*, 9.
13 Silberberger, *Against and for Method*.
14 See, for instance, Brenner and Schmid, "Towards a New Epistemology of the Urban?"; Angelo and Wachsmuth, "Urbanizing Urban Political Ecology"; Gururani, "Cities in a World of Villages"; Balakrishnan, *Shareholder Cities*; Bathla, "Delhi without Borders."

imagination rather than working with imaginative processes themselves. However, while conducting ethnographic and historiographic research, it often becomes apparent that our ways of knowing and thus our writing practices are shaped by the affective and the sensorial.

In addition to the disciplinary and Cartesian boundaries of knowing, researchers often encounter a third, ontoepistemological border, which is deeply entrenched in how coloniality has shaped and continues to shape ways of knowing. The knowing subject in a discipline is not transparent and disincorporated from or untouched by the geopolitical configuration of the world in which people and regions have and continue to be ranked and configured racially.[15] For instance, it is often assumed that non-Western researchers have to be a token of their culture; that is, they have to research the places they come from and the developmental challenges related to urbanization and landscape change in the countries of their origin. Such expectations, however, often do not arise for Western scholars, who are assumed to be beholders of a universal knowledge system. This essentially constitutes an attempt at epistemic privileging in the name of upholding a singular global or one-world ontology of modernity that the West sits at the center of. In response, scholars from decolonial and postcolonial studies have highlighted how a large number of social theories are located at the very borders of the colonial matrix of power. They have thus argued for moving beyond simply situating knowledge in landscapes and spaces that have been made peripheral by also actively thinking of and engaging with other modernities and ways of becoming—for instance, in how to think of subaltern lives and their urban popular economies and territories of operation that make lives worth living.[16] Further in this sense, Walter Mignolo and Gloria Anzaldúa have proposed border thinking as a method to politically and epistemically de-link from the web of imperial knowledge, which has energized several disobedient and anarchic traditions of researching otherwise.[17]

15 See Mignolo, "Epistemic Disobedience, Independent Thought and Decolonial Freedom," 160.
16 See Urban Popular Economy Collective, "Urban Popular Economies."
17 Anzaldúa, *Borderlands;* Mignolo, *Local Histories.*

A Methodological Pluriverse

Researching otherwise: disobedience and anarchy

The title of this book, *Researching Otherwise*, pays homage to Arturo Escobar's call for thinking worlds and knowledges "otherwise." Drawing upon Escobar, Feyerabend, and a diversity of other methodologically disobedient and anarchic thinkers, this book attempts to undo the methodological borders and boundaries that have constrained landscape and urban research by discouraging it from a transdisciplinary dialogue, stymieing an engagement with sensuousness and affect, and blocking the ability to draw upon pluriversal worlds. *Researching Otherwise* is therefore a call "to craft another space for the production of knowledge—another way of thinking, *un paradigma otro*, the very possibility of talking about 'worlds and knowledges otherwise'."[18] It posits that such ways of decolonial, pluriversal, and more-than-human knowing can offer tools and ways for reimagining and reconstructing local worlds and transcending developmental paradigms of researching and operating.[19] Rather than rigid and closed epistemologies of knowing the landscape and the urban, this book promotes fluid epistemologies that respond to the incommensurabilities, radical alterities, and other ways of knowing the environment.

In exploring the pluriversality of postcolonial and more-than-human worlds, researchers are increasingly concerned with the questions of restitution of knowledge to the communities that they research with. Moreover, researchers increasingly confront questions of how to fill in, unmask, and unearth the silences in archives and the ways of knowing and researching the present.[20] For instance, in answering the persistent question "Why am I in academia?" that researchers transitioning from landscape and urban practice to academia often ask themselves, Ihnji Jon ruminates upon the radical planning tradition espoused by scholars such as John Friedmann.[21] Jon asks what makes academic research different from

[18] Escobar, "Worlds and Knowledges Otherwise," 179.
[19] See Escobar, *Designs for the Pluriverse*.
[20] See Bertschi, Lafontaine Carboni, and Bathla, *Unearthing Traces*; Kennedy, "Infrastructures of 'Legitimate Violence'."
[21] Jon, "The City We Want."

Nitin Bathla

journalism or, say, consultancy work. Friedmann famously argued that "planners are not journalists who can dispassionately observe the passing scene. They have to ask themselves, given the reality of what is happening now, can planning powers intervene to shift the balance of forces toward goals of social justice and inclusion in the ongoing processes of urban and regional restructuring, and with what tools at hand?"[22] For Jon, the banality of academic research can be overcome by centering on the methodological question of who and what are we producing knowledge for and what are the implications of revealing these facts. Thus, in *researching otherwise* researchers should resist the neoliberal urge to concern themselves primarily with citations and publishing in impact-factor journals, and instead drive their research practice towards building collectives and spaces of solidarity for realizing *worlds otherwise*.[23] Similarly drawing upon decolonial and pluriversal thought, Catalina Ortiz vigorously proposes storytelling as one such entry point for *planning otherwise:* "The decolonial turn calls for a practice of imagining and acknowledging alternative ways of knowing, sensing and being," leading Ortiz to propose theory generation as a counter-storytelling project.[24]

As Eduardo Viveiros de Castro so presciently highlights, today "Anthropocene-thinking requires the practice of a radical form of ontological pluralism" through paying "attention to the many ways of living and thinking the Anthropocene by different peoples in different places, differently affected by capitalism's processes of material extraction and spiritual sorcery" and the unearthing of different Earths.[25] Following this line of thought, ontological anarchy is a way and method of being open to ontological pluralism by acting in defiance of the one-world ontology of modernity. Taking another example, Walter Mignolo—drawing upon the work of postcolonial scholars such as Partha Chaterjee—forces us to rethink the universality of modernity and pay attention to pluriversal ways of knowing and becoming. Here epistemological disobedience does away with the understanding of epistemology with a capital E and instead constitutes an invitation for discovering "worlds and

22 Friedmann, "Uses of Planning Theory," 250.
23 See Oldfield, *High Stakes, High Hopes*.
24 Ortiz, "Storytelling Otherwise," 3.
25 Viveiros de Castro, "On Models and Examples," S298.

knowledge otherwise." To borrow from Maan Barua, researching otherwise is the rendition of research practice that does not reject established forms of research methods, but rather imparts a decentered, runaway, fugitive character to research practice.[26]

Transductive movement

The advancement and development of grounded theory since the 1960s has attempted to decenter and deconstruct the notions of deducing the world through "grand theory" and one-world epistemology by proposing to close the gap between theory and empirical research through grounding or induction.[27] Grounded theory calls for theory to be generated rather than verified, which is proximate and intersectional with William J. T. Mitchell's call to go against theory. Mitchell's idea of "theory" is a special project that attempts to govern interpretations of particular texts by appealing to an account of interpretation in general.[28] Going against theory is thus not a call to abandon theory but to find pluriversal ways of interpreting and knowing the world through embracing methodological anarchy. While the various strands of grounded theory have provided a much-established way of enacting disobedience through knowing inductively and theorizing the plurality of worlds that we inhabit,[29] there is a third way, namely transduction, a method proposed by French philosopher Henri Lefebvre that allows for a dialectical movement between induction and deduction.[30] Through its dialectical movement, transduction allows for the critique of theory through practice and practice through theory, thus helping destabilize hegemonic theoretical positions while still operating within a pluriverse. Scholars such as Gillian Hart have powerfully employed transductive movement in the methodology of relational comparison, and I myself have deployed this through what I term "critical transductive methodology."[31]

Imagination

Imagination is an active component of experience and perception, engaged in a constant interchange with the material textures of the existing world—one that

26 Barua, *Lively Cities*, 36.
27 See Glaser and Strauss, *Discovery of Grounded Theory*.
28 Mitchell, *Against Theory*.
29 See Charmaz, *Constructing Grounded Theory*; Allen and Davey, "Value of Constructivist Grounded Theory."
30 See Stanek, Schmid, and Moravánszky, "Theory Not Method"; Hart, "Relational Comparison Revisited."
31 Bathla, "Delhi without Borders."

→ Figure 1

Nitin Bathla

can help account for what is forgotten, disappeared, hidden, and lost. Imagination as a pedagogy has the potential to reveal the unknown.[32] For Feyerabend imagination is a crucial aspect of enacting methodological anarchy—*"we need a dream world in order to discover the features of the real world we think we inhabit."*[33] Researchers usually deploy imagination in the formal aspects of their writing, for instance through expressing themselves more freely and poetically. However, it is pertinent to think of the ways in which imagination can be deployed as a research methodology. Fabulation, for instance, has emerged as an important feminist method that allows for researching otherwise and living differently in the present. Donna Haraway, in exercising what she calls "speculative fabulation," immerses herself in the works of feminist science fiction.[34] These include the extraplanetary worlds of author Ursula K. Le Guin, where exploitative socio-spatial differentiation is reproduced on the other planets of the universe colonized by space-faring races,[35] or the works of Black feminist author Octavia E. Butler that transpose readers back in time to situate contemporary experiences of blackness.[36] Haraway's conclusion:

> It matters what matters we use to think other matters with; it matters what stories we tell to tell other stories with; it matters what knots knot knots, what thoughts think thoughts, what ties tie ties. It matters what stories make worlds, what worlds make stories.[37]

Such fabulations allow researchers to think of worlds through imagined other worlds. Alternatively, and drawing upon the work of Saidiya Hartmann and Donna Haraway, Daniela K. Rosner proposes critical fabulations as a design method for "ways of storytelling that rework how things that we design come into being and what they do in the world."[38]

Architectural historians such as Anne Hultzsch have similarly deployed imaginative methodologies in an attempt to close the absence of gendered voices in architectural historiography. Hultzsch claims that looking for women who may have been missed from the historiographic canon is futile because women at the time were barred from receiving architectural

32 See Culhane and Elliott, *A Different Kind of Ethnography*, 15.
33 Feyerabend, *Against Method*, 22 (emphasis in the original).
34 Haraway, "SF."
35 See Le Guin, *Language of the Night*.
36 See Butler, Mehaffy, and Keating, "'Radio Imagination'."
37 Haraway, "SF," 4.
38 Rosner, *Critical Fabulations*, 48.

education in the first place. In her attempts at gendering architecture history, she instead attempts to imagine architecture through the eyes of women travelers.[39] Historian Ariella Aïsha Azoulay, on the other hand, proposes the method of potential histories, which deploys imagination as a means of unlearning imperialism. Here potential history is an ontoepistemic refusal to recognize violence as irreversible in its outcome and the categories, statuses, and forms under which it materializes:

> Potential history refuses to inhabit the position of the historian who arrives after the events are over, that is, after the violence was made into part of the sealed past, dissociated in time and space from where we are. Violence against people and their worlds is not history, and the work of potential history is to argue that this violence can be reversed, brought to a closure, mended.[40]

In imagining potential histories, Azoulay attempts to offer potential futures that are different from what we have today. Or, as another example, Maja and Reuben Fowkes, who in their curatorial project on potential agrarianisms cast a look at marginal agrarian histories for the reparation of highly urbanized and industrialized agrarian landscapes of the present.[41]

Creative embodiment

Research is a highly embodied act: "Something happens differently when your body must move and adjust to the rhythms, structures, rules, dangers, joys and secrets of a unique location. Ethnography *and historiography, if I may*, is as much, or more, about bodily attention—performing in and against a circumscribed space—as it is about what is told to you in an interview."[42] In comparison to imaginative methodologies, creative methodologies are transdisciplinary, collaborative, embodied, and critical approaches to research that bridge ethnography or historiography, anthropology, and the arts. It is often this anticipatory, creative, and uncertain potential of research—of not really knowing where we are headed—that makes it exhilarating. Creativity is actively intermingled with imaginative practices, everyday life, and social relationships. They can deepen

39 Hultzsch, *Architecture, Travellers and Writers*.
40 Azoulay, *Potential History*, 286.
41 Fowkes and Fowkes, "Politics and Ecology of Invasive Species."
42 Ethnographer D. Soyini Madison, cited in Culhane, "Imagining," 11, emphasis added.

Nitin Bathla

our understandings, enrich our analyses, and facilitate our communication with diverse audiences both within the academy and outside of it. Walking, for instance, as I will detail below, is one such creative embodiment, offering a collaborative methodology that as a practice provides an opportunity for co-imagining as a way of inhabiting the landscape, thinking of the past and of the future, and engaging in collective projects.[43] It does not simply entail following people in their footsteps but also pays attention to how they theorize the city, their ideas, memories, and strategies.[44]

Doing sensory ethnography provides a further means for creative embodiment in research, allowing researchers to transcend privileging the visual experiences of sights, words, and texts over other senses and producing polysensorial accounts of the pluriversal worlds they research. It helps record, analyze, and transmit the liminal sensations of what we research through its sounds, smells, tastes, and textures. While historians might be tempted to dismiss creative embodiment and the sensory as an ethnographic tendency, too intimate to make any reasonable scientific, theoretical, or philosophical meaning, some of them try to visit sites and landscapes that they are writing about to make sense of, and to sense, the voices and places that they are reading about in the archives. Therefore, in a way, this book itself follows the imaginative logic of discovery.

> Doing sensory ethnography provides a further means for creative embodiment in research, allowing researchers to transcend privileging the visual experiences of sights, words, and texts over other senses and producing polysensorial accounts of the pluriversal worlds they research.

The subsequent section provides three guiding pathways along which the contributions in this book have been grouped. These sections on transdisciplinary, sensory, and restitutive approaches cover several original contributions from a diversity of researchers—both those who have contributed to this book and those beyond its bounds. Rather than being divergent and self-contained, these approaches are convergent and intersectional. Together they illustrate revisable and open-ended methodologies for *researching otherwise*.

43 See Streule, "Doing Mobile Ethnography."
44 See further Tümerdem, "Recording the Landscape."

A Methodological Pluriverse

Transdisciplinary methods

Given the challenges and uncertainties posed by the Anthropocene and its corollaries, researchers have called for *researching with* or doing "science with society."[45] Contrary to cross- and multi-disciplinarity, which insist on knowing through collaborations between specialists across disciplines, transdisciplinarity, a term initially introduced by the Swiss psychologist Jean Piaget in the 1970s, challenges the subject-object separation by going beyond (trans-) disciplines and by researching in collaboration with communities that have conventionally been treated as passive research subjects.[46] Research by design, in particular, has emerged as an important direction in landscape and urban research practice, whereby researchers have attempted to deploy design as a means to transdisciplinarity. Participatory action research (PAR)[47] and transdisciplinary action research (TDAR)[48] are two important streams of transdisciplinary research where researchers from across a number of disciplines participate with people in improving and understanding the world by changing it. While PAR and TDAR are established forms of creative research, other forms of collaborative and transdisciplinary research also exist, such as socially engaged art,[49] that can enable researchers to transcend the theory-practice and research-activism divides. Theater is one such form of performance ethnography that can be deployed for transdisciplinary research, as Metaxia Markaki illustrates in her chapter in this volume.

Action research

As a research tradition, PAR emerged in Latin America in the 1970s in research conducted with exploited groups and classes. PAR offers a radical methodology that combines theory, action, and participation to initiate constructive grassroots change through nonviolent means.[50] While research and practice in landscape and urban studies has always relied on cross- and multidisciplinary collaborations with sociologists, historians, biologists, cultural researchers, and practitioners, as well as other design disciplines, PAR and TDAR allow researchers a methodology by

45 See Seidl et al., "Science with Society."
46 Bernstein, "Transdisciplinarity," 2.
47 See Kemmis, McTaggart, and Nixon, "Introducing Critical Participatory Action Research."
48 See McIntyre, *Participatory Action Research*; Stokols, "Transdisciplinary Action Research."
49 See Bishop, *Artificial Hells*; Bathla and Garg, "Radical Encounters."
50 See Fals-Borda, "Application of Participatory Action-Research."

which to actively collaborate with non-specialists. Furthermore, TDAR allows for "systematic coordinating and reconciling of local environmental interests with broader societal concerns [that] can make landscape scholarship more responsive to the 'ecological and cultural urgencies' of our time."[51] Based on the importance allotted to specific tools of transdisciplinarity in research, several important renditions of PAR and TDAR can be encountered, with one great example being the design-in-dialogue approach adopted by Newrope Studio that privileges dialogue as a means to transdisciplinarity.[52]

Drawing

"Drawing is discovery," as the British painter and poet John Berger famously put it. "It is the actual act of drawing that forces the artist to look at the object in front of him, to dissect it in his mind's eye and put it together again; or, if he is drawing from memory, that forces him to dredge his own mind, to discover the content of his own store of past observations."[53] On the one hand, drawing has served as an important tool for planners to drain and discipline landscapes and the urban.[54] On the other, drawing offers "textility of making," as Tim Ingold so powerfully points out,[55] or an opportunity for drawing from the stream of everyday life, as Michael Taussig so beautifully highlights in his ethnographic notebooks.[56] However, drawing is not merely a tool of visual ethnography, for it is not just the artist, the practitioner, or the researcher that holds the ability to draw but also the communities and groups that we research with. It offers the opportunity to open a dialogue; it has been central to transdisciplinary methodologies through what has been termed "the method of rapid appraisal."[57] In his collaborative research with homeless migrants in Italy, for instance, Michele Lancione highlights how drawings and graphics in novels in particular offer an activist mode of existence beyond the bounds of the research-activist divide.[58] In their contribution in this volume, Luke Harris, Cara Turett, and Bonnie Kate Walker emphasize the use of drawing as a tool of transdisciplinary research and relational thinking on landscape and the urban with the communities who dwell in them.

51 McIntyre, *Participatory Action Research*, 2.
52 See De Blust, Persyn, and Schaeben, *5IN4E*.
53 Berger, "Drawing Is Discovery."
54 See Bhattacharyya, "Discipline and Drain."
55 Ingold, "Textility of Making."
56 Taussig, *I Swear I Saw This*.
57 Beebe, "Basic Concepts and Techniques of Rapid Appraisal."
58 Lancione, "Ethnographic Novel."

→ Figure 2

Radical and socially engaged art

Radical and socially engaged art has emerged as an important tool for transdisciplinarity in landscape and urban research. Whether it be the Turner-Prize-winning *Granby Four Streets* project in Liverpool, the *Refugee Heritage* project by the Decolonizing Architecture Art Research (DAAR) in Palestine, or the work of Oda Projesi (Room Project), a women's collective in Istanbul, art has opened possibilities for radical change.[59] However, in her critically acclaimed book *Artificial Hells*, Claire Bishop also illustrates how the recent "social turn" in art practice is actually only a return to the social, highlighting how avant-garde art movements since circa 1917, such as the Dadaists, always responded to the social and political potentials of doing and knowing through art in urban space.[60]

Set against this background, landscape and urban researchers have been driven by similar impulses to socially engage with communities for over a century at least. In my own case, I actively collaborated with the artist Sumedha Garg and the women-workers collective Saat Saheliyan (Seven Sisters) while conducting my doctoral research in the peripheries of Delhi. The long-term socially engaged art project, Otherworlds, not only afforded me intimate insights into the gendered nature of labor and rental violence within clusters of garment manufacturing, but also helped catalyze change through collaboration with the community that I was researching with. It thus offers a pluriversal and transdisciplinary methodology of knowing and transforming the urban. In her contribution in this volume, Andreea-Florentina Midvighi similarly illuminates the collaborative potential of visual ethnography through research conducted with doubly displaced Palestinian refugees in Yarmouk Camp in Damascus.

→ Figure 3

Sensory methods

Landscapes and urban spaces are highly sensuous environments with a wide range of sensory impulses emanating from human and more-than-human sources, such as tactile inducements, smells, warmth of light and coolness of shade, voices, automobile

59 See Vilenica, *Radical Housing*; Bathla and Garg, "Radical Encounters."
60 Bishop, *Artificial Hells*.

Nitin Bathla

noises, singing and chirping of birds, music, as well as other sensations that lie beyond the human sensorium. Therefore senses mediate a researcher's engagement with urban life, rendering insights into the multisensory character of urbanity, place, and the social actors entangled with it. The emergence of sensory ethnography has opened up a research methodology for engaging with polysensorial environments through acknowledging that landscapes and urban spaces are also sites of human experience that comprise social relationships, memories, emotions, and how they are negotiated on an everyday basis. Sensory ethnography accounts for and takes as its starting point the multisensoriality of experience, perception, knowing, and practice in not only how it is integral for ethnographers but also for people who participate in research.[61] *Doing Sensory Ethnography* by Sarah Pink provides an excellent guidebook for researchers looking to engage with the sensuousness of landscape and the urban.[62] Meanwhile, the beautifully haunting films of the Sensory Ethnography Lab (SEL) at Harvard University immerse us into the sensoriums of more-than-human worlds across the planet, allowing us to make sense of the sensual and multisensory.[63] However, the task at hand for researchers engaging with sensory methodologies is to transcend beyond the human sensorium and elucidate how environments that are beyond the horizon are being disrupted through imperial violence. The 2012 SEL film *Leviathan* highlights this paradigm of transcending beyond the human through immersing us into the sensorium of the ocean and how industrial fishing shapes the more-than-human worlds of the oceanscape beyond what can be humanly known.[64] Similarly, in her contribution in this volume, Nancy Couling highlights ways of knowing ocean worlds beyond the perceptual abilities of the human.

Walking

In recent years walking has increasingly emerged as an important methodology of both creating new, embodied ways of knowing and of producing scholarly narratives. Walking forces researchers to focus their

[61] See Low, "Sensuous City."
[62] Pink, *Doing Sensory Ethnography*.
[63] See Nakamura, "Making Sense of Sensory Ethnography." For further information on SEL, see their website: https://sel.fas.harvard.edu/.
[64] See Lapworth, "Sensing."

attention on the kinesthetic, mobile, and sensory dimensions of the lived experience.[65] Jo Lee and Tim Ingold presciently remind us that walking has always been an important aspect of participation in fieldwork. However, one should be cautious that "to participate is not to walk into but is rather to walk with—where 'with' implies not a face-to-face confrontation, but heading the same way, sharing the same vistas, and perhaps retreating from the same threats behind."[66] Researchers often trace the origin of walking as a research practice back to the figure of the *flaneur* in Walter Benjamin's *Das Passagen-Werk*.[67] For Benjamin, the *flaneur*, or the strolling subject, is the detective of street life seeking clues about the social physiognomy of the streets through walking or *flânerie*. Here *flânerie* emerges as a crowd practice and part of a social process of inhabiting and appropriating urban space.[68] Benjamin's influences are rife in Michel de Certeau's understanding of walking as a practice through which the ordinary practitioners of the city, who he calls *"Wandersmänner"* (wandering men), write the text of the city. It is a method of exploring how the city is made and remade from below.[69] A parallel modality of walking as a methodology for knowing the landscape and the urban can be found in the work of the Swiss sociologist Lucius Burckhardt. His method of strollology, part of what he termed *"Spaziergangswissenschaft"* (literally, the science of walking) provides a way of experiencing the aesthetics of landscape. "Strollology examines the sequences in which a person perceives his surroundings,"[70] and its task "is to gather impressions and string them together, a tool with which previously unseen parts of the environment can be made visible as well as an effective means of criticizing conventional perception."[71] Since then, walking has, for instance, been employed in the work of the Italian collective Stalker, which came together in the mid-1990s to develop a methodology for participative tools to construct a "collective imaginary" for a place.[72] In her own contribution in this volume, Johanna Just explores walking as a method of knowing multispecies and more-than-human landscapes in the Lower Rhine Valley.

65 See Pink et al., "Walking across Disciplines."
66 Lee and Ingold, "Fieldwork on Foot," 67.
67 See Buck-Morss, "Benjamin's Passagen-Werk."
68 See Shields, "Fancy Footwork."
69 de Certeau, "Walking in the City."
70 Burckhardt, *Why Is Landscape Beautiful?* 225.
71 Burckhardt, *Why Is Landscape Beautiful?* 238.
72 For further details on Stalker/ *Osservatorio Nomade*, see the website https://www.spatialagency.net/database/stalkerosservatorio.nomade.

→ Figure 4

Nitin Bathla

Sonic research

"Listening is a political act,"[73] therefore there have been calls for paying attention and incorporating sound and expanded listening into the methodological apparatus of landscape and urban research, to the extent that they are involved in the construction and mediation of human and more-than-human environments.[74] These methods challenge the predominance of verbal-textual methods of knowing, helping to come to grips with the sounding of more-than-human, more-than-textual, and multisensual worlds.[75] This in turn has led to generative crossovers of sound studies and sonic geographies and the use of phonography and multisensory methodologies for landscape and urban research. The development of acoustemology, in particular by Steven Feld, "conjoins 'acoustics' and 'epistemology' to theorize sound as a way of knowing," whereby Feld describes the methodology as an inquiry "into what is knowable, and how it becomes known, through sounding and listening."[76] This constitutes a knowing-with and knowing-through the audible. In his contribution in this volume, Ludwig Berger immerses us in a similarly diverse soundscapes, partially through what he describes as audio walks, a method that combines the sensory approaches of walking and listening.[77]

Ethnographic filmmaking

When we record in the field, in the multiple ways we do, we do so corporeally—we produce corporeal images, drawings, etc. Therefore, recording allows the anthropologist to develop an acute sensorial approach. Recording, regardless of the media we choose, then becomes a way of paying attention. Similarly, editing of media—be it film, image, sound, drawing, or text—forces the researcher to select what is meaningful to a specific situation or a place. It is a form of analyzing, and as such film is also a form of writing. Researchers from physical and social sciences, such as ethnography and geography, have employed film as a means of doing sensory research. The first ever ethnographic film, *Nanook of the North*, directed by Robert Flaherty, was released over a century ago in 1922, capturing the everyday life of the indigenous

[73] Alexandra, "Are We Listening Yet?" 45.
[74] See Gallagher and Prior, "Sonic Geographies"; Gallagher, Kanngieser, and Prior, "Listening Geographies."
[75] See Lorimer, "Cultural Geography."
[76] Feld, "[1] Acoustemology," 12.
[77] See also Berger, Fischer, and von Bowen, "Only Dogs Walk."

Inuit people of Canada's northern Quebec region.[78] While ethnographic film, like the discipline of ethnography itself, has been historically plagued by the coloniality of a Euro-American gaze on the cultures of the world, it has nonetheless gradually undergone a similar reframing as used in research into landscape and the urban.

Current ethnographic films such as *Homo Urbanus* by architecture and urban filmmakers Ila Bêka and Louise Lemoine have provided polysensorial ways of knowing the urban,[79] while the film *Natura Urbana* by Matthew Gandy and Sandra Jasper has employed the cinematic medium to not only sense and analyze the ruderal landscapes of Berlin but also transmit these sensory experiences to the viewers.[80] The latter film was screened at many important conferences, film festivals, and radical theaters around the world, opening up important discussions on wastelands to audiences around the world.[81] My own film *Not Just Roads*, produced in collaboration with Klearjos Eduardo Papanicolaou in the context of my doctoral research at ETH Zurich in 2020, similarly attempts to center the sensory beneath the contested urbanization of state-led highway programs in India.[82] Similar to *Natura Urbana*, the use of the cinematic method in *Not Just Roads* does not become a way of narrating something that I already knew as a researcher, but rather centers on the cinematic imagination.[83] It is a process that entails recording (as in paying attention), editing (as in analyzing), and then later narrating everything to the reviewer as set of sequences. As another example, the acclaimed 2022 documentary film *All That Breathes* by the Indian filmmaker and researcher Shaunak Sen deploys the cinematic medium to bring to life the sensorium of the more-than-human world of the city of Delhi. Following from this, Klearjos Eduardo Papanicolaou's contribution in this book further explores the history of cinema and the development of ethnographic film.

78 See Bathla and Papanicolaou, "Reframing the Contested City."
79 See Bêka and Lemoine, *Emotional Power of Space*. See also the film series *Homo Urbanus* by Bêka and Lemoine.
80 *Natura Urbana: The Brachen of Berlin*, Documentary, 2017.
81 Matthew Gandy recently released an eponymous book, which is based on the reflections from the film but also serves as an extension to it. See Gandy, *Natura Urbana*.
82 *Not Just Roads*. See also El-Husseiny et al., "Not Just Roads."
83 For the term, see MacDougall, *Looking Machine*.

→ Figure 5

Restitutive methods

Restitution, from the Latin *restitutio*, is an act of return or restoration to a previous state. The term has become increasingly used in the fields of museology and

Nitin Bathla

archival science to denote the return of cultural and natural history objects to the places that they were colonially looted from. Various European museums are caught in this current, for instance in the scramble to find an appropriate means to restitute the Benin Bronzes stolen during the colonial plunder of West Africa.[84] However, as discussed earlier in this introduction, restitution should not necessarily operate on a neutral, one-world ontoepistemology, because citizenship and belonging has been differently constructed through the forces of colonialism and imperialism. Moreover, this vitally opens prescient questions regarding restitution and research across the pluriversality of more-than-human worlds.[85] The method of potential histories is one such way of restituting history. Rather than being an established category of methods, like those discussed in the previous two sections, this book proposes that restitutive methods, in research terms, are emergent methods. Restitutive methods, as explained below, obligate researchers to investigate relationships of power and hegemony in more-than-human worlds and catalyze steps for the restitution of the objects of their research to the communities that have been affected by them. The three methodological orientations that I have grouped here are only illustrative of a larger canon of restitutive approaches that is yet to come, and as such represent an invitation for the readers of this book to identify and propose further methods that center their attention on restitution of knowledge.

Radical cartography

Far from being a neutral image of an objective reality, cartography is a contested practice, with maps serving the language of power and biopolitical control. Cartography, maps, and terrestrial lessons have allowed for colonial conquests through the abstraction of the Earth as the globe.[86] As William Rankin presciently highlights, this has led to the construction of a territoriality without borders, making us inhabitants of a global grid and projection system.[87] The legal power that cartographic projections enable have assisted in the appropriation of land, expulsions, and the destruction of the lifeworlds of

[84] See, for instance, the Swiss Benin Initiative at the Rietberg Museum in Zurich under https://rietberg.ch/en/research/the-swiss-benin-initiative.
[85] See Schneider, "Expanded Visions."
[86] See Ramaswamy, *Terrestrial Lesson*.
[87] Rankin, *After the Map*.

communities that dwell on the Earth. Artists, social collectives, and radical and critical cartographers have therefore variously attempted to subvert the power of the map and its cartographic conventions. David Pinder, for instance, highlights how during the 1950s and 1960s the radical art and political group Situationist International sought to appropriate urban maps and cartographic discourses to develop a new form of "psychogeographical mapping" as a means of exploring and changing the city.[88] Often, indigenous and marginalized groups who face cartographic violence, such as forest-dwelling tribes in Kalimantan, Indonesia, themselves exercise a form of counter-cartography to resist expulsions.[89] Critical and radical cartography as a research methodology then links geographical knowledge with power and attempts to subvert this power.[90] The radical and tantalizing maps of Philippe Rekacewicz, who was one of the lecturers at the seminar out of which this book emerged, provides a great illustration of how cartography can be subverted through the use of metaphors.[91]

Forensics

Forensics draws its roots from the Latin word *forensis* and translates into "pertaining to the forum." In architecture, landscape, and urban studies, forensics has emerged as a generative field and methodology of study, bringing together aesthetics, legal studies, truth regimes, evidencing, and the tensions between the field and forum, in the process also turning to the study of architecture, the urban, and landscapes. In this sense forensics has been described as an operative concept of critical practice committed to investigating the actions of states and corporations and critically reflecting on the investigation of how the scales of bodies, buildings, territories, and their digital representation are currently undertaken.[92] It is an especially pertinent methodology in a world that is increasingly shrouded in the tensions caused by transmuting forms of state violence. Forensics here goes beyond critical cartography in that it tries to deconstruct the forums of justice and reassemble them around new aesthetic frameworks and evidence.[93]

88 Pinder, "Subverting Cartography."
89 See Peluso, "Whose Woods Are These?"
90 See Crampton and Krygier, "Introduction to Critical Cartography."
91 Rekacewicz, "Frontiers, Migrants and Refugees."
92 See Franke et al., *Forensis*.
93 Bathla, "Complexities and Contradictions."

→ Figure 6

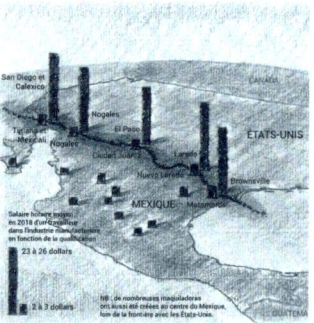

→ Figure 7

Nitin Bathla

While there has been a broader "forensic turn" in the humanities and environmental and legal studies attuned to material investigation, within the fields of architecture, landscape, and urban studies *forensic* has been pioneered and exemplified in the work of Forensic Architecture, an agency established at the Goldsmiths in London in 2011.[94] While in its various investigations Forensic Architecture has mostly used architecture as a material witness of state and corporate violence against individuals and communities, other researchers have attempted to deploy its methods at ever larger scales of the landscape and the urban. Shoudireh Molavi, for instance, deploys this forensic methodology to investigate the "slow violence"[95] and colonial control over the landscape of the Gaza Strip.[96] Her findings examine how toxic herbicides exert control over the productive agrarian landscapes of the Gaza Strip and the Palestinians residing there. Charles Heller and Lorenzo Pezzani have similarly extended this forensic methodology to investigate the humanitarian violence against refugees that unfolds in the seascape, often beyond the human sensorium.[97] In his contribution in this volume Ludo Groen deploys the forensic methodology to unearth and unmask the architecture of gold vaults in Switzerland, mapping it onto territorial exceptions such as Special Economic Zones and how it helps Switzerland to install itself at the center of global monetary flows. Touching upon a similar topic of mapping architectural traces of the Swiss–South African gold trade in Johannesburg, in this volume Denise Bertschi deploys film as a methodology of investigative spatial research.

94 See Dziuban, "Mapping the 'Forensic Turn'"; Forensic Architecture, *Forensis*.
95 See Nixon, *Slow Violence*.
96 Molavi, *Stateless Citizenship*.
97 Heller and Pezzani, "Forensic Oceanography."

Multispecies and more-than-human ethnography

Last, multispecies, and more-than-human ethnography have emerged as generative methodologies, located at the "species turn" in anthropological research that decenter and destabilize conceptual questions about culture and species by including the history of anthropology of animals, plants, and other organisms. Multispecies ethnography focuses on how a multitude of organisms' livelihoods shape and are shaped by political, economic, and cultural forces.[98] "Unlike multispecies ethnography, the emphasis in more-than-human ethnography is transversal. It focuses on polyvalent connections between the living and material world rather than the dyadic human-non-human relations."[99] Together, these modes of ethnographic research provide possibilities to identify biocultural hope amid the apocalyptical tales of environmental destruction that surround research into landscape and urban studies. Projects such as the Feral Atlas by Anna Tsing and colleagues have provided imaginative and creative ways of visibilizing the more-than-human Anthropocene and for identifying radical hope within it.[100]

[98] See Kirksey and Helmreich, "Emergence of Multispecies Ethnography."
[99] Barua, "Plantationocene."
[100] The Feral Atlas project is curated and edited by Anna L. Tsing, Jennifer Deger, Alder Keleman Saxena, and Feifei Zhou. For further information see https://feralatlas.org/ (accessed Dec. 19, 2023).

Nitin Bathla

Figure 1 View of the 2021 exhibition *Potential Agrarianisms: Will There Still Be Sugar After the Rebellion?* at Kunsthalle Bratislava

Figure 2 Students in a NEWROPE Studio session using the design-in-dialogue methodology to collectively draw and imagine alternative design futures in sand at ETH Zurich, 2019

A Methodological Pluriverse

Figure 3   A tapestry of the planetary map of fast fashion and the other worlds that exist within it, produced by the women-workers collective Saat Saheliyan (Seven Sisters) as part of the Otherworlds art project on the peripheries of Delhi

Nitin Bathla

Figure 4 A mobile zebra-striped carpet crosswalk being laid out by participants of a walk organized by Gerhard Lang close to the Tempelhof Airport in Berlin. The project was inspired by Lucius Burckhardt's idea of strollogy and the science of walking.

Figure 5 A still from the critically acclaimed 2021 film *All that Breathes*, directed by Shaunak Sen. The film follows the multispecies bonds between kites and caregivers in Delhi, India, and how they are affected by Delhi's air crisis.

A Methodological Pluriverse

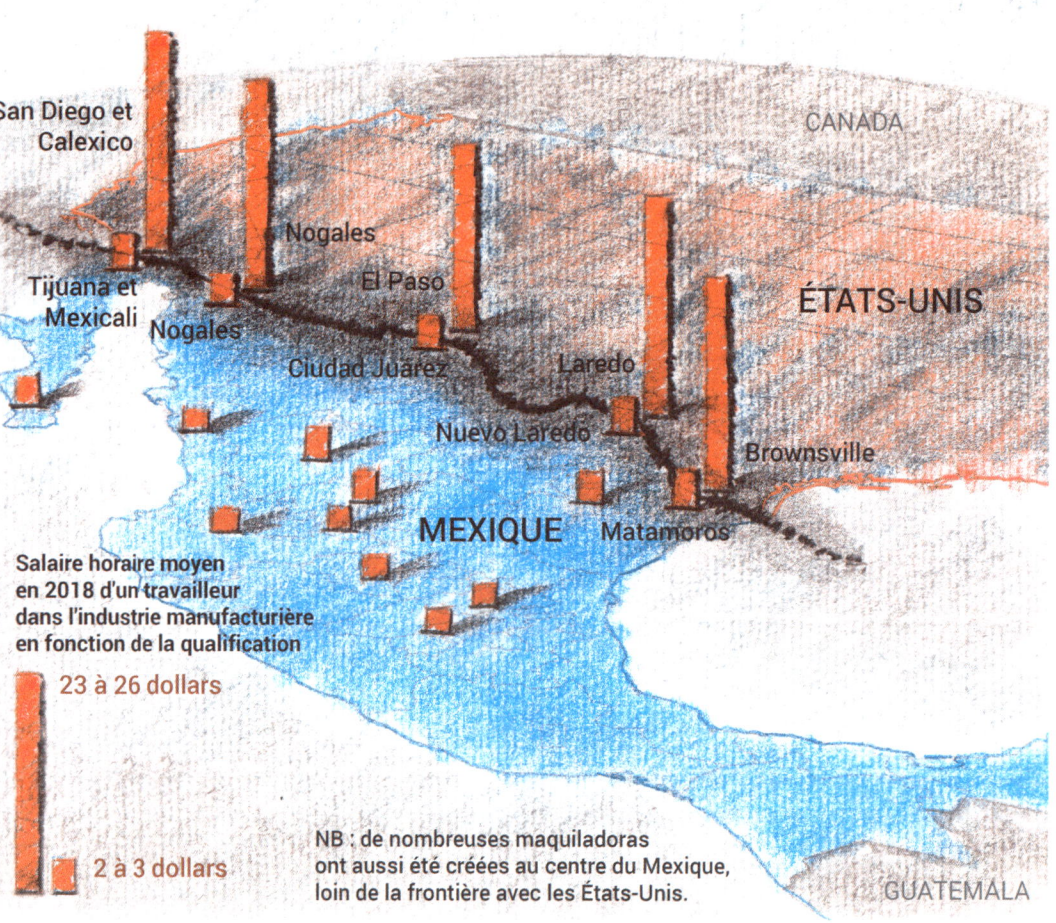

Figure 6   "The fractured border between the United States and Mexico," Philippe Rekacewicz, 2008 (updated 2018): A hand-drawn map comparing hourly wages on both immediate sides of the US-Mexico border to contextualize human migration

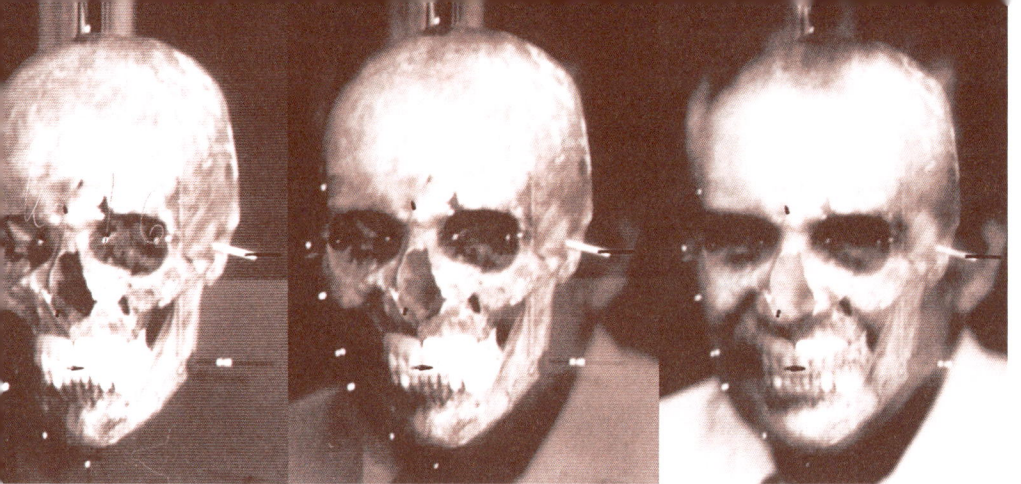

Figure 7 — A still from the 2012 film *Mengle's Skull*, directed by Eyal Weizman and Thomas Keenan. The film highlights how the forensic technique of image superimposition was used aesthetically as a presentational form at the posthumous trial of the infamous Nazi physician and war criminal Josef Mengele, who had fled to Brazil.

A Methodological Pluriverse

BIBLIOGRAPHY

A

Alexandra, Darcy. "Are We Listening yet? Participatory Knowledge Production through Media Practice: Encounters of Political Listening." *Participatory Visual and Digital Research in Action*, 2015, 41–55.

Allen, Natalie, and Mark Davey. "The Value of Constructivist Grounded Theory for Built Environment Researchers." *Journal of Planning Education and Research* 38, no. 2 (2017): 222–32. https://doi.org/10.1177/0739456X17695195.

Angelo, Hillary, and David Wachsmuth. "Urbanizing Urban Political Ecology: A Critique of Methodological Cityism." *International Journal of Urban and Regional Research* 39, no. 1 (2014): 16–27. https://doi.org/10.1111/1468-2427.12105.

Anzaldúa, Gloria. *Borderlands/La Frontera*. 5th edition. San Francisco: Aunt Lute Books, [1987] 2022.

Azoulay, Ariella. *Potential History: Unlearning Imperialism*. London, New York: Verso Books, 2019.

B

Balakrishnan, Sai. *Shareholder Cities: Land Transformations Along Urban Corridors in India*. Philadelphia: University of Pennsylvania Press, 2019.

Barua, Maan. *Lively Cities: Reconfiguring Urban Ecology*. Minneapolis: University of Minnesota Press, 2023.

Barua, Maan. "Plantationocene: A Vegetal Geography." *Annals of the American Association of Geographers* 113, no. 1 (2022): 13–29. https://doi.org/10.1080/24694452.2022.2094326.

Bathla, Nitin. "Complexities and Contradictions in Forensic Architecture." *trans* 36, *Spannung* (February 2020): 103–8.

Bathla, Nitin. "Delhi without Borders: A Critique of Everyday Life under Extended Urbanisation." Doctoral thesis, ETH Zurich, 2021.

Bathla, Nitin, and Sumedha Garg. "Radical Encounters: Housing and Socially-Engaged Art: An Experiment from a Tenement Town at the Periphery of Delhi." *Radical Housing Journal* 1, no. 2: *The Drawing in Landscape Architecture and Urbanism* (October 2020): 10–25.

Bathla, Nitin, and Klearjos Eduardo Papanicolaou. "Reframing the Contested City through Ethnographic Film: Beyond the Expository on Housing and the Urban." *International Journal of Housing Policy* 22, no. 3 (2022): 351–70. https://doi.org/10.1080/19491247.2021.1886028.

Beebe, James. "Basic Concepts and Techniques of Rapid Appraisal." *Human Organization* 54, no. 1 (1995): 42–51.

Bêka, Ila, and Louise Lemoine. *The Emotional Power of Space*. Venice, 2023.

Berger, John. "Drawing Is Discovery." [*The New Statesman* 1 (1953).] Reprint in *New Statesman America* (May 1, 2013).

Berger, Ludwig, and Florian Fischer. "Only Dogs Walk as if They Knew Where They're Going: Retracing an Audio Walk to the Empty City Center of Braunschweig." Audio paper. Seismograph: 2019. https://doi.org/10.48233/seismograf2102.

Bernstein, Jay. "Transdisciplinarity: A Review of Its Origins, Development, and Current Issues." *Journal of Research Practice* 11, no.1 (2015): article R1.

Bertschi, Denise, Julien Lafontaine Carboni, and Nitin Bathla, eds. *Unearthing Traces: Dismantling Imperialist Entanglements of Archives, Landscapes, and the Built Environment*. Lausanne: EPFL Press, 2023. https://doi.org/10.55430/6638VA01.

Bhattacharyya, Debjani. "Discipline and Drain: Settling the Moving Bengal Delta." *Global Environment* 11, no. 2 (2018): 236–57.

Bishop, Claire. *Artificial Hells: Participatory Art and the Politics of Spectatorship*. London, New York: Verso Books, 2012.

Brar, Dhanveer Singh. "Blackness, Radicalism, Sound: Black Consciousness and Black Popular Music in the USA (1955–1971)." Goldsmiths, University of London, 2013.

Brenner, Neil, and Christian Schmid. "Towards a New Epistemology of the Urban?" *City* 19, no. 2–3 (May 4, 2015): 151–82. https://doi.org/10.1080/13604813.2015.1014712.

Buck-Morss, Susan. "Benjamin's Passagen-Werk: Redeeming Mass Culture for the Revolution." *New German Critique*, no. 29 (1983): 211–40.

Burckhardt, Lucius. *Why Is Landscape Beautiful? The Science of Strollology*. Basel: Birkhäuser, 2015.

C

Charmaz, Kathy. *Constructing Grounded Theory: A Practical Guide Through Qualitative Analysis*. Sage, 2006.

Corboz, André. "The Land as Palimpsest." *Diogenes* 31, no. 121 (1983): 12–34.

Crampton, Jeremy W., and John Krygier. "An Introduction to Critical Cartography." *ACME: An International Journal for Critical Geographies* 4, no. 1 (March 3, 2015): 11–33.

Culhane, Dara, and Denielle Elliott. *A Different Kind of Ethnography: Imaginative Practices and Creative Methodologies*. Toronto: University of Toronto Press, 2016.

D

De Blust, Seppe, Freek Persyn, and Charlotte Schaeben. *51N4E, Denkstatt, Endeavour: Design in Dialogue*. Vol. 2. Berlin: Ruby Press, 2021.

De Certeau, Michel. "Walking in the City." In *Beyond the Body Proper: Reading the Anthropology of Material Life*, edited by Margaret Farquhar and Judith Lock, 249–58. Durham, NC: Duke University Press, 1984.

Dicks, Bella, Bambo Soyinka, and Amanda Coffey. "Multimodal Ethnography." *Qualitative Research* 6, no. 1 (2006): 77–96.

Dziuban, Zuzanna. "Mapping the 'Forensic Turn'." *Engagements With Materialities of Mass Death in Holocaust Studies and Beyond*. Vienna: New Academic Press, 2017.

E

El-Husseiny, Momen, AbdouMaliq Simone, Llerena Guiu Searle, D. Asher Ghertner, and Sandra Jasper. "Not Just Roads." *The AAG Review of Books* 9, no. 4 (2021): 39–52. https://doi.org/10.1080/23255 48X.2021.1960094.

Escobar, Arturo. *Designs for the Pluriverse: Radical Interdependence, Autonomy, and the Making of Worlds*. Durham, NC: Duke University Press, 2018.

Escobar, Arturo. "Worlds and Knowledges Otherwise." *Cultural Studies* 21, no. 2–3 (2007): 179–210. https://doi.org/10.1080/09502380601162506.

F

Fals-Borda, Orlando. "The Application of Participatory Action-Research in Latin America." *International Sociology* 2, no. 4 (1987): 329–47.

Farías, Ignacio, and Thomas Bender. *Urban Assemblages: How Actor-Network Theory Changes Urban Studies*. London: Routledge, 2012.

Feld, Steven. "[1] Acoustemology." In *Keywords in Sound*, 12–21. Durham, NC: Duke University Press, 2015.

Feyerabend, Paul. *Against Method*. London, New York: Verso, 1993.

Forensic Architecture, ed. *Forensis: The Architecture of Public Truth*. Berlin: Sternberg Press, 2014.

Fowkes, Maja, and Reuben Fowkes. "The Politics and Ecology of Invasive Species: A Changing Climate for Pioneering Plants." In *The Routledge Companion to Contemporary Art, Visual Culture, and Climate Change*, 332–41. London: Routledge, 2021.

Friedmann, John. "The Uses of Planning Theory: A Bibliographic Essay." *Journal of Planning Education and Research* 28, no. 2 (2008): 247–57.

G

Gallagher, Michael, Anja Kanngieser, and Jonathan Prior. "Listening Geographies: Landscape, Affect and Geotechnologies." *Progress in Human Geography* 41, no. 5 (2017): 618–37.

Gallagher, Michael, and Jonathan Prior. "Sonic Geographies: Exploring Phonographic Methods." *Progress in Human Geography* 38, no. 2 (2014): 267–84.

Gandy, Matthew. *Natura Urbana: Ecological Constellations in Urban Space*. Cambridge, MA: MIT Press, 2022.

Glaser, Barney G., and Anselm L. Strauss. *Discovery of Grounded Theory: Strategies for Qualitative Research*. London: Routledge, 2017.

Gururani, Shubhra. "Cities in a World of Villages: Agrarian Urbanism and the Making of India's Urbanizing Frontiers." *Urban Geography* 41 (2020): 971–89. https://doi.org/10.1080/02723638.2019.1670569.

H

Haraway, Donna J. "SF: Science Fiction, Speculative Fabulation, String Figures, so Far." *Ada: A Journal of Gender, New Media, and Technology*, no. 3: Feminist Science Fiction (November 2013). Available at https://scholarsbank.uoregon.edu/xmlui/bitstream/handle/1794/26308/ada03-sfsci-har-2013.pdf?sequence=1&isAllowed=y.

Hart, Gillian. "Relational Comparison Revisited: Marxist Postcolonial Geographies in Practice." *Progress in Human Geography* 42, no. 3 (2018): 371–94.

Heller, Charles, and Lorenzo Pezzani. "Forensic Oceanography." *Moving Images: Mediating Migration as Crisis*. Bielefeld, Germany: Transcript Verlag, 2020, 95–126.

Homo Urbanus. Ten-film series, edited and directed by Bêka and Lemoine. 2017–2022. http://www.bekalemoine.com/homo_urbanus.php.

Hultzsch, Anne. *Architecture, Travellers and Writers: Constructing Histories of Perception 1640–1950*. London: Routledge, 2017.

I

Ingold, Tim. "The Textility of Making." *Cambridge Journal of Economics* 34, no. 1 (2010): 91–102.

J

Jon, Ihnji. "The City We Want: Against the Banality of Urban Planning Research." *Planning Theory & Practice* 22, no. 2 (2021): 321–28. https://doi.org/10.1080/14649357.2021.1893588.

K

Kemmis, Stephen, Robin McTaggart, and Rhonda Nixon. "Introducing Critical Participatory Action Research." Chapter 1 in *The Action Research Planner*, 1–31. Singapore: Springer, 2014. https://doi.org/10.1007/978-981-4560-67-2_1.

Kennedy, Hollyamber. "Infrastructures of 'Legitimate Violence': The Prussian Settlement Commission, Internal Colonization, and the Migrant Remainder." *Grey Room* (2019): 58–97.

Kirksey, S. Eben, and Stefan Helmreich. "The Emergence of Multispecies Ethnography." *Cultural Anthropology* 25, no. 4 (2010): 545–76.

L

Lancione, Michele. "The Ethnographic Novel as Activist Mode of Existence: Translating the Field with Homeless People and Beyond." *Social & Cultural Geography* 18, no. 7 (October 3, 2017): 994–1015. https://doi.org/10.1080/14649365.2016.1231336.

Lapworth, Andrew. "Sensing." *Transactions of the Institute of British Geographers* 44, no. 4 (2019): 657–60.

Le Guin, Ursula K. *The Language of the Night: Essays on Fantasy and Science Fiction*. New York: Ultramarine Publishing, 1979.

Lee, Jo, and Tim Ingold. "Fieldwork on Foot: Perceiving, Routing, Socializing." In *Locating the Field*, edited by Simon Coleman and Peter Collins: 67–85. London: Routledge, 2020. https://doi.org/10.43 24/9781003085904.

Lorimer, Hayden. "Cultural Geography: The Busyness of Being More-than-Representational." *Progress in Human Geography* 29, no. 1 (2005): 83–94.

Low, Kelvin E.Y. "The Sensuous City: Sensory Methodologies in Urban Ethnographic Research." *Ethnography* 16, no. 3 (2015): 295–312. https://doi.org/10.1177/1466138114552938.

M

MacDougall, David. *The Looking Machine: Essays on Cinema, Anthropology and Documentary Filmmaking*. Manchester: Manchester University Press, 2019.

McIntyre, Alice. *Participatory Action Research*. Newcastle upon Tyne: Sage, 2007.

Mehaffy, Marilyn, and Ana Louise Keating. "'Radio Imagination': Octavia Butler on the Poetics of Narrative Embodiment." *Melus* 26, no. 1 (2001): 45–76.

Mignolo, Walter. *Local Histories/Global Designs: Coloniality, Subaltern Knowledges, and Border Thinking*. Princeton: Princeton University Press, 2012.

Mignolo, Walter D. "Epistemic Disobedience, Independent Thought and Decolonial Freedom." *Theory, Culture & Society* 26, no. 7–8 (2009): 159–81. https://doi.org/10.1177/0263276409349275.

Mitchell, William John Thomas. *Against Theory: Literary Studies and the New Pragmatism*. Chicago: University of Chicago Press, 1985.

Molavi, Shourideh C. *Stateless Citizenship: The Palestinian-Arab Citizens of Israel*. Leiden: Brill, 2013.

Moten, Fred, and Stefano Harney. "The University and the Undercommons: Seven Theses." *Social Text* 22, no. 2 (2004): 101–15.

N

Nakamura, Karen. "Making Sense of Sensory Ethnography: The Sensual and the Multisensory." *American Anthropologist* 115, no. 1 (2013): 132–35. https://doi.org/10.1111/j.1548-1433.2012.01544.x.

Nijhuis, Steffen, and Jeroen de Vries. "Design as Research in Landscape Architecture." *Landscape Journal* 38, no. 1–2 (January 1, 2019): 87–103. https://doi.org/10.3368/lj.38.1-2.87.

Nixon, Rob. *Slow Violence and the Environmentalism of the Poor*. Cambridge, MA: Harvard University Press, 2011.

O

Oldfield, Sophie. *High Stakes, High Hopes: Urban Theorizing in Partnership*. Vol. 60. Athens, GA: University of Georgia Press, 2023.

Ortiz, Catalina. "Storytelling Otherwise: Decolonising Storytelling in Planning." *Planning Theory* 22, no. 2 (2022), 177–200. https://doi.org/10.1177/14730952221115875.

P

Peluso, Nancy Lee. "Whose Woods Are These? Counter-Mapping Forest Territories in Kalimantan, Indonesia." *Antipode* 27, no. 4 (1995): 383–406. https://doi.org/10.1111/j.1467-8330.1995.tb00286.x.

Pinder, David. "Subverting Cartography: The Situationists and Maps of the City." *Environment and Planning A: Economy and Space* 28, no. 3 (March 1, 1996): 405–27. https://doi.org/10.1068/a280405.

Pink, Sarah. *Doing Sensory Ethnography*. Newcastle upon Tyne: Sage, 2015.

Pink, Sarah, Phil Hubbard, Maggie O'Neill, and Alan Radley. "Walking across Disciplines: From Ethnography to Arts Practice." *Visual Studies* 25, no. 1 (March 23, 2010): 1–7. https://doi.org/10.1080/1472586100360670.

R

Ramaswamy, Sumathi. *Terrestrial Lessons: The Conquest of the World as Globe*. Chicago: University of Chicago Press, 2017.

Rankin, William. *After the Map: Cartography, Navigation, and the Transformation of Territory in the Twentieth Century*. Chicago: University of Chicago Press, 2016.

Rekacewicz, Philippe. "Frontiers, Migrants and Refugees: Cartographic Studies." *TRIALOG, Borders and Migration* 2, no. 101 (2009): 27–31.

Reyes, Paulina de los, and Markus Lundström. "Researching Otherwise? Autoethnographic Notes on the 2013 Stockholm Riots." *Critical Sociology* 47, no. 7–8 (2021): 1159–70. https://doi.org/10.1177/0896920520978482.

Robinson, Jennifer. "Comparative Urbanism: New Geographies and Cultures of Theorizing the Urban." *International Journal of Urban and Regional Research* 40, no. 1 (January 1, 2016): 187–99. https://doi.org/10.1111/1468-2427.12273.

Rosner, Daniela K. *Critical Fabulations: Reworking the Methods and Margins of Design*. Cambridge, MA: MIT Press, 2018.

Roy, Ananya, and Emma Shaw Crane, eds. *Territories of Poverty: Rethinking North and South*. Athens, GA: University of Georgia Press, 2014.

S

Schneider, Arnd. "Expanded Visions: Rethinking Anthropological Research and Representation through Experimental Film." Chapter 12 in *Redrawing Anthropology: Materials, Movements, Lines*, edited by Tim Ingold, 177–94. London: Routledge, 2016.

Nitin Bathla

Seidl, Roman, Fridolin Simon Brand, Michael Stauffacher, Pius Krütli, Quang Bao Le, Andy Spörri, Grégoire Meylan, Corinne Moser, Monica Berger González, and Roland Werner Scholz. "Science with Society in the Anthropocene." *Ambio* 42 (2013): 5–12.

Shields, Rob. "Fancy Footwork: Walter Benjamin's Notes on Flânerie." Chapter 4 in *The Flâneur*, edited by Keith Tester, 61–80. London: Routledge, 2014.

Silberberger, Jan, ed. *Against and for Method: Revisiting Architectural Design as Research*. Zurich: gta Verlag, 2021. https://doi.org/10.54872/gta/4550.

Stanek, Lukasz, Christian Schmid, and Ákos Moravánszky, eds. "Theory Not Method: Thinking with Lefebvre." Introduction to *Urban Revolution Now: Henri Lefebvre in Social Research and Architecture*. Farnham: Ashgate, 2014.

Stokols, Daniel. "Transdisciplinary Action Research in Landscape Architecture and Planning: Prospects and Challenges." *Landscape Journal: Design, Planning, and Management of the Land* 30, no. 1 (2011): 1–5.

Streule, Monika. "Doing Mobile Ethnography: Grounded, Situated and Comparative." *Urban Studies* 57, no. 2 (2019): 421–38. https://doi.org/10.1177/0042098018817418.

T

Taussig, Michael T. *I Swear I Saw This: Drawings in Fieldwork Notebooks, Namely My Own*. Chicago; London: The University of Chicago Press, 2011.

Tilley, Lisa. "Resisting Piratic Method by Doing Research Otherwise." *Sociology* 51, no. 1 (2017): 27–42.

Tümerdem, Nazlı. "Recording the Landscape: Walking, Transforming, Designing." *A | Z ITU Journal of the Faculty of Architecture* 15, no. 2 (2018): 83–106.

U

Urban Popular Economy Collective (Solomon Benjamin, Alioscia Castronovo, Luci Cavallero, Cristina Cielo, Véronica Gago, Prince Guma, Rupali Gupte, Victoria Habermehl, and Lana Salman). "Urban Popular Economies: Territories of Operation for Lives Deemed Worth Living." *Public Culture* 34, no. 3 (2022): 333–57.

V

van den Brink, Adri, Diedrich Bruns, Hilde Tobi, and Simon Bell. *Research in Landscape Architecture*. London: Routledge, 2016.

Vilenica, Ana, ed. *Radical Housing: Art, Struggle, Care*. Amsterdam: Institute of Network Cultures, 2021.

Viveiros de Castro, Eduardo. "On Models and Examples: Engineers and Bricoleurs in the Anthropocene." *Current Anthropology* 60, no. S20 (2019): S296–308.

IMAGE CREDITS

Figure 1: Maja and Reuben Fowkes
Figure 2: Newrope, ETH Zurich
Figure 3: Bhavyaa Parashar
Figure 4: VG Bild-Kunst, Bonn, 2020, Helmut Aebischer
Figure 5: HBO Documentary Films
Figure 6: Philippe Rekacewicz, visionscarto.net
Figure 7: International Documentary Film Festival Amsterdam (IDFA)

Bathla, Nitin. "A Methodological Pluriverse: An Introduction." In Nitin Bathla, ed., *Researching Otherwise: Pluriversal Methodologies for Landscape and Urban Studies*. Zurich: gta Verlag, 2024, 11–43. https://doi.org/10.54872/gta/4692-0.

Transdisciplinary Methods

Luke Harris, Cara Turett, Bonnie Kate Walker

The Dirt on Drawing: A Method for Relational Thinking

Researching Otherwise
Nitin Bathla, ed.

Drawing as research methodology

From in-depth analyses of urban natures to tracing mushrooms from the forest to the global commodity market, researchers in the humanities and social sciences are increasingly concerned with charting the diverse entanglements and dependencies between human and nonhuman life.[1] Analyzing these relationships necessarily brings different disciplines into conversation, and these sites of contact between disparate ways of knowing produce innovative research methodologies. One such novel methodology is the recent emergence of drawing as a form of research in collaborative projects between scientists, social scientists, and designers.[2]

While these projects demonstrate the unique power of drawings to integrate multiple perspectives and allow for nonlinear interpretations, we believe that this approach has much yet to offer, especially in the use of architectural drawing methods that incorporate scale, materiality, and temporality. Not only does drawing open the possibility for transdisciplinary dialogue, as Nitin Bathla articulates in the introduction to this volume, drawings themselves are operative. They can be critical devices for seeing, imagining, and constructing pluriversal worlds. Though emerging from a different disciplinary tradition, in this way the practice of drawing resembles what Bathla describes as "radical cartography," in that it can actively critique and undermine representations which serve to reproduce dominant power dynamics.[3]

In the interest of furthering this conversation, this article describes a drawing-based research methodology that allows researchers to trace otherwise hidden socio-ecological relations across diverse spatial and temporal scales. Drawing is particularly adapted to landscape research, which must link multiple corresponding timescales, interdependent ecological processes, a robust hierarchy of actors past and present, and constantly changing material conditions. Accordingly, there is a rich lineage of innovative drawing-based research practices in the field of landscape architecture. This work builds on Lawrence and Anna Halprin's movement notations,[4]

1. A brief list of well-known examples includes Tsing, *Mushroom at the End of the World*; Gandy and Jasper, *Botanical City*; Elkin, *Plant Life*.
2. Two examples of this tendency are Tsing, et al., *Feral Atlas*; Arènes, Latour, and Gaillardet, "Giving Depth to the Surface."
3. Nitin Bathla and Sumedha Garg provide a compelling example of how a drawing-based counter cartography can enable those who lack access to dominant forms of representation to lay claims to space. They also note that these "community-authored drawings" are typically missing from standard accounts of drawing in landscape architecture and urbanism. See Bathla and Garg, "Drawing as Counter-Cartography."
4. The drawings of the Halprins provided a framework for diagramming movements through time and space, allowing the complexity of urban and environmental transformations to catalyze design. The DAPL work takes inspiration from the way the Halprins created an abstract drawing language to both analyze and transform spatial conditions. See Hirsch, *City Choreographer*.

or Motations, James Corner's diagrams of ecological succession and experimental maps,[5] Jane Wolff's powerful and idiosyncratic drawings of the Sacramento River Delta,[6] Anu Mathur and Dilip da Cunha's critique of static representations of water,[7] and recent experiments with dynamic diagrams by Brian Osborn and Teresa Galí-Izard.[8] Common to these diverse practices is a conviction that drawings are not just tools for communication that illustrate and provide evidence for predeveloped ideas. Instead, analysis and conceptualization occur through a process of representation that is uniquely spatial and nonlinear.[9] This link between drawing and thinking should be obvious to designers, who understand that each drawing opens certain possibilities and forecloses others.[10]

The methodology for relational drawing described in this article emerges from the field of landscape architecture, which provides the tools, techniques, and analytical frame for the project. Practitioners and researchers must be deeply attuned to relations, as landscapes are composed not only of the constant interaction of living and nonliving entities and the systems that support them but also, inextricably, by social logics such as extraction, settlement, and urbanization.[11] At the messy interface between intentional human constructions and unfolding ecological processes, drawing can trace otherwise hidden relations through time and physical space. Paul Klee describes that drawing "can 'make visible' relations between things that would otherwise remain invisible."[12] Such relations can be hidden because the cause is temporally or spatially distant from the effect, or because the distinction between cause and effect is ambiguous.[13] The relations can also be invisible to the naked eye, rendering traditional forms of documentation such as photography or film difficult.[14] By making them visible, drawing not only reveals those relationships to the viewer but to the drawer herself. The act of determining which relationships are meaningful in a particular context reveals possible pathways for transformation. Each drawing contains a seed of a possible future.

This article describes a methodology for drawing-based research developed through a collective

5   Reed and Lister, "Ecology and Design"; Corner and MacLean, *Taking Measures*.
6   By deftly negotiating spatial and temporal scales, Wolff's drawings highlight the regional transformations and political tensions over water and land. They are a direct inspiration for the relational drawings described below. See Wolff, *Delta Primer*.
7   Mathur and da Cunha, *Soak*.
8   Galí-Izard, *Same Landscapes*; Geffel, Osborn, and Raxworthy, "Viridic Disturbance."
9   The practice of cartography provides a clear example of the potential connection between research and representation. Radical cartographers undermine the supposed objectivity of the map by incorporating situated perspectives and innovative representational techniques. See Nitin Bathla's introduction to this volume. Further examples include Campos-Delgado, "Counter-Mapping Migration," and the work of Philippe Rekacewicz at https://visionscarto.net/_philippe-rekacewicz_.
10 On how a particular relationship between drawing and thinking is linked to the birth of architecture as a discipline, see Brothers, *Michelangelo*.
11 For a discussion of relational materiality, see Krzywoszynska and Marchesi, "Relational Materiality of Soils." For its relevance to landscape research, see Cho, "Permafrost Politics."
12 Paul Klee, quoted in Anderson, *Drawing as a Way of Knowing*, 19.
13 This corresponds to what Rob Nixon describes as "slow violence," where harm is distributed across space and, crucially, time, making it difficult to trace the source of the violent action. Drawing can represent these intentionally obscured relations. See Nixon, *Slow Violence*.
14 See Fischer and Kirkwood, "Seeing the Petrochemical Landscapes."

investigation conducted along the Dakota Access Pipeline (DAPL) in 2017. The DAPL is a 1,886-kilometer underground oil pipeline designed to bring oil from the Bakken Oil Fields in western North Dakota across the Great Plains to a distribution plant in Patoka, Illinois, and ultimately to the Gulf of Mexico. The pipeline is owned by a private company, Energy Transfer Partners, and was under construction between 2016 and 2017. Contested from the start, it continues to face intermittent legal, environmental, and property rights battles in the US court system.[15] The DAPL became internationally known in the fall of 2016 when members of the Standing Rock Sioux Tribe launched a resistance movement to the planned construction of the pipe under the Missouri River and across tribal lands, continuing a long struggle against the settler state.[16] The movement gained international support and attention, drawing thousands of indigenous and non-indigenous supporters to the reservation where protest camps were constructed alongside the path of the pipeline crossing the river.[17]

In the summer of 2017, six months after the camps at Standing Rock had been bulldozed, five of us (the authors plus Batul Abbas and Claire Casstevens), all recent landscape architecture graduates back then, embarked on a research project that sought to explore the DAPL as a politically and ecologically contested landscape. In the process, we traveled across the length of the pipeline for a month. Our research focused on three main zones of study: in North Dakota, where the pipeline began; the site of the Standing Rock protests adjacent to the Standing Rock Indian Reservation; and, last, in northeastern Iowa, which was at the epicenter of opposition to the pipeline by land-owning farmers. This article focuses on the research methodology developed through this investigation. It first discusses field drawings, produced from a direct encounter with a condition, and then introduces the concept of relational drawings, which contain a spatiotemporal structure and emerge from a collaborative process of reflection.

15 See Fortin and Friedman, "Dakota Pipeline."
16 See Gilio-Whitaker, *As Long as Grass Grows.*
17 For more information on the Standing Rock Movement, the DAPL, and its wide-reaching impact on indigenous land rights, climate activism, and public perception of oil and gas infrastructure projects, see Estes, *Our History Is the Future.*

Field drawing: note-taking, morphological thinking and situated speculations

Right after leaving for the oil fields of North Dakota, the van we were driving already started having engine issues. One fieldwork technique that we had decided on in advance was the shared use of 15-by-20-centimeter orange sketchbooks to document our trip. We began by drawing the van. While waiting outside the mechanic in Ohio, we each drew how we thought the engine worked. The engine was metabolically linked to the primary subject of our research: oil extracted from the shale plays of North Dakota and sent through a 3,200-kilometer pipeline across the middle of the US for domestic and international consumption. These drawings of the inner workings of the van highlighted an unresolved tension in our project, which attempts to critique the construction of an oil pipeline while consuming its product. Throughout the time that we were on the road, the van served as a mobile studio, hosting our tools, our bodies, our food, and our shelter. The month-long fieldwork was not only an exercise in field research but also a collective practice of eating, drawing, and living together. Our drawings in the orange notebooks speak to the creation of collective life and work that occurred through the many hours spent in and around our vehicle-cum-studio. In retrospect, it is fitting that all our notebooks began with an expository study of our temporary home.

Reflecting on this intuitive practice of drawing-as-notetaking, we realized that these drawings played three important roles: they created a necessary space to process impressions and observations, encouraged morphological thinking, and supported situated speculations. In our research along the pipeline, we made over one thousand field drawings which formed a composite of things seen, heard, and noticed by us en route. Instead of seeking to capture a whole, each of these field drawings is a partial record of a discovery; the first step in the process of sifting through information to understand what matters.[18] In this way, they are what John Berger calls "working drawings," which he describes as "an autobiographical record of one's discovery of an event—seen, remembered or imagined,"

18 For an excellent reflection on the potential of field drawing relative to other forms of documentation, see Taussig, *I Swear I Saw This*.

→ Figure 1 (a–d)

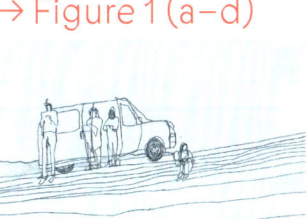

and which are distinguished from a "finished work," which is "an attempt to construct an event in itself."[19] Drawing in the field engenders a process of "continuous selective decision-making over time, and a feedback between the drawer and the drawn."[20] As a result, each of these drawings is an extended mode of attention, attempting to discover "the idea in the observation."[21] They contain the progression of thought over time, allowing it to be accessed later.

A field drawing also allows the drawer to explore her subject through its morphological development. Artist Gemma Anderson describes morphological drawing as a key feature in her practice, and one she recognizes in the work of Paul Klee: "Like Klee, I endeavor to move closer to the dynamic nature of nature through art and find it helpful to think of a plant as an instance or a slice of reality, and rather than represent this slice I aim to represent this slice within a continuum, as 'life represented alive.'"[22]

If we take the geological layer holding the Bakken oil as the slice of reality that Anderson describes, then the formation of 3,000 meters of stone above it by deposition, erosion, the life and death of plants and animals, the movement of mountains, the appearance and disappearance of glaciers and seas, is the continuum in which that slice can be represented. In a project about the extraction and transport of 375-million-year-old petrified organic matter as fossil fuels, the reality of that collapse of timescales lies in the geological section. Drawing a geological section in the field simultaneously "reckons with the reality" of the distance between the surface of the ground and Bakken oil, while speculating about the landscape's morphological development.[23] This is an example of how field sketches can do something that is difficult using other forms of documentation.[24] They can speculate. Guesses, idle musings, and daydreams contain ideas about alternative pasts, presents, and futures. Such speculations are hypothetical and projective yet grounded in the time and place one is observing. As a result, these situated speculations will be different from the ideas that come later, elsewhere.

19 Berger, *Permanent Red*, 24.
20 Anderson, *Drawing as a Way of Knowing*, 18.
21 Johann Wolfgang von Goethe, quoted in Daston and Galison, *Objectivity*, 69.
22 Anderson, *Drawing as a Way of Knowing*, 164.
23 Taussig, *I Swear I Saw This*, 13.
24 See Holmes, "Problem with Solutions."

→ Figure 2 (a–b)

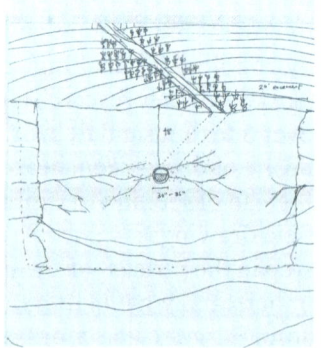

Drawing is a form of recording that can incorporate events that happened in the distant past, unlike, for example, a photograph. In comparing drawing and photography, Berger describes that "a photograph is static because it has stopped time. A drawing or painting is static because it encompasses time."[25] The capacity to encompass time through drawing links the practice with the scope and timescale of landscape subjects, often vast and variable, sometimes contradictory. This is the case with the Bakken shale deposits, which were formed hundreds of millions of years ago and extracted within half a century. This ability to encompass time and think morphologically through drawing is integral to landscape research, which must reckon with the changing nature of subjects and the spaces that they make. Morphological drawing allows the researcher to examine the formation of a landscape across deep time, but she can also analyze the growth of a tree and how it has responded to various environmental cues over its life,[26] or the development of a pattern of settlement. Drawing morphologically encourages the researcher to wonder about the historical formation of what is present at any given moment, opening new lines of investigation.

    These examples illustrate how drawing raises questions about relations, growth, and change occurring beneath surficial appearances. The notebooks that we filled in the field formed the foundation of our ongoing research. But, as the project continued, we realized that each of us drawing separately on 6-by-8-inch pieces of paper limited our ability to collectively synthesize and abstract from the lived experience.

Relational drawings: finding a structure

Our first stop on the research project was a small town in North Dakota called Watford City. Situated within the Bakken Oil Fields, which are the source of the pipeline, the town has been shaped by the fluctuating fate of the local oil industry.[27] After several days in Watford City meeting pipeline workers, agronomists, educators, and activists, our notebooks were

25 Berger, "Drawn to That Moment," 149.
26 See Hallé, Oldeman, and Tomlinson, *Tropical Trees and Forests*.
27 See Becker, "Paradox of Plenty," 14.

> The capacity to encompass time through drawing links the practice with the scope and timescale of landscape subjects, often vast and variable, sometimes contradictory.

overflowing with sketches and notes. We spent the evenings discussing what we had seen and heard, parsing through stories and often-conflicting information. In an effort to sort this material in real time and develop a hierarchy of importance, we drew the people we met on a large roll of paper, as if they were seated together at a long table, with each figure surrounded by the stories they shared. The form of the drawing achieved two main goals. First, it linked the story to the teller, which situated their knowledge. In this way, the drawing held "partial, locatable, critical knowledges sustaining the possibility of webs of connections."[28] Second, it brought each story into relation with other, often contradictory, accounts, attempting to create the "webs of connections" that Donna Haraway describes. We called this preliminary structure the "table drawing," and we continued develop it as we moved along the pipeline, adding people we met and stories that we found relevant or revealing. In this way the long table stood in for the pipeline as the material link connecting disparate people together.[29]

On our way to and from Watford City every day, we drove on the same road, passing drilling rigs with their wells reaching to the layer of oil-impregnated Bakken shale over 4 kilometers below the surface. Through conversations, we came to understand how the territory was shaped by cycles of boom and bust, driven by the global price of oil. When oil prices were high or new advancements were made in extraction technology, such as the introduction of horizontal drilling or hydraulic fracking, workers came from across the US, attracted by the promise of high wages. In boom times, they were met by housing shortages, often paying rents that were higher than in New York City to live in so-called man-camps, temporary neighborhoods of trailer homes occupied by men working in the oil fields.[30] These temporal cycles of boom and bust and the spatial scale of the oil extraction emphasized that the "site" we were investigating extended far beyond the political boundaries of the town.[31]

These complex relationships did not fit in the field drawings or the table drawing. To further our analysis of the condition, we had to find a different way of

28 Haraway, "Situated Knowledges," 584.
29 For additional discussion of the fieldwork and drawing method of the table drawing, see Office of Living Things, "Reciprocity."
30 Barkdull, Weber, and Geigle, "Extractive Industries," 200.
31 Jane Hutton has developed an expanded understanding of site through her research on material connections between spatially disparate landscapes in Hutton, *Reciprocal Landscapes*.

→ Figure 3

drawing. To this end, we developed a drawing method with a spatial and temporal structure that allowed us to think about relationships at multiple scales. We manipulated and reinterpreted the standard architectural drawing types: plan, section, and axonometric. Traditionally, landscape architects make use of representational techniques developed in the field of architecture, which confidently show the built elements at a certain scale and a single moment in time.[32] This inheritance generates a productive tension, where the standard drawing conventions are descriptive of spatial realities, such as scale and materials, but are never enough to capture the emergent elements, the links beyond the scale of the site, and the growth of the living elements over time.

In our fieldwork, it became clear that typical architectural drawings were unable to represent relationships that were necessary to understand this condition. We had to construct another structure for drawing that allowed these relationships to emerge. Berger writes that a drawing can create a "space" where disappearance is countered by assemblage.[33] By playing with the temporal and spatial frame of the drawing, we consciously developed the structure of this "space" in order to bring elements into relation. To distinguish these drawings from the field drawings described above, we began to call them "relational drawings" in reference to the complex interactions of living and nonliving entities that are emphasized in each of them.

Using a rigorous yet experimental drawing method, we attempted to make drawings that approximated the complexities and interdependencies of a site by defining relevant relationships and giving a structure to their intermingling. Structure in a drawing is the establishment of a set of rules of analysis, which allow the drawers to create hierarchies of information and depict relationships between elements. Landscape subjects are mutually influential, and drawing can explore those reciprocal influences. Teasing out the relationships that matter is a necessary task for those who hope to work with the complexity and autonomy of landscapes, because, as anthropologist Anna Tsing writes, "relationships are potential vectors of transformation."[34]

[32] See Davis and Oles, "From Architecture to Landscape."
[33] Berger, "Drawn to That Moment," 150.
[34] Tsing, "On Nonscalability," 507.

Defining a structure is necessarily a different kind of work than the field drawing discussed above. It supports another way of thinking. As Anderson writes, "drawing enables the development of abstract thinking and allows previously unperceived relations between objects to be discovered."[35] The drawing of Watford City was made collectively by five people after long conversations processing our experiences. We started the drawing by hand at our campsite at night and finished it on computers half a year later. It is thus synthetic and collective, bringing together fragments of our fieldwork and research into a coherent structure, but steadfastly resisting a comprehensive view. We attempt to link our subjective experience with processes unfolding across larger temporal and spatial scales, generating a tension between what can be found through "being there" and what is visible only at a distance.

Above ground, the drawing shows the road on which we drove to and from town, the pattern of urbanization driven by oil extraction, the changing weather, and the oil rigs themselves.[36] At one of the rigs, a section shows an oil well descending through the geological strata to the layers of Bakken shale. Here the scale shifts to bring the short boom-and-bust cycles of Watford City's economy in relation with the extended geologic time of the oil on which the whole territory rests. The section is populated by drawings of creatures that were once alive but whose bones now make up the geological strata upon which the surface rests, troubling the geontological boundary of life and nonlife which fuels the ongoing extraction.[37]

We continued to develop this method further and produced two more relational drawings as part of the research project, each trying to understand a certain situation along the pipeline. One of these addressed the site of the major protests against the DAPL at the edge of the Standing Rock Sioux Reservation. Here, where the Cannonball River meets the Missouri River, members of the Standing Rock Sioux Tribe established three camps—the Sacred Stone, Oceti Sakowin, and Rosebud—to protest the pipeline's construction through their territory. When we arrived

35 Anderson, *Drawing as a Way of Knowing*, 64
36 This settlement pattern can be seen as a form of "fossil urbanism," as described in Bathla, "Urban Autopia."
37 See Povinelli, *Geontologies*.

→ Figure 4

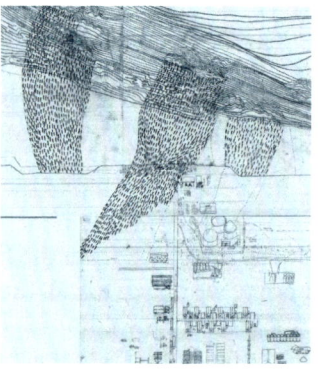

in June 2017, the camps had been dismantled through waves of conflict between the water protectors who organized to halt the pipeline and North Dakota state police and military forces. Walking through the site, we found the traces of the resistance movement that were brought back to life through interviews and conversations. In recounting her experience as a founding member of Sacred Stone, the first camp of the movement, Ladonna Bravebull Allard discussed the erasure of indigenous footprints by the bulldozing of a sacred Arikara site by Tiger Swan, a private security contractor hired by the entity constructing the pipeline, Energy Transfer Partners.[38] We went to Standing Rock to find and draw the footprints of the movement.

We organized the relational drawing of this condition into three circular plans and corresponding sections at three scales. The central circle, at a scale of 1:2, shows in plan the ground as we found it in 2017, shortly after the snow that had blanketed the ground during the protests the previous fall hand melted. The ground revealed traces of the encampments: tent stakes, scissors, a pocketknife, ropes, canned food lids, footprints, and animal tracks. The section shows details of *Achillea millefolium, Cornus sericea,* and *Artemisia cana,* all plants described as culturally important in the ethnobotanical garden of Sitting Bull College, a tribal college near the protest site.

The next scale, 1:120, cuts a section around the Sacred Stone Camp, the site of the beginning of the protest. In plan, this portion of the drawing shows a detailed aerial of the camps, drawn from drone footage held by the Sitting Bull College Library.[39] When speaking with people about the camp, the events of the protest movement were often entangled with past struggles, such as resistance to the construction of the Oahe Dam, as well as with fears and hopes for the future. The drawing needed a language to hold these distinct but intimately linked events. The section surrounding the middle circle uses shades of gray to communicate different moments in time (the construction of the camp and its facilities, their operation and their demolition) as narrated to us by a Standing Rock Sioux Tribe member.[40] The section also includes

38 Estes, "They Took Our Footprint," 44.
39 Sitting Bull College, Cannonball, North Dakota, USA, https://www.sittingbull.edu/about/community/library/ (accessed Dec. 21, 2023).
40 In a personal conversation with Standing Rock Sioux Tribe member and Sacred Stone Camp resident who introduced himself as "Uncle Buck." We are extremely grateful to Uncle Buck for his generosity and creativity in describing the spatial details of the camp on site, which was critical to the production of these drawings. His first-person accounts allowed us to time-travel on the site, creating the potential for that possibility in our drawings.

→ Figure 5

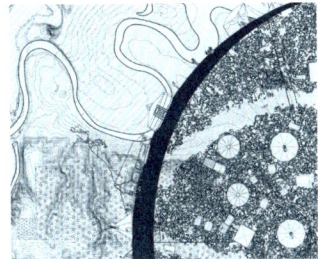

our visit six months after the demolition of the camps, as well as visions of the future shared with us by people we interviewed, such as the monitoring of the water of the Missouri River to test for oil spills; the harnessing of wind power; the continuation of the Standing Rock Movement; and, far into the future, the seventh generation—here, recalling a conversation we had, represented as an astronaut—looking back.[41]

The largest circle, drawn at 1:6000, shows the protest camps and the pipeline in the context of the contemporary Sioux land, including not only the current reservation but parts of the territory granted to the Sioux in the 1851 and 1868 treaties of Fort Laramie, both of which the US government broke.[42] It also depicts the flooding of the Missouri River in 1962 after the construction of the Oahe Dam, which inundated the majority of the Sioux's fertile agricultural land and many sacred sites.[43] By drawing the meandering, flexible contours of the Cannonball-River, it became clear that this landscape was once dominated by intermittent flooding, with the land used collectively for agriculture in floodplain soils. By contrast, the much wider, rectified edge of present-day Lake Oahe represents a different political-ecological organization. The pipeline, built across the Missouri River and shown in the upper part of the drawing, echoed this conflict between energy infrastructure and the fluvial landscape. In this saturated floodplain of alluvial soils, an oil spill would distribute quickly and widely, with effects felt throughout the Standing Rock Reservation and the entire Mississippi River floodplain.[44] Last, this scale also documents the process of fractionation, a legacy of settler governance in the landscape where property held by tribal members is divided into successively smaller pieces with each generation, rendering it economically unproductive.[45]

After we returned from our trip, we began sorting through our field notes to compose a relational drawing of Standing Rock. In the assorted ephemera and documents we brought home, there was a map of the stars with a circular cross section around the edge. Using this drawing as inspiration, we developed the

[41] The discussion of the long-term future as existing in continuum with the past and present was a common thread in our conversations in the Standing Rock Sioux Reservation. Nick Estes discusses this idea, which reappears in the title of his book: "Settler narratives use a linear conception of time to distance themselves from the horrific crimes committed against Indigenous peoples and the land. ... But Indigenous notions of time consider the present to be structured entirely by our past and by our ancestors. There is no separation between past and present, meaning that an alternative future is also determined by our understanding of our past. Our history is the future." Estes, *Our History Is the Future*, 24.

[42] Ells, "Centering Sovereignty," 182.

[43] Ostler and Estes, "Supreme Law of the Land."

[44] For documentation of leaks along the pipeline and their effects, see Brown, "Five Spills, Six Months in Operation."

[45] See Bagley and Whyte, "At Standing Rock."

multi-scaled series of circular sections and plans, hypothesizing that this structure could explore and bring together many of the experiences of our fieldwork, each at the scale and drawing method most appropriate to them. Each of these embedded scales tells a story that is integral to understanding the landscape of Standing Rock and the DAPL more broadly. But the drawing was not primarily made to "tell a story"; it was made to discover it. A drawing can hold contradictions without needing to resolve them. In this way it can resist linear narratives, allowing for unanticipated readings and discoveries. With this structure in place, we were able to represent relationships between seemingly unrelated events. For example, the 1962 flooding of the Missouri River by the US Army Corps of Engineers was an important backdrop for Energy Transfer Partners' later use of an eminent domain clause to construct the pipeline. These two acts of federal governmental authority were deeply connected in the minds of the Standing Rock Sioux members with whom we spoke. Both the dam and the pipeline were built without consent of the Tribal Council, and both caused direct harm to the tribe. They were both acts with devastating consequences for the ecosystem of the Missouri River and its watershed, both of principal importance in the tribe's worldview. During the protests in 2016, the phrase *"Mni Wiconi,"* meaning "Water is Life," became a rallying cry worldwide.

> Each of these embedded scales tells a story that is integral to understanding the landscape of Standing Rock and the DAPL more broadly. But the drawing was not primarily made to "tell a story"; it was made to discover it.

Where does drawing lead?

These kinds of drawings encourage thinking to follow certain pathways: pathways that have the potential to be spatial and precise. Like a radio dial, they attune attention to a certain frequency, picking up faint signals and latent potentials, raising questions that could otherwise be ignored. The drawing creates a space that allows thinking to unfold rather than fixing a thought. Designers often work with layers of trace paper atop previous drawings, and in this way a drawing produced as part of a research project can become the "base" for future thinking. This can be literal, in the sense that anyone can draw over it, or it can be conceptual, where the drawing stimulates lines of thought that lead to future change. Building on an existing drawing is a projective action. The potential that is latent in all drawing invites others into the process of imagining and conceiving of possible futures. In this way, the processes set in motion through the making of a drawing do not stop with the drawing's completion. For Berger, "drawing is discovery. … A line, an area of tone, is not really important because it records what you have seen, but because of what it will lead you on to see."[46] The drawer is changed by the act of drawing, but additionally the drawing itself as an independent object also continues to evolve through encounter. In this way, a drawing can continue to accumulate "dirt" as it is made and remade through ongoing engagement with people and place.

As a sustained way of looking, the field drawing practice we described encourages researchers to engage with material conditions and their histories. If one has the goal of producing a relational drawing of a given situation after the fact, then the researcher must attend to spatial relationships while in the field. The relational drawings, with a structure and distance, support a mode of research that moves beyond Cartesian logics of cause and effect, instead representing mutually influential connections, which are especially important for socio-ecological investigations.[47] These drawings provide a way of analyzing situations that cross spatial and temporal scales, where the crucial connections are hidden and the boundaries between objects are blurry and contested.

46 Berger, Permanent Red, 23.
47 See Harvey, *Justice*, 54.

ACKNOWLEDGEMENTS

The research team consisted of Batul Abbas, Claire Casstevens, Luke Harris, Cara Turett, and Bonnie Kate Walker, and all the drawings are collectively produced. This article was written by three of the team members, but many of the ideas and methods described were developed as a group during the fieldwork and exhibition of the project. Our ongoing collaboration continues through our landscape research and design collective, Office of Living Things. The research project was generously funded by the Benjamin C. Howland Fellowship from the University of Virginia School of Architecture. We would like to thank the many people who generously shared their time and stories with us as part of this research project. We are also indebted to Nitin Bathla, Jan Silberberger as peer reviewer, and Thomas Skelton-Robertson and Jennifer Bartmess at gta Verlag for their insightful comments.

Figure 1 (a–b)   Van sketches: Field drawings enabled quick visual notetaking. This selection is focused on the van that was our transportation and mobile studio. Each drawing is 15×20 cm.

The Dirt on Drawing

Figure 1 (c–d) Van sketches: Field drawings enabled quick visual notetaking. This selection is focused on the van that was our transportation and mobile studio. Each drawing is 15×20 cm.

Figure 2 (a–b)   Geology sketches: By using the same pens and notebooks, the five drawers generated a diversity of comparable interpretations of the same conditions. These drawings focus on the geological condition driving oil extraction in North Dakota.

The Dirt on Drawing

Harris, Turett, Walker

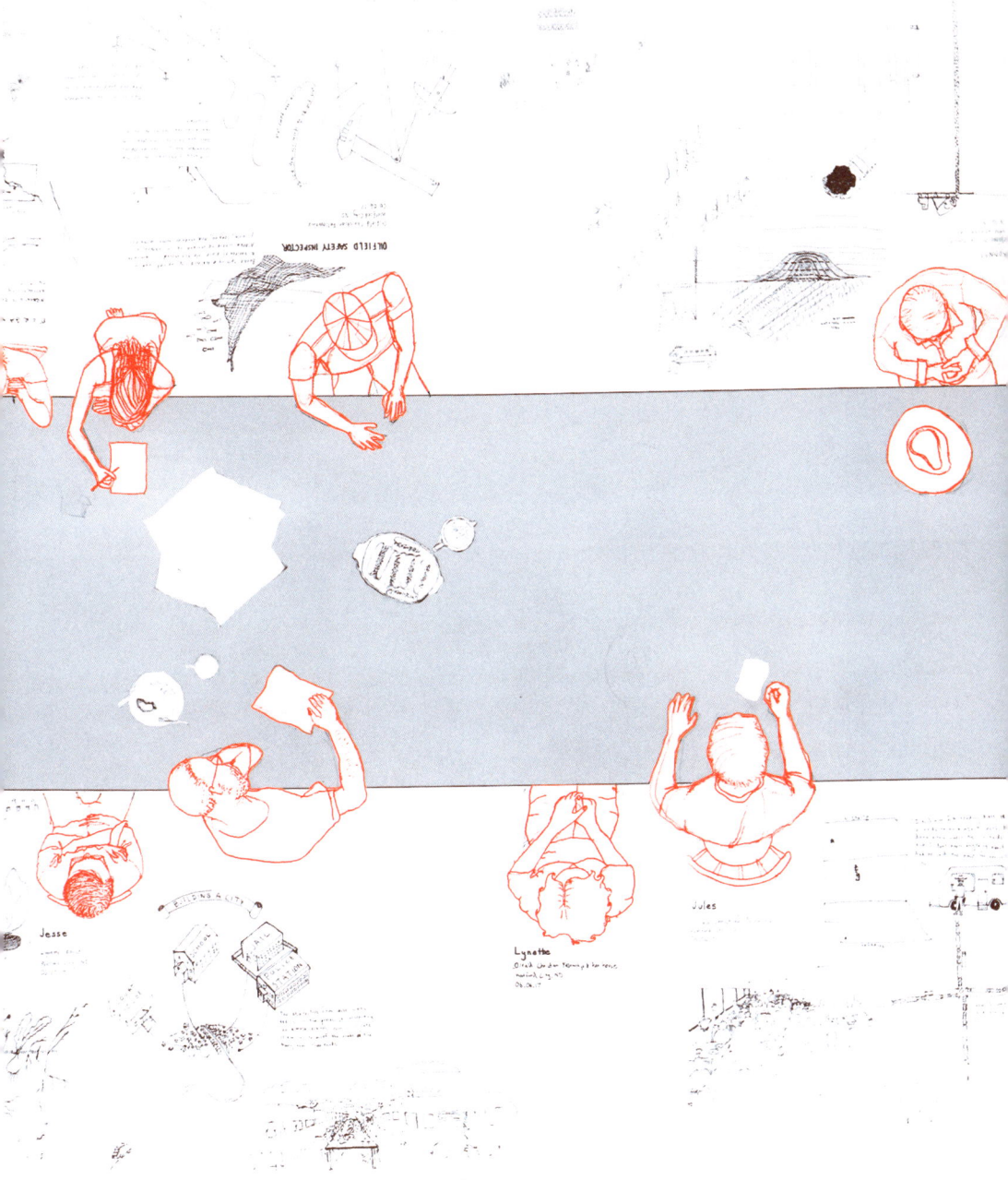

Figure 3 Table drawing: made collectively in the field to keep track of information. Each story was linked to the teller, resulting in a long table hosting the key informants from our fieldwork. 210 × 90 cm

The Dirt on Drawing

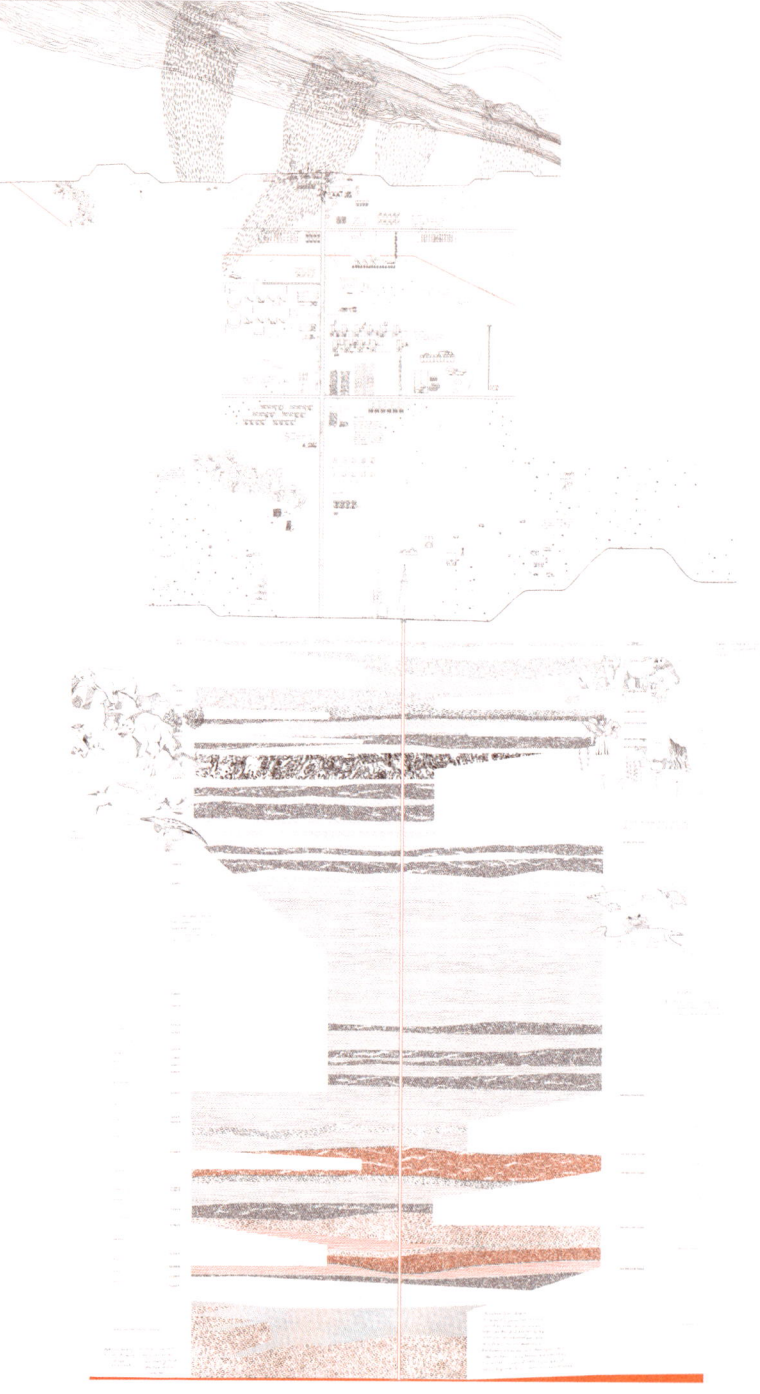

Figure 4   Watford City drawing: A relational drawing cataloguing the extractive landscape around Watford City, North Dakota, at the origin of the Dakota Access Pipeline. 115×190 cm

Figure 4 (detail) Watford City drawing: Detail showing the urban fabric of Watford City situated in the broader landscape of oil production. The drawing combines elements completed by hand in the field with digital linework added later.

The Dirt on Drawing

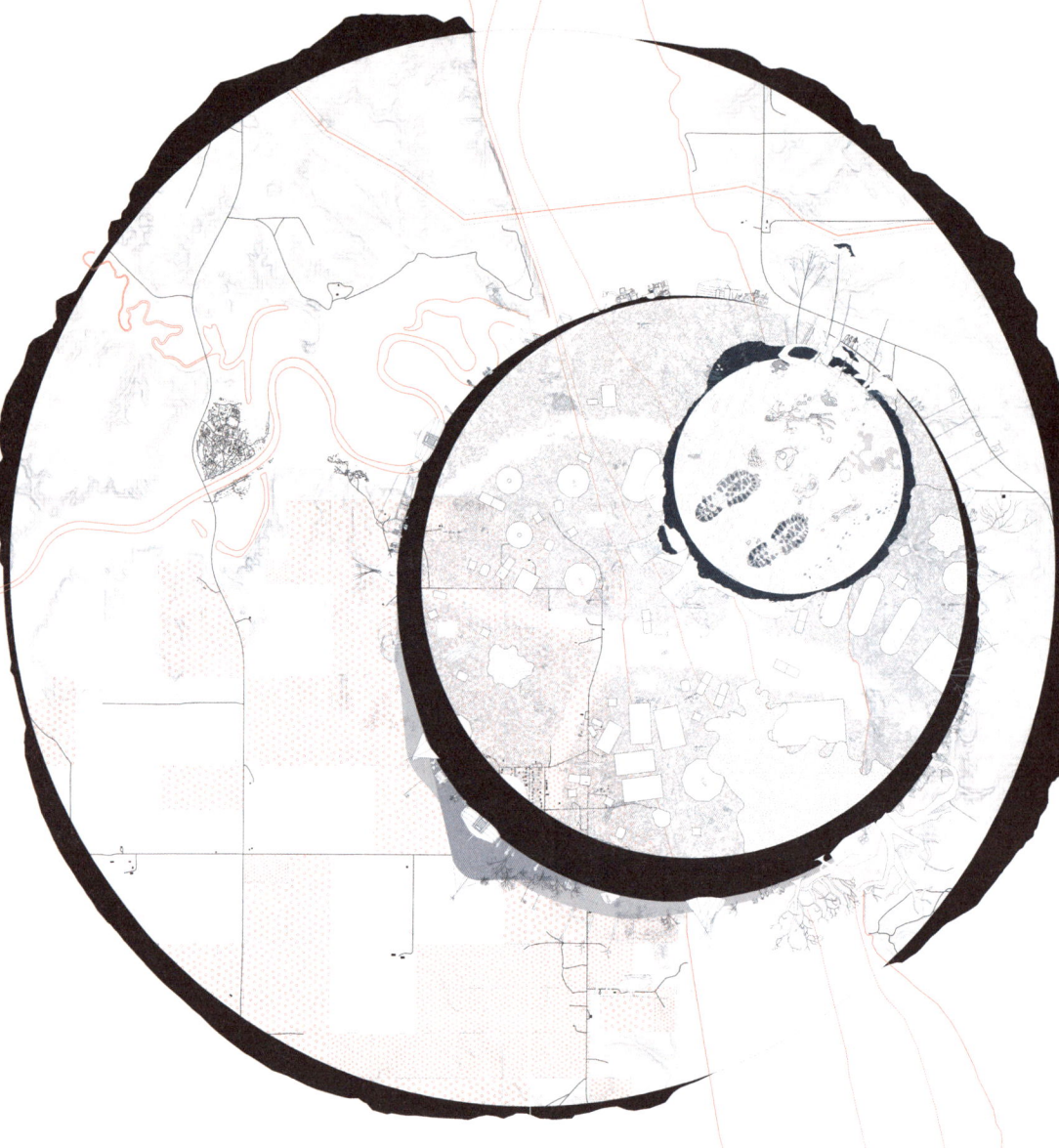

Figure 5 Standing Rock drawing: The drawing depicts our visit to the Sacred Stone camp in June 2017 in relation to broader geographies of extraction and displacement. 180×180 cm

Harris, Turett, Walker

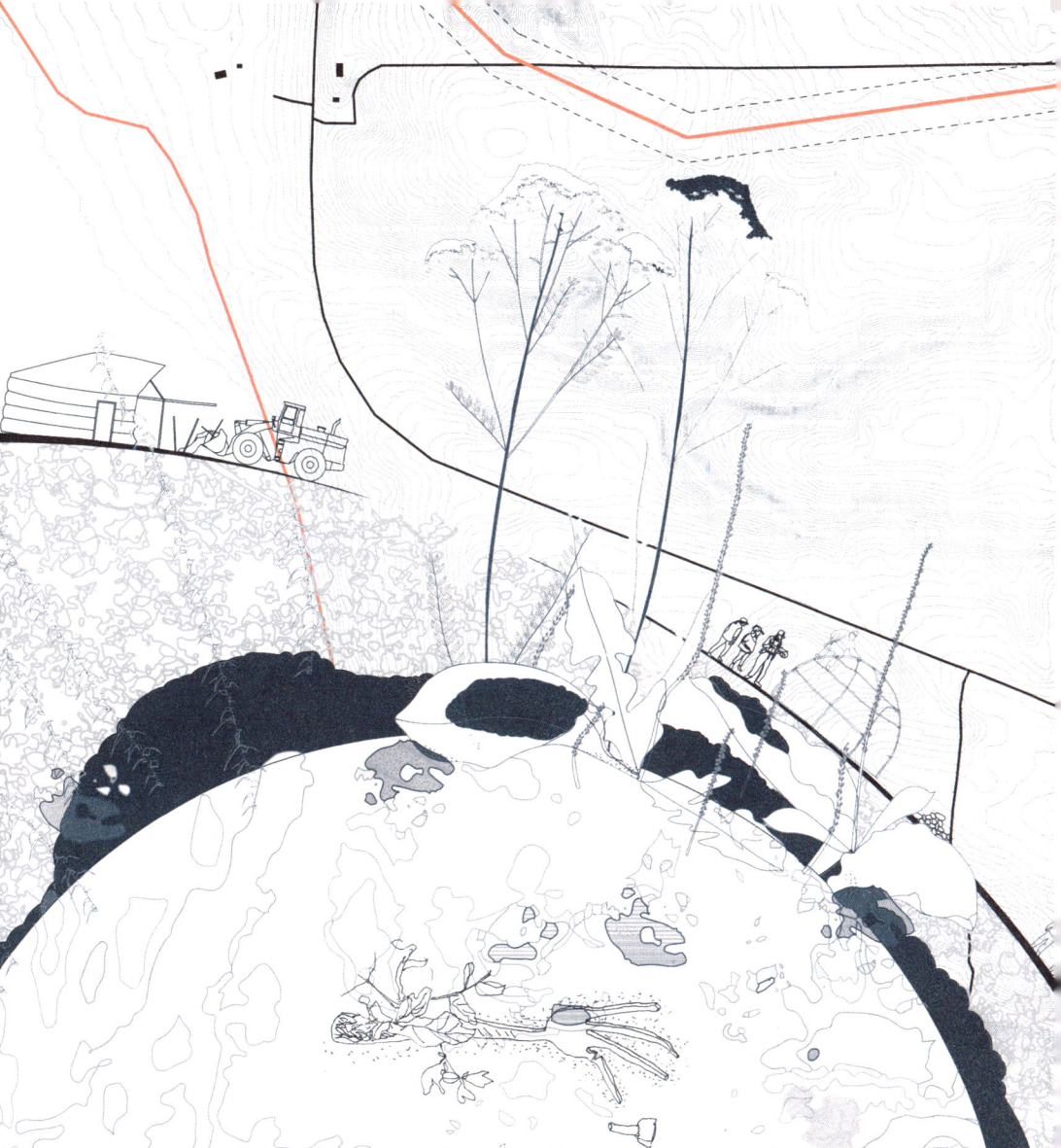

Figure 5 (detail) Standing Rock drawing: Detail showing the ground with the material residue of the Sacred Stone camp one year after the protest, a section showing the camp's demolition, and the path of the pipeline and the Missouri River near their intersection.

The Dirt on Drawing

BIBLIOGRAPHY

A

Anderson, Gemma. *Drawing as a Way of Knowing in Art and Science*. Bristol: Intellect Ltd., 2019.

Arènes, Alexandra, Bruno Latour, and Jérôme Gaillardet. "Giving Depth to the Surface: An Exercise in the Gaia-Graphy of Critical Zones." *The Anthropocene Review* 5, no. 2 (August 2018): 120–35. https://doi.org/10.1177/2053019618782257.

B

Bagley, Katherine, and Kyle Powys Whyte. "At Standing Rock, A Battle Over Fossil Fuels and Land." *Yale E360*, November 10, 2016. https://e360.yale.edu/features/at_standing_rock_battle_over_fossil_fuels_and_land (accessed March 22, 2023).

Barkdull, Carenlee, Bret A. Weber, and Julia C. Geigle. "Extractive Industries and Temporary Housing Policies: Man Camps in North Dakota's Oil Patch." In *The Bakken Goes Boom: Oil and the Changing Geographies of Western North Dakota*, edited by William Caraher and Kyle Conway, 199–224. Grand Forks: Digital Press @ The University of North Dakota, 2016.

Bathla, Nitin, "Urban Autopia: The Architecture of Car-Oriented Capitalism." *Architectural Review* 1495: Energy (October 2022): 84–88.

Bathla, Nitin, and Sumedha Garg. "Drawing as Counter-Cartography: Reflections on a Socially-Engaged Art Project." OASE 107: *The Drawing in Landscape Design and Urbanism* (December 2020): 49–62.

Becker, Karin L. "The Paradox of Plenty: Blessings and Curses in the Oil Patch." In *The Bakken Goes Boom: Oil and the Changing Geographies of Western North Dakota*, edited by William Caraher and Kyle Conway, 11–30. Grand Forks: Digital Press @ The University of North Dakota, 2016.

Berger, John. *Permanent Red: Essays in Seeing*. London: Methuen, 1960.

Berger, John. "Drawn to That Moment." In *The White Bird: Writings by John Berger*, edited by Lloyd Spencer, 146–151. London: Chatto & Windus, 1985.

Brothers, Cammy. *Michelangelo, Drawing, and the Invention of Architecture*. New Haven: Yale University Press, 2008.

Brown, Alleen, "Five Spills, Six Months in Operation: Dakota Access Track Record Highlights Unavoidable Reality — Pipelines Leak." *The Intercept*, January 9, 2018. https://theintercept.com/2018/01/09/dakota-access-pipeline-leak-energy-transfer-partners/.

C

Campos-Delgado, Amalia. "Counter-Mapping Migration: Irregular Migrants' Stories through Cognitive Mapping." *Mobilities* 13, no. 4 (2018): 488–504. https://doi.org/10.1080/17450101.2017.1421022.

Cho, Leena. "Permafrost Politics: Toward a Relational Materiality and Design of Arctic Ground." *Landscape Research* 46, no. 1 (2021): 25–35.

D

Daston, Lorraine, and Peter Galison. *Objectivity*. New York: Zone Books, 2010.

Davis, Brian, and Thomas Oles. "From Architecture to Landscape: The Case for a New Landscape Science" *Places Journal* (October 2014), online. https://doi.org/10.22269/141013.

E

Elkin, Rosetta S., *Plant Life: The Entangled Politics of Afforestation*. Minneapolis: University of Minnesota Press, 2022.

Ellis, Elizabeth. "Centering Sovereignty: How Standing Rock Changed the Conversation." In *Standing with Standing Rock: Voices from the #NoDAPL Movement*, edited by Nick Estes and Jaskiran Dhillon, 172–97. Minneapolis: University of Minnesota Press, 2019.

Estes, Nick. *Our History Is the Future: Standing Rock Versus the Dakota Access Pipeline, and the Long Tradition of Indigenous Resistance*. London and New York: Verso, 2019.

Estes, Nick. "'They Took Our Footprint Out of the Ground': An Interview with LaDonna Brave Bull Allard." In *Standing with Standing Rock: Voices from the #NoDAPL Movement*, edited by Nick Estes and Jaskiran Dhillon, 43–55. Minneapolis: University of Minnesota Press, 2019.

F

Fischer, D. L., and Meghan L. E. Kirkwood. "Seeing the Petrochemical Landscapes of the Bakken." Landscape Journal 41, no. 1 (May 2022): 61–76. https://doi.org/10.3368/lj.41.1.61.

Fortin, Jaycey, and Lisa Friedman. "Dakota Pipeline Is Ordered Shut Down During Environmental Reviews." *New York Times*, July 7, 2020, Section B, 5.

G

Galí-Izard, Teresa. *The Same Landscapes: Ideas and Interpretations*. Barcelona: Editorial Gustavo Gili, 2005.

Gandy, Matthew, and Sandra Jasper, eds. *The Botanical City*. Berlin: JOVIS, 2020.

Geffel, Michael, Brian Osborn, and Julian Raxworthy. "Viridic Disturbance: Reprogramming the Tools of Landscape Maintenance." *LA+ Interdisciplinary Journal of Landscape Architecture* 15: Green (Spring 2022): 46–51.

Gilio-Whitaker, Dina. *As Long as Grass Grows: The Indigenous Fight for Environmental Justice, from Colonization to Standing Rock*. Boston: Beacon Press, 2020.

H

Hallé, Francis, Roelof A. A. Oldeman, and P. B. Tomlinson. *Tropical Trees and Forests: An Architectural Analysis.* New York: Springer-Verlag, 1978.

Haraway, Donna. "Situated Knowledges: The Science Question in Feminism and the Privilege of Partial Perspective." *Feminist Studies* 14, 3 (Autumn 1988), 575–99.

Harvey, David. *Justice, Nature and the Geography of Difference.* Cambridge, MA: Blackwell, 1996.

Hirsch, Alison Bick. *City Choreographer: Lawrence Halprin in Urban Renewal America.* Minneapolis: University of Minnesota Press, 2014.

Holmes, Rob. "The Problem with Solutions." *Places Journal* (July 2020), online. https://doi.org/10.22269/200714.

Hutton, Jane. *Reciprocal Landscapes: Stories of Material Movements.* New York: Routledge, 2019.

K

Krzywoszynska, Anna, and Greta Marchesi. "Toward a Relational Materiality of Soils." *Environmental Humanities* 12, 1 (May 2020): 190–204.

M

Mathur, Anuradha, and Dilip da Cunha. *Soak: Mumbai in an Estuary.* New Delhi: Rupa & Co, 2009.

N

Nixon, Rob. *Slow Violence and the Environmentalism of the Poor.* Cambridge, MA: Harvard University Press, 2011.

O

Office of Living Things. "Reciprocity." *LUNCH* 14 (Fall 2020): 167–76.

Ostler, Jeffrey, and Nick Estes. "The Supreme Law of the Land: Standing Rock and the Dakota Access Pipeline." In *Standing with Standing Rock: Voices from the #NoDAPL Movement*, edited by Nick Estes and Jaskiran Dhillon, 96–100. Minneapolis: University of Minnesota Press, 2019.

P

Povinelli, Elizabeth A. *Geontologies: A Requiem to Late Liberalism.* Durham, NC: Duke University Press, 2016.

R

Reed, Chris, and Nina-Marie Lister. "Ecology and Design: Parallel Genealogies." *Places Journal* (April 2014), online. https://doi.org/10.22269/140414.

T

Taussig, Michael. *I Swear I Saw This: Drawings in Field work Notebooks, Namely My Own.* Chicago: University of Chicago Press, 2011.

Tsing, Anna Lowenhaupt. *The Mushroom at the End of the World: On the Possibility of Life in Capitalist Ruins.* Princeton, NJ: Princeton University Press, 2015.

Tsing, Anna Lowenhaupt. "On Nonscalability: The Living World Is Not Amenable to Precision-Nested Scales." *Common Knowledge* 18, 3 (Fall 2012): 505–24. https://doi.org/10.1215/0961754X-1630424.

Tsing, Anna Lowenhaupt, Jennifer Deger, Alder Keleman Saxena, and Feifei Zhou. *Feral Atlas: The More-Than-Human Anthropocene.* Stanford: Stanford University Press, 2020.

W

Wolff, Jane. *Delta Primer: A Field Guide to the California Delta.* San Francisco: William K Stout, 2003.

IMAGE CREDITS

Figures 1–5: Batul Abbas, Claire Casstevens, Luke Harris, Cara Turett, and Bonnie Kate Walker

Andreea-Florentina Midvighi

Recovering Evidence of Existence through Collaborative Visual Ethnography

Researching Otherwise
Nitin Bathla, ed.

Although large numbers of people are being displaced around the world due to the destruction of their homes, there is always something that outlives such attempted erasures of the built environment. Refugee camps are usually meant to be temporary settings for people and infrastructure but often end up accommodating multiple generations of families. Once those camps are destroyed or closed, how can we uncover those decades of existence when there is almost no official archival material to root them in history? In such contexts, research can only draw on methodologies that help uncover ways in which such stories continue to exist in the imaginaries and practices of the ones that survived them.

A growing body of writings reflect on the necessity of employing decolonial, embodied, and relational methodologies and the importance of researching otherwise.[1] Refugees' imaginaries are also receiving increased attention, as are innovative conceptualizations of what constitutes heritage.[2] Asserting that colonial relations survived juridical and administrative decolonization, the decolonial approach emphasizes their ongoing role "in processes of political intervention, economic exploitation and epistemological patronage exercised by the West on the Rest."[3] In unpacking such power relations, it also empowers occluded indigenous knowledges subjected to epistemicide and memoricide.[4] In the case of (double) refugees,[5] such an approach reveals the forces at play that produce them and the knowledge that enables such production to "inspire and inform alternative political subjectivities and collective political visions of another world beyond colonialism, imperialism, interventionism, war, capitalist expansion and environmental degradation."[6]

In my work, I apply a collaborative visual ethnography together with Palestinian double refugees from the Yarmouk refugee camp in Syria by looking at forms of transnational heritage and cultural resistance as a counter-archive. The destruction of the unofficial refugee camp of Yarmouk left the refugees who had lived there as producers of knowledge. Reflections on visual ethnography and a forthcoming collaborative film serve to advocate for a decolonial epistemology of camps.

1. See, for instance, Smith, *Decolonizing Methodologies;* Choi, Selmeczi, and Strausz, *Critical Methods;* Thanem and Knights, *Embodied Research Methods;* Boatcă, "Counter-Mapping as Method."
2. See Cox, Durrant, Farrier, and Woolley, *Refugee Imaginaries;* Sharp and Panetta, *Beyond the Square,* 121; Hilal and Petti, *Photographic Documentation.*
3. Boatcă, *Global Inequalities,* 116.
4. See, for instance, Santos, *Epistemologies of the South;* Hawari, "Erasing Memories of Palestine."
5. Double refugees are people (and their descendants) who have been displaced multiple times. The Palestinian double refugees discussed in this paper were often first displaced during the founding of the state of Israel in 1948 and subsequently during various conflicts in the Middle East. See Fraihat, "What About the Palestinian Double Refugees?"
6. Arat-Koç, "Decolonizing Refugee Studies," 373.

Andreea-Florentina Midvighi

Yarmouk and its destruction

Yarmouk was established in 1957 as an unofficial refugee camp located on a site some 8 kilometers south of Damascus to house Palestinians displaced as a result of the Israeli settler-colonial occupation and the 1948 *Nakba*.[7] It became the largest Palestinian refugee camp, a major commercial center well connected to Damascus's infrastructure and was colloquially referred to as "the capital of the Palestinian diaspora." In addition to about 150,000 Palestinian refugees, around 300,000 Syrians also inhabited the camp before the Syrian revolution, while in 2012 the number of people doubled.[8]

At the beginning of the Syrian revolution Yarmouk's geographical position placed it between the regime's army in Damascus and the rebel forces in the south of the city targeted by the regime. Inhabitants of the camp helped surrounding areas with the provision of food, fuel, and medicine. Although it initially tried to maintain a neutral position, Yarmouk soon became militarized and was drawn into the fighting.[9] A series of massacres and attacks starting in July 2012 were followed by airstrikes which prompted the exodus of the vast majority of the camp's inhabitants.[10]

The concept of "urbicide,"[11] indicating the deliberate destruction of the built environment in an instrumental attempt to create "homogenous, exclusionary political programs,"[12] strongly applies to Yarmouk. Between July 2013 and May 2018, Yarmouk was under a nearly continuous siege, which "had the harshest impact, and has caused the largest number of deaths from starvation."[13] As a result of intense bombing, about 80 percent of its buildings now are destroyed. Out of about formerly one million residents, only around 4,000 who cannot afford to live anywhere else are now still there.[14] The camp has no infrastructure, and of the houses still standing many have no windows or doors.

In the context of the Damascus area, Andy Bernard-Moulin emphasizes the weaponization of urbicide in modern urban warfare and further elaborates on the role played by urban planning.[15] Entire neighborhoods suffered large-scale demolitions with the double aim of eliminating communities resisting the

7 "Catastrophe" in Arabic, the term refers to the massacres and expulsion of about 900,000 Palestinians during the establishment of the state of Israel.
8 Salameh, "Unacknowledged Syrians," 50–51.
9 For an account of Yarmouk's involvement in the Syrian revolution, see Salameh, "Unacknowledged Syrians"; Gabiam, *Politics of Suffering*, 160–61.
10 See AlSahli's (former member of Reaction) short 2013 movie *MiG* for a poetic illustration of its impact during the events.
11 The term "urbicide" was coined by Michael Moorcock in "Dead God's Homecoming." The concept became popular in connection to the massacres committed against the Bosnian Muslims during the war in former Yugoslavia between 1992 and 1995 and is now a key concept in Middle Eastern Studies. "In no other region of the world," writes Bruce Stanley, "have more cities experienced urbicide over the past half century than in the Middle East." Stanley, "City-Logic of Resistance," 12.
12 Coward, *Urbicide*, xiii.
13 Gabiam, Politics of Suffering, 171.
14 UNRWA, "Yarmouk (Unofficial camp*)."
15 Bernard-Moulin, "Urbicide in Syria."

regime while bringing economic gains. For decades, the camp had been a center of resistance to ongoing settler-colonialism in Palestine, which also served the regime's political interests. When it could not be controlled anymore, however, it was razed to the ground. The end goal of the regime's urbicidal practices was "to transform the whole society, sociologically and physically speaking."[16]

Analyses of prior urban planning in Syria[17] have revealed the ways in which the war benefited previous plans by the Al-Assad regime to capitalize on urban destruction and homogenize Syria for political purposes, causing radical demographic changes and vast displacements as a result.[18] Although such legal instruments were officially described within a framework of "social justice" or development,[19] studies have shown a logic of particularly targeting spaces of resistance occupied by different religious or ethnic groups instead of the ruling elite.[20] Nurhan Abujidi's account of urbicide in Palestine as *"the assault on urbanity that attempts to destroy shared spatiality as a political and social body and as a place of identity"*[21] also pertains to Yarmouk. Particularly in the context of Syria, Sawsan Abou Zainedin and Hani Fakhani argue that "urban arrangements in the conflict have been manipulated by the regime to enforce political homogeneity that would further consolidate the regime's power in the post-conflict phase."[22]

Urbicide has also enabled the materialization of urban planning projects that capitalize on foreign investments. In the case of Yarmouk, the camp's outskirts would be drawn into the Basilia City project, which is intended to cover 900 hectares and has already drawn massive international investments.[23] Laws allowing the Syrian Republic to seize property for which ownership cannot be proven implicitly exclude half of the country's former population. This includes Palestinian refugees, who are now displaced abroad and cannot claim such ownership, have lost their documents, or do not have access to Syrian embassies.[24]

As the obliteration of the space of Yarmouk by the Syrian regime and the displacement of its population with no right of return draws stark parallels with

16 Bernard-Moulin, "Urbicide in Syria," 7.
17 This refers in particular to Decree 66, passed in Sept. 2012, and Law No. 10, which came into effect in April 2018. Plan No. (105) to "renovate" and "reconstruct" Yarmouk and Qaboun regions was also approved on June 25, 2022.
18 See Rollins, "Decree 66"; Nasr, "Assad's Property Law."
19 Hanna, "The Politics of Urban Reconstruction in Syria," July 2, 2018.
20 Rollins, "Decree 66."
21 Abujidi, *Urbicide in Palestine*, 39 (italics in original).
22 Abou Zainedin and Fakhani, *Syria's Urbicide*, 1.
23 See al-Aswad, "Palestinians' Homes Stolen"; see also "Damascus Governorate."
24 See Nasr, "Assad's Property Law."

Andreea-Florentina Midvighi

the 1948 expulsion from Palestine, refugees often call it "a second Nakba."[25] In the context of the siege and the weaponization of urban planning schemes that followed its destruction, Yarmouk "acquired a visceral centrality precisely as a symbol of the ongoing Palestinian catastrophe."[26]

Refugees as producers of knowledge

Although camps tend to be portrayed as markers of spaces of exclusion, the refugees that inhabit them are also producers of knowledge, keepers of memories, and embodied manifestations of a culture outside the state.[27] After the physical destruction of a camp, the people forced into exile continue to maintain the basis of the social relationalities built in its specific space, which undergoes a deterritorialization, continuing to undermine colonial formations of the present. Equally, after multiple inherited, unrecognized, lived dislocations, refugees embody particular forms of emplacement. Following Elena Fiddian-Qasmiyeh, "even the 'erasure' or 'closure' of a camp at a particular time does not mark their end, as these remain as traces, or even as camps *in potentia*."[28]

As Palestinian intellectual Yousif M. Qasmiyeh illustrates in one of his poems, the legitimate keepers of the camp's embodied archive cannot be governed by institutions:

> Only refugees can forever write the archive. The camp owns the archive, not god.
> For the archive not to fall apart, it weds the camp unceremoniously.
> The question of a camp-archive is also the question of the camp's survival beyond speech.
> Circumcising the body can indicate the survival of the place. Blessed are the pending places that are called camps.[29]

Established in 2008 in Yarmouk, and running until the beginning of the Syrian revolution when members were either forced to flee or were taken by regime forces, a cultural resistance group called Reaction worked with video, photography, posters, theater, comic sketches, and other means to tackle various forms of injustice in the camp. The group had a large number of followers on social media and was involved

25 For instance, Fouad Mohamedyye, interview by the author and Abed Alnaji, May 15, 2023, Stockholm; Alaa Al Arifi, interview by the author and Abed Alnaji, March 3, 2023, Uppsala; Abed Alnaji, interview by the author, March 19, 2023, Uppsala.
26 Fiddian-Qasmiyeh, "Memories and Meanings," 298.
27 See Agamben, *State of Exception;* Agamben, *Homo Sacer;* Agier, *Managing the Undesirables.*
28 Fiddian-Qasmiyeh, "Memories and Meanings," 292.
29 Qasmiyeh, "Writing the Camp-Archive."

in different forms of community organizing, which helped it connect with other groups in Palestine and the diaspora.

Reaction had long been doing visual ethnography through their practices of documenting the lives and stories of the camp, although there was no need to call it as such. Their actions were driven by the urgency to document, preserve, and reproduce life in the camp for the future, especially when the attacks from the Al-Assad regime intensified after the first bombing of Yarmouk in December 2012. Although the group is officially now dissolved and its members are now in different countries, they are still connected and continue to work with various art forms.

Protest as preliminary research

Today, Sweden hosts the largest Palestinian refugee community from Yarmouk in Europe. Although there is no exact data on this—Palestinian refugees are not registered as such in the databases, but as "stateless" persons from Syria—it is generally believed that around 15,000 Palestinians from Yarmouk became double refugees there.

I personally became aware of Reaction's work during a 500-kilometer walk that I joined in June 2020 from Gothenburg to Stockholm, initiated in protest against an increase in the number of deportations.[30] I was working with Cultures of Resistance Films on documentaries about various resistance movements around the world. Having a strong belief in walking as an anticapitalist practice and its power to raise awareness,[31] I quit my job and joined the walk.

With its slowness, long discussions, and the many people we collaborated with on the way, the walk became my entry point into the history and afterlife of the Yarmouk camp. Among refugees from Syria, Palestine, Lebanon, Iraq, and Afghanistan, there were also three double refugees from Yarmouk, two of whom had also been part of Reaction. They were documenting the walk and the stories of the refugees, and each day distributed footage or short videos they had edited from it the prior day in the hope of attracting media attention to the march and the protest planned for the parliament building in Stockholm

30 One refugee from Lebanon had decided initially to walk 10 km. As more and more people joined, the walk grew in length and scope.

31 See, for instance, Solnit, *Wanderlust*.

Andreea-Florentina Midvighi

once we reached our destination. Although I had myself lived in the Jenin refugee camp in the West Bank and had been in many Palestinian refugee camps in the West Bank, Jordan, and Lebanon, I realized that I knew very little about Palestinian refugee camps in Syria, let alone Yarmouk, its largest.

For the walk, we chose visibility instead of comfort. We walked on large, paved streets or highways that were hard on our feet and sometimes took longer than village or forest trails but made us and our big flags visible to passersby. In collectively walking, we challenged the injustices and alienation refugees feel in Sweden—as well as the disconnection trauma and alienation enforced in one's body and one's sense of self—when occupying the streets, squares, cities, villages, or lake areas; taking agency, using our bodies in motion to draw attention to the country's lack of accountability of the plight of its refugees. We were being and doing otherwise than expected; sharing tastes, dreams, and memories, fears of deportations, bureaucratic deadlocks, family stories, news from dear ones left behind.

After the walk, I became increasingly interested in forms of transnational heritage and the ways in which the former inhabitants of the Yarmouk camp continue to keep the camp alive. What I learned about Yarmouk during this experience, and during the two years spent in Sweden formed the basis of my ongoing research. In the fourteen semi-structured interviews that I conducted, I experienced firsthand how "the idea of a collective imagination is itself tricky, especially if an ethnographer seeks to share it," and that only through "verbal projections and through embodied practices" can an ethnographer try to understand it.[32] My conversations and engagements with Palestinians displaced from Yarmouk helped to identify patterns: the ways in which Yarmouk is refracted through Palestinians' place-making in Sweden; the city as an extension of the camp; the importance of meaningful places, such as rooftops, crossroads, or cemeteries; the camp as a structure, a memoryscape, a spatial and political imaginary; Yarmouk as a way of being; how Palestinian refugees negotiate what is rendered visible and what

32 Pink, "Urban Tour," 182–83.

→ Figure 1

is invisibilized; or how not knowing or not saying has an impact in constructing refugees' subjectivity.

Archival silences

To investigate these patterns, my initial plan was to gather whatever official archival material I could find in terms of documents, photographs, videos, maps, or reports from the library of the American University of Beirut, the UMAM Archives and Research Centre, the Institute for Palestine Studies, the digital archives of the United Nations Relief and Works Agency for Palestine Refugees (UNRWA), and elsewhere and review them in Sweden together with groups of Palestinian double refugees from Yarmouk. I wanted to then film these encounters and take photographs together with members of Reaction and other former inhabitants of the camp, and also work on forms of counter-mapping. Moreover, I intended to analyze the ways in which Reaction engages with and reflect the space of the camp through its artwork.

Yet, as common in dictatorial regimes, Syria is notorious for its control of its archives and the silencing, obliteration, and fabrication of materials.[33] The status of Yarmouk as an unofficial camp under the control of a Syrian municipality where UNRWA had a limited influence made it even more difficult to store and archive a history of the camp. My inquiries also came to a halt for security reasons. The UNRWA digitized photography collection, the UN online library, and the University Museum of Bergen collections were the only ones where I was able to find a few photographs of Yarmouk from before 2011. At the archives of the American University of Beirut, the Institute for Palestine Studies in Beirut, and the UMAM Archives and Research Centre, I could not find much either.

In the absence of official archives, I decided as a result of conversations with members of Reaction and other Palestinian refugees to instead investigate patterns of displacement through photographing personal objects, analyzing the photos that the refugees brought with them when leaving the camp, and filming the stories around these traveling memories.[34] Many people either did not take much with

33 See, for instance, Hussein Moustafa, "Research Without Archives?"

34 See Bertschi, Lafontaine Carboni, and Bathla, *Unearthing Traces*.

→ Figure 2

→ Figure 3

Andreea-Florentina Midvighi

them when leaving the camp, thinking that they would soon return, or whatever they managed to take was lost on the way. Whatever was left then became even more important in their struggle to keep memories of the camp alive, as well as their connection with Palestine.

As the very identity of Yarmouk's inhabitants was profoundly enmeshed in the space of the camp, the physical and existential void its destruction left behind demands for building an archive that tells the story of the built environment of Yarmouk and of the many ways in which it was more than a physical place. Employing visual ethnography renders visible the embodied heritage of displaced peoples, such as Palestinian refugees. It helps answer calls such as Nurhan Abujidi's for the urban to "be approached from a different perspective in urbicide discourse, by empowering its hidden but major characteristics, the political dimension and its link with shared place/spaces and its bond with identity."[35]

While writing this text, I am in the process of finding out where the communities of Palestinian double refugees from Yarmouk currently live in Sweden in order to investigate forms of sociality, transnational heritage, and ways in which the Yarmouk refugee camp continues to be reproduced in the diaspora. I am photographing and filming interviews in collaboration with former members of the Reaction group.

In addition to doing slow research, I am taking time to learn and think together with the refugees about how their displacement, everyday subjectivities, and embodied presence of the camp should be represented. For example, I collaborate closely with Abed Alnaji, one of the members of Reaction. We discuss the questions together prior to the interviews and decide who will ask them. It has been very interesting to witness the conversations he develops with the interviewees while they are drawing maps of Yarmouk explaining their daily routes in the camp and the places most important to them. I have talked more to women, and when they choose not to be on camera, we still record the audio to capture their voice inflections.

35 Abujidi, *Urbicide in Palestine*, 37.

→ Figure 4

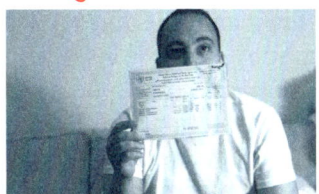

→ Figure 5

→ Figure 6

Recovering Evidence of Existence

One collaboration has led to another, connecting us with photographers or poets from different cities in Sweden who are also getting involved in and collaborating with the project in various ways—for sound, translations, or editing, for instance. Many of our collaborators are also involved in maintaining transnational heritage and solidarity. For instance in a videography called "Message From The Absence," Iyad Alhasan recites a poem over film shots of the destroyed Yarmouk camp taken by his cousin, followed by shots from Jerusalem and the West Bank.[36] In doing so, memories and scenes of Yarmouk are superimposed with lived (Sweden), remembered (Yarmouk before 2012), recorded (Yarmouk in 2021), visualized, and imagined urban landscapes. To extend this idea of superimposition, we plan to project our final documentary onto the buildings in Sweden where the people we collaborated with now live.

Visual ethnography

> When approached as a process or practice, as something relational and productive, imagination leads to new spaces of inquiry, spaces that are dependent on the collaborative nature of anthropological knowledge. Such an approach situates imagination as a pedagogy, and one with the potential to open up and to make visible the unknown.[37]

Current debates in visual ethnography emphasize the power inequalities in representation, the potency of film and photography to bring together "the scientific and the aesthetic,"[38] and its capability to allow "sensorial, observational, relational, and liminal possibilities that transcend beyond the violence of abstraction in text."[39] Although the act of representation itself can be considered intrinsically violent,[40] film, it has been claimed, can potentially challenge abstracted representations of place.[41] Before the establishment of urban studies as a field, photography was an important instrument to document and memorize heritage buildings at risk of being destroyed due to increased changes in the urban environment.[42]

It was not until the 2000s that photography became a recognized method for researching urban

36 Alhasan, "Message From The Absence."
37 Culhane, "Imagining," 15.
38 Heider, *Ethnographic Film*, 4.
39 Bathla and Papanicolaou, "Reframing the Contested City," 366.
40 Noys, "Violence of Representation," 12. For a discussion around the "aesthetic violence" of the camera when representing refugees, see, for instance, Burgoyne, "Abstraction."
41 Stickells and Monsley, "Film/Architecture/Narrative," 176.
42 Conord and Cuny, "Towards a 'Visual Turn,'" 2.

changes.⁴³ Although its roots go back to the 1920s, it was only in the 1960s that the potential of doing film and ethnography together started to be consistently explored. In this sense, Karl G. Heider's reflections on the beginnings of the methodology and the implications of technological innovations also account for the gradual move towards an embodied and sensorial approach.⁴⁴ Or again expressed in concrete examples, Sergei Eisenstein's 1938 *Montage and Architecture* and Le Corbusier's *promenade architecturale* have been influential in starting a tradition of using montage in film, photography, architecture, and urban research.⁴⁵

Significantly, Sarah Pink highlights the significance of "theorizing collaborative ethnographic methods as place-making practices," in that "we can generate understandings of both how people constitute urban environments through embodied and imaginative practices and how researchers become attuned to and constitute ethnographic place."⁴⁶ In *Sensuous Scholarship*, Paul Stoller also moves beyond the idea of the body as a text in Eurocentric anthropological endeavors and accounts for the necessity of building "sensuous epistemologies."⁴⁷ Engaging in such practices could lead to "lost biographies, memories, words, pains and faces which cohere into a vast secret museum of historical absence."⁴⁸ By encompassing various senses, visual ethnography proves a powerful method of surfacing and representing embodied archives and mobilized imaginaries.

Although there is an increased recognition of the relevance of "sensorial experience and embodied memory," Palestinians have yet to gain their rightful place in writing the camp.⁴⁹ Granting them such a position would imply "that camp life has intrinsic value, a cultural rootedness and integrity of its own," and that "refugees experience identity and belonging not just at the ideological level of symbol and doctrine but at the visceral level of embodied practice."⁵⁰ Employing visual ethnography as a methodology in exploring these issues then becomes even

> By encompassing various senses, visual ethnography proves a powerful method of surfacing and representing embodied archives and mobilized imaginaries.

43 Conord and Cuny, "Towards a 'Visual Turn,'" 2.
44 Heider, *Ethnographic Film*, 15. See also Bathla and Papanicolaou, "Reframing the Contested City."
45 See Buckley, *Graphic Assembly;* Hallam, et al., *Cities in Film* (n.d.); Treiber, Meireis, and Franke, *Essentials of Montage in Architecture*.
46 Pink, "Urban Tour," 176.
47 Stoller, *Sensuous Scholarship*.
48 Stoller, *Sensuous Scholarship*, 83.
49 Allan, *Refugees of the Revolution*, 215.
50 Allan, *Refugees of the Revolution*, 215.

more relevant, having a higher potential to reflect such embodiment, multivocality, agency, as well as representations of relationality.

Referring to Yarmouk in particular, Bernard-Moulin argues that "cultural resistance is very interesting because it directly challenges the logics of Urbicide of denying a communal identity"—impunity, he continues, can be challenged by tactics such as *"resistance-as-documentation."*[51] I therefore incorporate a decolonial approach using visual ethnography to inquire how we think about camps and refugees, starting with connecting the ongoing colonialities both on the ground—as in land occupation and the multiple displacements of the Palestinian population—and in knowledge production in the Global North.[52]

Towards a decolonial perspective of camps

Diasporic communities' ties cannot be underestimated. "Camps, it seems," writes Diana Allan, "are spawning their own diasporas, creating cross-currents of attachment that unsettle our understanding of how Palestinian identity and affiliation should now be conceived," engendering "other conceptions of home, identity, and belonging that have developed in exile."[53] As Walter Mignolo points out, everyday acts of resistance and of coming together, as well as cultural and art practices, become tools to "delink from the Colonial Matrix of Power and to engage in epistemic … and aesthetic … reconstitutions."[54]

The streets of Yarmouk, for instance, bore the names of the villages in Palestine where the refugees came from. In addition to speaking a particular Yarmouk dialect, people continued to speak within their families the dialects of the regions in Palestine they were displaced from. "Indigeneity," I argue following Ahmad Amara and Yara Hawari, "offers a way to rethink the Palestinian political project as a more encompassing one that understands all Palestinians, wherever they may be, as indigenous people facing attempted erasure."[55]

To follow Kirsten McConnachie, pointing to the parallels and continuities between prisoner-of-war camps (from the 1790s to the present), internment

51 Bernard-Moulin, "Urbicide in Syria," 11 (italics in the original).
52 See Santos, *Epistemologies of the South*, 48.
53 Allan, *Refugees of the Revolution*, 188–89.
54 Mignolo, Politics of Decolonial Investigations, 31.
55 Amara and Hawari, "Using Indigeneity."

Andreea-Florentina Midvighi

camps (1890s onward), and the ubiquitous refugee camps (which have been the main response to forced migration since 1915) is a necessary gesture in understanding colonial trajectories.[56] In Sweden and Europe at large, Palestinian and other refugees are represented as "figures of economic dependency, violations of property, and threats to Western culture," reworking—as Arun Kundani writes—"older forms of racism to produce images that are distinctive to the neoliberal era."[57] Writing on racial capitalism as well, Jodi Melamed reminds us that in addition to being "expropriation of labor, land and resources," capitalism is also "a system of expropriating violence on collective life itself."[58] What is needed to counter "the current structure of domination" entailed by neoliberalism and ongoing colonialities is "to bring indigeneity into representation."[59] Additionally, the concept of "humanity" instrumentalized in the imaginaries produced in the Global North becomes—following human rights lawyer Stamar Mann—"a mask in the world trade in migrants."[60]

Apart from having been a place where people lived, now Yarmouk is also people living in different parts of the world. Through active place-making, and the reproduction of the camp as a structure, a memoryscape, a spatial and political imaginary, a way of being, and of themselves as producers of cultural resistance, Palestinian refugees from Yarmouk are undermining such a "technology of antirelationality."[61] A focus on refugees' imaginaries and practices in the diaspora counters such a humanitarian "semiotics of suffering" by enabling a "transformatory aesthetics, or reworlding."[62] By complementing textual representations and by engaging the bodies, senses, and imaginaries of researchers, collaborators, interviews, and viewers, visual ethnography is potentially powerful in distributing agency and opening collective spaces and collaborations.

"Contesting the coloniality of established knowledge and the coloniality of power behind it," writes Walter Mignolo, "requires changing the terms of the conversation in both spheres: the sphere of state-directed de-Westernization and the sphere of the political society's decolonial drive to reconstituting the

56 McConnachie, "Camps of Containment."
57 Kundani, "What is Racial Capitalism?"
58 Melamed, "Racial Capitalism," 78.
59 Melamed, "Racial Capitalism," 83.
60 Cox, et al., *Refugee Imaginaries*, 2.
61 Ruth Wilson Gilmore in Jodi Melamed, "Racial Capitalism," 78.
62 Cox, et. al, *Refugee Imaginaries*, 8.

communal."[63] The history of activism, resistance, and solidarity in Yarmouk are indices of the "communal" referred to by Mignolo. Munir Fasheh, Palestinian mathematician and educator, refers to a similar notion of the communal "as the most basic 'building block' of community, and as the deepest medium of learning and community work."[64]

Colonization implies an epistemicide—"the massive destruction of ways of knowing that did not fit the dominant epistemological canon,"[65] a production of displacement and destruction of knowledges and memories. By acknowledging the space of the Yarmouk refugee camp as heritage and building a counter-archive, we are challenging these structural inequalities, also concerning reception of art and its valorization. Notably, the term urbicide was used by Ada Louise Huxtable refer to "the killing of history and memory through the destruction of the built form."[66] In this context, forms of infrastructural sociality such as those developed in Palestinian refugee camps become potential disrupters. After more than seven decades, Palestinian refugee camps are products of the modernity/coloniality paradigm.[67] The ways in which the inhabitants of the camps appropriate and reorganize their space both constitute and reflect their identity, kinship relations, the villages they were forced to leave, and the dialects they refuse to forget. Heritage in and of Palestinian refugee camps takes many forms: spatial practices, memoryscapes, embodied practices, longings, knowledge production, different aesthetics and aesthesis, symbols mobilized for political action.[68] This research will contribute to a recent trend in ethnic studies concerned with indigenous geographies of solidarity and decolonial practices of sociality, continuing post-displacement in the diaspora.

Conclusion

Despite urbicide, Yarmouk continues to exist in the imaginary and practices of its former inhabitants as immaterial heritage, as a way of being, as embodied sociality. Refugee camps, according to Alessandro Petti, "reconstruct, in a sense, the demolished villages [they were initially displaced from] by re-assembling

63 Mignolo, *Politics of Decolonial Investigations*, 13.
64 Quoted in Sukarieh, "Decolonizing Education," 191.
65 Santos, *Epistemologies of the South*, 238.
66 Sharp, "Urbicide and the Arrangement of Violence in Syria," 121.
67 See McConnachie, "Camps of Containment"; Walsh and Mignolo, *On Decoloniality*.
68 See Bshara, "Marvels of Despair."

Andreea-Florentina Midvighi

their people and the social relations that bind them."⁶⁹ Exploring how this process continues in the diaspora after displacement by using collaborative visual ethnography enhances the recognition that images indeed play a huge part in how we experience and represent knowledge, and they help bridge different disciplines. It would also encourage more interventional research and more connection with current societal issues.

By building a counter-archive for Yarmouk with artistic works, photos, videos, and documents from former inhabitants of the camp now living in Sweden, as well as filming these encounters and reflecting on forms of immaterial heritage, we are attempting to provide fuller representation and analysis of the spatial, social, and imaginary dynamics constitutive of the relations with the materiality of the camp and its symbolic and embodied reconfigurations. Visual ethnography thus becomes a powerful decolonial structure that enables us to "gain deeper insights that get under the surface of what is visible, to share our findings and to engage others in our arguments and in the stories of those people who participate in our research."⁷⁰ Although displaced multiple times, Palestinian double refugees from Yarmouk can thus continue to not only exist but also reclaim their evidence of existence.

69 Petti, "Architecture of Exile."
70 Pink, *Doing Visual Ethnography*, 12.

ACKNOWLEDGMENTS
I am extremely grateful for the huge help, patience, and care I received from Jennifer Bartmess, editor at gta Verlag, and Nitin Bathla, the editor of this book, without whom the publishing of this chapter would not have been possible.

Recovering Evidence of Existence

Figure 1   On the walk from Gothenburg to Stockholm, trying to get the attention of the passers-by. July 2020

Andreea-Florentina Midvighi

89

Figure 2 — Mohamad Mohammadieh, drawing a map of Yarmouk illustrating the places most important to him (screenshot from interview for the forthcoming documentary). April 20, 2023, Uppsala

Figure 3 — Shadi Diab showing a family photo (screenshot from interview) for the forthcoming documentary. May 2, 2023, Uppsala

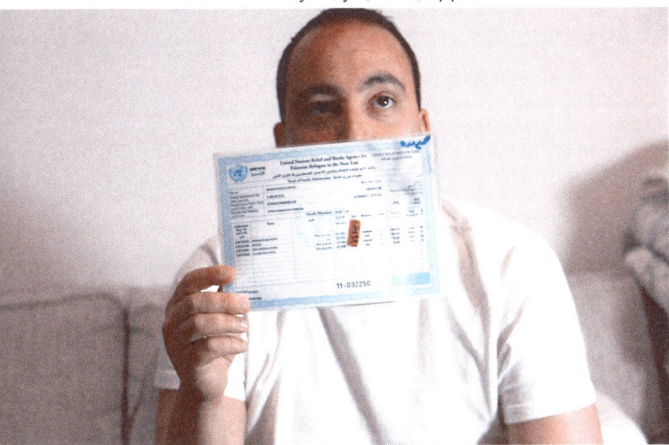

Figure 4 — Alaa Al Arifi showing his UNRWA card, one of the things he managed to take with him from Yarmouk (screenshot from interview for the forthcoming documentary). March 3, 2023, Uppsala

Recovering Evidence of Existence

Figure 5 Fouad Mohammadieh, talking about his latest painting representing Yarmouk (screenshot from interview for the forthcoming documentary). May 15, 2023, Stockholm

Figure 6 — Abed Alnaji of Reaction during an interview for the forthcoming documentary and showing objects he brought with him from Yarmouk: books, a photo of his mother, who was a first-generation Palestinian refugee, and the house keys. March 19, 2023, Uppsala

Recovering Evidence of Existence

BIBLIOGRAPHY

A

Abou Zainedin, Sawsan, and Hani Fakhani. *Syria's Urbicide: The Built Environment as a Means to Consolidate Homogeneity.* The Aleppo Project, July 2019. https://www.thealeppoproject.com/wp-content/uploads/2019/07/SyriasUrbicideSawsanAbouZainedinHaniFakhani2019.pdf (accessed November 25, 2023).

Abujidi, Nurhan. *Urbicide in Palestine: Spaces of Oppression and Resilience.* London: Routledge, 2014. https://doi.org/10.4324/9781315819099.

Agamben, Giorgio. *Homo Sacer: Sovereign Power and Bare Life.* Stanford: Stanford University Press, 1998. https://doi.org/10.1515/9780804764025.

Agamben, Giorgio. *State of Exception.* Chicago: University of Chicago Press, 2005. https://doi.org/10.1515/9780822386735-014.

Agier, Michel. *Managing the Undesirables: Refugee Camps and Humanitarian Government.* Translated by David Fernbach. Cambridge and Malden, MA: Polity Press, 2020.

Al-Aswad, Harun. "Palestinians' Homes Stolen Once Again as Assad Eyes Syria's Yarmouk Camp." Middle East Eye, August 4, 2020. https://www.middleeasteye.net/news/syria-palestinians-assad-homes-stolen-yarmouk-camp (accessed August 27, 2023).

Alhasan, Iyad. "Message From The Absence." Facebook, June 16, 2021. https://t.ly/TxKOj (accessed August 25, 2023).

Allan, Diana. *Refugees of the Revolution: Experiences of Palestinian Exile.* Stanford: Stanford University Press, 2013.

AlSahli, Thaer. *Mig,* 2013. https://www.youtube.com/watch?v=omgJovb65HU&t=1s (accessed August 27, 2023).

Amara, Ahmad, and Yara Hawari. "Using Indigeneity in the Struggle for Palestinian Liberation." *Al-Shabaka,* August 8, 2019. https://al-shabaka.org/commentaries/using-indigeneity-in-the-struggle-for-palestinian-liberation/ (accessed August 28, 2023).

Arat-Koç, Sedef. "Decolonizing Refugee Studies, Standing up for Indigenous Justice: Challenges and Possibilities of a Politics of Place." *Studies in Social Justice* 14, no. 2 (2020): 371–390. https://doi.org/10.26522/ssj.v14i2.2271.

B

Bathla, Nitin, and Klearjos E. Papanicolaou. "Reframing the Contested City through Ethnographic Film: Beyond the Expository on Housing and the Urban." *International Journal of Housing Policy* 22, no. 3 (2022), 351–70. https://doi.org/10.1080/19491247.2021.1886028.

Bernard-Moulin, Andy. "Urbicide in Syria: An Updated Case-Study on the Politics of Urban Destruction in the Damascus Area." Unpublished paper for the conference "Mediterranean and Middle-East Metropolis," Paris, May 2018. https://www.researchgate.net/publication/330598626_URBICIDE_in_Syria_An_updated_Case-Study_on_the_politics_of_urban_destruction_in_the_Damascus_Area#fullTextFileContent (accessed November 25, 2023).

Bertschi, Denise, Julien Lafontaine Carboni, and Nitin Bathla, eds. *Unearthing Traces: Dismantling Imperialist Entanglements of Archives, Landscapes, and the Built Environment.* Lausanne: EPFL Press, 2023. https://doi.org/10.55430/6638VA01.

Boatcă, Manuela. "Counter-Mapping as Method: Locating and Relating the (Semi-)Peripheral Self." *Historical Social Research / Historische Sozialforschung* 46, no. 2: Reflexivity Between Science and Society (2021), 244–63. https://doi.org/10.12759/hsr.46.2021.2.244-263.

Boatcă, Manuela. *Global Inequalities Beyond Occidentalism.* Farnham: Ashgate, 2015. https://doi.org/10.4324/9781315584867.

Bshara, Khaldun. "Marvels of Despair: The Status of Cultural Heritage in Palestine." *This Week in Palestine* 277 (May 2021). https://thisweekinpalestine.com/marvels-of-despair/ (accessed November 25, 2023).

Buckley, Craig. *Graphic Assembly: Montage, Media, and Experimental Architecture in the 1960s.* Minnesota: University of Minnesota Press, 2019. https://doi.org/10.5749/j.ctvpwhdbd.

Burgoyne, Robert. "Abstraction, Bare Life, and Counternarratives of Mobility in the Refugee Films of Richard Mosse and Ai Weiwei, Incoming and Human Flow." In *Refugees and Migrants in Contemporary Film, Art and Media,* edited by Deniz Bayrakdar and Robert Burgoyne, 73–88. Amsterdam: Amsterdam University Press, 2022. http://doi.org/10.5117/9789463724166_ch03.

C

Choi, Shine, Anna Selmeczi, and Erzsébet Strausz, eds. *Critical Methods for the Study of World Politics: Creativity and Transformation.* London and New York: Routledge, 2020. https://doi.org/10.4324/9781315104997.

Conord, Sylvaine and Cécile Cuny. "Towards a "Visual Turn" in Urban Studies? Photographic Approaches." *visual ethnography* 3, no. 1 (June 2014), 1–6. http://dx.doi.org/10.12835/ve2014.1-0028.

Coward, Martin. *Urbicide: The Politics of Urban Destruction.* London: Routledge, 2008. https://doi.org/10.4324/9780203890639.

Cox, Emma, Sam Durrant, David Farrier, Lyndsey Stonebridge and Agnes Woolley, eds. *Refugee Imaginaries: Research Across the Humanities.* Edinburgh: Edinburgh University Press, 2020. https://doi.org/10.1515/9781474443210.

Culhane, Dara. "Imagining: An Introduction." In *A Different Kind of Ethnography: Imaginative Practices and Creative Methodologies*, edited by Danielle Elliot and Dara Culhane, 1–22. Toronto: University of Toronto Press, 2017.

D

DAAR (Sandi Hilal and Alessandro Petti), photographic documentation by Luca Capuano. *Refugee Heritage*. Stockholm: Art and Theory Publishing, 2021.
"Damascus Governorate Receives an Organizational Plan for the Yarmouk Camp That Allows the Return of Only 40% of Its Residents." *Palestinian Refugees Portal*, 26 June 2020. https://refugeesps.net/post/14444 (accessed August 28, 2023).

E

Elia, Nada. *Greater Than the Sum of our Parts: Feminism, Inter/Nationalism & Palestine*. London: Pluto Press, 2023. https://doi.org/10.2307/j.ctv36cj888.

F

Fiddian-Qasmiyeh, Elena. "Memories and Meanings of Refugee Camps (and more-than-camps)." In *Refugee Imaginaries: Research Across the Humanities*, edited by Emma Cox, Sam Durrant, David Farrier, Lyndsey Stonebridge and Agnes Woolley, 289–310. Edinburgh: Edinburgh University Press, 2020. https://doi.org/10.1515/9781474443210.
Fraihat, Ibrahim. "What About the Palestinian Double Refugees?" *Brookings*, February 25, 2014, Commentary OP-ED. https://www.brookings.edu/articles/what-about-the-palestinian-double-refugees/ (accessed August 1, 2023).

G

Gabiam, Nell. *The Politics of Suffering: Syria's Palestinian Refugee Camps*. Bloomington and Indianapolis: Indiana University Press, 2016.

H

Hallam, Julia, Robert Kronenburg, Richard Koeck and Les Roberts, eds. *Cities in Film: Architecture, Urban Space and the Moving Image*. Conference proceedings, *An International Interdisciplinary Conference, University of Liverpool*, 26–28th March 2008. https://www.liverpool.ac.uk/media/livacuk/architecture/images-research/cityinfilm/downloads/Cities_in_Film_2008_Proceedings.pdf (accessed August 27, 2023).
Hanna, Edwar. "The Politics of Urban Reconstruction in Syria." The Bartlett Development Planning Unit, UCL, July 2, 2018. https://blogs.ucl.ac.uk/dpublog/tag/conflict-in-cities/ (accessed November 25, 2023).
Hawari, Yara. "Erasing Memories of Palestine in Settler-Colonial Urban Space." In *Routledge Handbook on Middle East Cities*, edited by Haim Yacobi and Mansour Nasasra. London: Routledge, 2019. https://doi.org/10.4324/9781315625164.

Heider, Karl G. *Ethnographic Film*. Revised ed. Austin: University of Texas Press, 2006. https://doi.org/10.7560/714588.
Hussein Moustafa, Laila. "Research Without Archives?: The Making and Remaking of Area Studies Knowledge of the Middle East in a Time of Chronic War." *Archivaria* 85 (May 2018), 68–95. https://archivaria.ca/index.php/archivaria/article/view/13631 (accessed December 5, 2023).

K

Kelliher, Diarmaid. "Historicising Geographies of Solidarity." *Geography Compass* 12, no. 9 (2018), e12399. https://doi.org/10.1111/gec3.12399.
Kundani, Arun. "What is Racial Capitalism?" Talk at Havens Wright Center for Social Justice, University of Wisconsin-Madison, October 15, 2020. https://www.kundnani.org/what-is-racial-capitalism/ (accessed August 28, 2023).

M

McConnachie, Kirsten. "Camps of Containment: A Genealogy of the Refugee Camp." *Humanity: An International Journal of Human Rights, Humanitarianism, and Development* 7, no. 3 (Winter 2016), 397–412. https://doi.org/10.1353/hum.2016.0022.
Melamed, Jodi. "Racial Capitalism." *Critical Ethnic Studies* 1, no.1 (Spring 2015), 76–85. https://doi.org/10.5749/jcritethnstud.1.1.0076.
Mignolo, Walter D. *The Politics of Decolonial Investigations*. Durham, NC, and London: Duke University Press, 2021. https://doi.org/10.2307/j.ctv1smjncs.
Moorcock, Michael. "Dead God's Homecoming." *Science Fantasy* 59 (June 1963), 2–46.

N

Nasr, Joseph. "Assad's Property Law Hits Hope of Return for Syrians in Germany." *Reuters*, June 14, 2018. https://www.reuters.com/article/us-mideast-crisis-syria-germany-insight-idUSKBN1JA1V1/ (accessed November 26, 2023).
Noys, Benjamin. "The Violence of Representation and the Representation of Violence." In *Violence and the Limits of Representation*, edited by Graham Matthews and Sam Goodman, 12–27. London: Palgrave Macmillan, 2013.

P

Petti, Alessandro. "Architecture of Exile IV.B." *Decolonizing Architecture Art Research*. 2017. https://www.decolonizing.ps/site/architecture-of-exile-iv-b/ (accessed August 28, 2023).
Pink, Sarah. "An Urban Tour: The Sensory Sociality of Ethnographic Place-making." *Ethnography* 9, no. 2 (June 2008), 175–96.
Pink, Sarah. *Doing Visual Ethnography: Images, Media and Representation in Research*. 4th edition Los Angeles, CA: Sage, 2021.

Q

Qasmiyeh, Yousif M. "Writing the Camp-Archive." *Refugee Hosts*. September 1, 2017. https://refugee-hosts.org/2017/09/01/refugees-are-dialectical-beings-part-one/ (accessed August 27, 2023).

R

Rollins, Tom. "Decree 66: The Blueprint for Al-Assad's Reconstruction of Syria?" *The New Humanitarian*, April 20, 2017. https://www.thenewhumanitarian.org/fr/node/259390 (accessed August 27, 2023).

S

Salim Salameh. "The Unacknowledged Syrians: Mobilization of Palestinian Refugees of Yarmouk in the Syrian Revolution." *Confluences Méditerranée* 4, no. 99 (2016), 47–60. https://doi.org/10.3917/come.099.0047.

Santos, Boaventura de Sousa. *Epistemologies of the South: Justice Against Epistemicide*. London and New York: Routledge, 2014. https://doi.org/10.4324/9781315634876.

Sharp, Deen. "Urbicide and the Arrangement of Violence in Syria," in Deen Sharp and Claire Panetta, eds. *Beyond the Square: Urbanism and the Arab Uprising*. New York: Terreform, 2016.

Solnit, Rebecca. *Wanderlust: A History of Walking*. London: Granta, 2014.

Stanley, Bruce. "The City-Logic of Resistance: Subverting Urbicide in the Middle East City." *Journal of Peacebuilding & Development* 12, no. 3 (2017), 10–24. https://doi.org/10.1080/15423166.2017.1348251.

Stickells, Lee, and Jonathan Monsley. "Film/Architecture/Narrative." In *Cities in Film: Architecture, Urban Space and the Moving Image, An International Interdisciplinary Conference, University of Liverpool, 26–28th March 2008*, Conference Proceedings, edited by Julia Hallam, Robert Kronenburg, Richard Koeck and Les Roberts, n.d., n.p. 171–76. https://www.liverpool.ac.uk/media/livacuk/architecture/images-research/cityinfilm/downloads/Cities_in_Film_2008_Proceedings.pdf (accessed December 5, 2023).

Stoller, Paul. *Sensuous Scholarship*. Philadelphia: University of Pennsylvania Press, 1997. https://doi.org/10.9783/9780812203134.

Sukarieh, Mayssoun. "Decolonizing Education, a View from Palestine: An Interview with Munir Fasheh." *International Studies in Sociology of Education* 28, no. 2 (2019), 186–99. https://doi.org/10.1080/09620214.2019.1601584.

T

Tatour, Lana. "Recognising Indigeneity, Erasing Palestine." *Assafir Al-Arabi* (AsA), 18 May, 2019. https://assafirarabi.com/en/25757/2019/05/18/the-naqb-bedouin-as-indigenous-people/ (accessed August 28, 2023).

Thanem, Torkild, and David Knights. *Embodied Research Methods*. London: SAGE Publications, 2019. https://doi.org/10.4135/9781529716672.

Treiber, Max, Sandra Meireis, and Julian Franke, eds. *Essentials of Montage in Architecture*. Dimensions: Journal of Architectural Knowledge 2, no. 4 (2022).

U

UNRWA, "Yarmouk (Unofficial camp*)." https://www.unrwa.org/where-we-work/syria/yarmouk-unofficial-camp (accessed August 29, 2023).

W

Walsh, Catherine E., and Walter Mignolo. *On Decoloniality: Concepts, Analytics, Praxis*. Durham, NC, and London: Duke University Press, 2018. https://doi.org/10.2307/j.ctv11g9616.

IMAGE CREDITS

Figure 1: Abed Alnaji
Figures 2–6: Andreea-Florentina Midvighi

Andreea-Florentina Midvighi

Midvighi, Andreea-Florentina. "Recovering Evidence of Existence through
Collaborative Visual Ethnography." In Nitin Bathla, ed., *Researching Otherwise:
Pluriversal Methodologies for Landscape and Urban Studies*.
Zurich: gta Verlag, 2024, 73–95. https://doi.org/10.54872/gta/4692-2.

Recovering Evidence of Existence

Metaxia Markaki

Who Owns the Land? On Research Poetics and Performance as Ways of Knowing

Researching Otherwise
Nitin Bathla, ed.

To research poetically means to explore in synthesis and in creative manners. How explicit and analytical can inquiry afford to be before restraining our ways of knowing? Can we imagine the power of a research occurring outside academic norms and textualities? A way of producing knowledge collectively, subversively, and poetically?

This essay brings forward the notion of *poetics*[1] to rethink possible ways of conducting research in landscape and urban studies. Delving into performance-sensitive ways of knowing and ethnotheatrical practices, it explores the possibility of a research which happens outside mere interpretative analysis, instead sublating it as it unfolds in the sphere of critical imagination and as an act of *poiesis*.[2] In *research poetics*, this essay searches for empowerment, emancipation, and for ways of countering power structures still adjacent to knowledge making.

In what follows I will narrate my creative encounter with the UrbanDig Project, a performance collective. After a few years of lonesome fieldwork for my doctoral dissertation on the depopulating mountain slopes of Arcadia in Greece, I met with the UrbanDig collective. They, too, had been working on similar topics, through other means, so they invited me to a transdisciplinary dialogue. From this exchange emerged a shared analytical lens, a script, and the performance *Who owns the land?* Soon after, I—the lonesome researcher—found myself together with UrbanDig on a stage, talking to an audience, introducing the performance, and initiating an open public dialogue in the format of a lecture series. Here I will recount this moment of creative encounter, when a multiplicity of "actors"—urban researchers, historians, artists, activists, performers, and their audience—crossed paths; fused the borders, roles, and tools of their disciplines; and performatively met around a stage. I will explore what kind of research and knowledge emerged from this: Who brought the data, who the analytical lens, and who the interpretation? Who learned from whom and who gets to decide what this knowledge is about? In this multivocality, where different perspectives and parallel voices intersect, where enactment, embodied knowl-

1 *Poetics*, meaning the art of making, derives from the Greek term ποιητική. The term was first introduced by the ancient Greek philosopher Aristotle in his work titled *Poetics*, where he explored the principles and elements that make up various forms of poetry, including tragedy and epic poetry. Throughout history, different scholars and theorists have engaged with the notion of poetics, offering perspectives on the creative process within various cultural, historical, and socio-political contexts. See further the section "research poetics" later in this chapter.

2 *Poiesis*, from the Greek ποιώ/ποιείν, means not only poetry but also *the making*—the act of creating, particularly in the context of artistic or creative endeavors. In philosophical and artistic discourse, the concept of *poiesis* goes beyond the mere act of physical creation; it involves bringing something into existence through intentional thought, inspiration, and artistic skill. It emphasizes the transformation of ideas, emotions, and experiences into tangible or perceivable forms that can be shared with others. In some philosophical contexts, poiesis is also contrasted with "praxis," which refers to practical action or ethical conduct. Poiesis is more concerned with the imaginative and creative aspects of human activity. The term has been explored by various philosophers, including Martin Heidegger, who discussed *poiesis* in the context of his philosophy of art and technology. Overall, *poiesis* encapsulates the idea of bringing something new and meaningful into existence through creative thought, imagination, and skillful craftsmanship.

Metaxia Markaki

edge, and orality prevail, I noticed the formation of a fertile ground. There, research was performed not as a single-authored monologue but as an ecology, in a dialogic manner.

The first part of this essay is written in an academic manner. It aims to locate the work in the epistemic context of performance ethnography and to discuss the potential of ethnodramatic practices in urban and landscape studies today. The second part is written in a dramaturgical manner. It narrates the research process I followed—from the field to the stage and to the public dialogue it triggered—through an ethnodramatic script composed of a "prelude," three research "acts," and an "exodus." The academically written part locates the work within existing literature and practice. The theatrical part employs dramaturgy of the autoethnographic analysis of the research-making itself.

The reader should not be confused. The ethnodramatic textuality presented in Part II is not the script of the performance *Who owns the land?* It is a new suggested textuality, composed of dialogues and analytical passages. It narrates all the stages of the research process I followed as an enacted, embodied performance, where a multitude of "actors" and "voices" meet and collectively perform. This approach aims to unveil the complexities of research-making through performance autoethnography and through a performance way of seeing.

Part I

Performance ethnography

"The performative turn has been taken in the social sciences. We have moved from textual ethnographies to performative [auto] ethnographies," write Norman Denzin and Yvonna Lincoln in 2005, drawing attention to an ongoing epistemological turn in social sciences driven by theater and performance studies.[3]

Performance emerged as an artistic practice in the 1960s and 1970s to challenge traditional artistic production, unmasking and countering its adjacent power structures. According to historians such as RoseLee Goldberg, performance art is linked to precedents such as the Futurists, Dadaists, and Surrealists. It makes central the process, the body, and the

[3] Denzin and Lincoln, "Series Editors' Foreword," 11.

enactment—the doing.[4] Outside institutionalized art spaces, artists use their bodies to challenge regimes of power and social norms, no longer using the object depicted in paintings, sculpture, film, or photography but "the living flesh and breath of the act itself."[5] Anti-institutional, anti-elitist, anti-consumerist performance art comes to constitute a provocation and a political social act, Diana Taylor explains, and as such it is used often by artivists (artist-activists) to intervene in political contexts, struggles, and debates.[6] Performance, however, exists only in relation to an audience. Rooted in the rudimentary principles of the theatrical praxis, and in ideas as old as the Platonian "politics of seeing" and the Aristotelian "theory of mimesis," performance invites the spectators to an active way of seeing. Addressing them as political subjects, it elevates them to the active role of social "actors," the "spect-actors" as Augusto Boal calls them in his *Theatre of the Oppressed*.

Eventually, performance transpires as and transcends to a form of knowing and understanding the world, able to challenge the prevalent epistemic violence in academia and to counter power structures adjacent to knowledge production. "More than a condition or ontology, performance emerges as an epistemology."[7] In its character of corporeal practice and in relation to other cultural practices and discourses, it offers a bodily way to transmit knowledge.[8] Parallel to its adoption by the arts since the 1960s, performance has broken institutional and cultural barriers: performance studies have emerged into the realm of scholarship, introducing bodily ways of knowing in inquiry and challenging epistemic disciplinary boundaries. Initiated within departments of theater, linguistics, communications, anthropology, sociology, and visual arts, performance studies seek counter-knowledge, introducing a post- or even counter-disciplinary approach. Taking seriously the idea that bodies (and not only books and documents) produce, store, and transfer knowledge, they transcend the established academic canons, textualities, methodologies, sources of knowledge, and systems of transmission, offering an inclusive theoretical paradigm for academics, artists, activists, and the public to

4 Goldberg, "Performance–Art for All?" 369.
5 Taylor, *Performance*, 1.
6 Taylor, *Performance*.
7 Halberstam, *Queer Art of Failure*, 87.
8 See Taylor, *Performance*.

Metaxia Markaki

meet. What is more, performance emerges as an episteme with a *poetic potential*. As Diana Taylor puts it: "Performance constitutes … *an act of doing with*. As an act of imagination, it allows to imagine (together) better scenarios and futurities. […] Performance is world-making, and we need to understand it."[9]

In his "Call to Performance," Norman Denzin envisions performance practices as embodied political acts able to not only challenge and reinvent the social world but also to revolutionize ethnographic praxis.[10] The emergence of performance ethnography thus introduces novel embodied ways of conducting, presenting, and representing fieldwork, while also reframing ethnographic textualities. Since the 1970s, social sciences have challenged the conventions and power relations within which academic knowledge production had been long delineated, resulting in the historic turn of critical ethnography towards qualitative research and art-based inquiry.[11] Art-based research in particular can help "open up multiplicity in meaning-making instead of pushing authoritative claims," for example.[12] Further, performance ethnography links tightly to postcolonial and feminist approaches. "Performance-sensitive ways of knowing contribute to an epistemological and political pluralism that challenges existing ways of knowing and representing the world."[13] Such formations are more inclusionary and better suited than existing ways for thinking about postcolonial or "subaltern" cultural practices. One of the reasons for this is that performance approaches to knowing insist on immediacy and involvement. "They consist of partial, plural, incomplete, and contingent understandings, not the analytic distance of detachment, the hallmarks of the textual and positivist paradigms."[14] As a result, they allow for inclusive and multivocal ways of making knowledge.

According to Foucault, the body is the site of power–knowledge relations, where the possibility of resistance against them co-exists.[15] Subversive knowledge and embodied, performance-sensitive ways of knowing disrupt and counter these relations.[16] They enable different bodies to produce knowledge and talk about themselves instead of others knowing

[9] Taylor, *Performance*, 208 (emphasis in the original).
[10] Denzin, "Call to Performance."
[11] See, for example, Denzin and Lincoln, *Sage Handbook of Qualitative Research*; Knowles and Cole, *Handbook of the Arts in Qualitative Research*; Leavy, *Handbook of Arts-Based Research*.
[12] McNiff, "Philosophical and Practical Foundations," 26.
[13] Conquergood, "Beyond the Text," 26.
[14] Salvatore, "Ethnodrama and Ethnotheatre," 267.
[15] See Foucault, *History of Sexuality*, vol 1: *Introduction*.
[16] Thanks to Maria Chassioti for articulating this during a discussion on her research thesis.

Who Owns the Land?

and talking on their behalf. They outline possibilities and the duty of self-creation (to create the subjectivity of one's own self) as an act of emancipation,[17] where *poetics* lies at its core. Performance ethnography emerges, thus, to occupy a seminal space in ethnographic discourse. Challenging the authorship, textuality, and the very format of the traditional ethnographic report, it incorporates performance genres, practices, and techniques. Within a broader field of performance ethnography, below I delve into the theatrically embodied inquiry—in the sense of its overt ambition to offer a "public voice ethnography" with exploratory and emancipatory potential—in the form of critical "ethnotheatre" and its textual format, "ethnodrama."

Critical ethnodrama

In his book *Ethnotheatre: Research from Page to Stage*, Johnny Saldaña identifies eighty unique terms that can all stand in academia under the broad umbrella of "ethnotheatre" or "ethnodrama."[18] These terms—which include terms such as oral history performance, performative inquiry, public voice ethnography, reality theater, research staging, scripted research, testimonial theater, theatrical research-based performance, transcription theater, and verbatim theater—show the vast possibilities and diversity for the genre. According to Saldaña:

> ethnotheatre, a word joining ethnography and theatre, employs the traditional craft and artistic techniques of theatre ... to mount for an audience a live or mediated performance event of research participants' experiences and/or the researcher's interpretations of data ... an ethnodrama, a word joining ethnography and drama is [a specific genre of dramatic literary writing], a written play script consisting of ... selected narratives collected from interview transcripts, participant observation field notes, journal entries, personal memories/experiences, and/or print and media artifacts.[19]

"Ethnodrama" and "ethnotheatre" are umbrella terms, constructed to establish academic legitimacy for scholars and researchers working within certain paradigms, explains Joe Salvator.[20] The terms embrace a

[17] See Foucault, "What is Enlightenment?"
[18] Saldaña, *Ethnotheatre*, 13–14.
[19] Saldaña, *Ethnotheatre*, 11.
[20] Salvator, "Ethnodrama and Ethnotheatre," 268–70.

wide and hybrid range of performance ethnography practices that employ the medium of theater to narrate various forms of creative, critical non-fiction. Emerging though a critique of Western academic ways of producing knowledge, their goal is the voicing of muted actors and democratizing knowledge in social science, aspiring to become a form of "public voice ethnography" with exploratory and emancipatory potential.

Ethnodramatic textuality plays a key role in this aspiration. Relying on qualitative data as its source material—ethnographic testimonies and documents, autoethnography, or collective devising—an ethnodrama aims to bring into the script a multiplicity of perspectives, mostly of subordinate/subjugated subjectivities. Dialogue replaces the traditional researcher's monologue, establishing a discursive, multivocal way of reporting. A dialectic manner of researching extends in different dimensions. Instead of a concrete outcome, the audience is presented with research findings and is invited to make an interpretation through their experience. What is more, as the format requires both rigorous research and skillful artistic adaptation, it calls for collaborative ventures between social scientists and various theater practitioners.

As a methodological inquiry avenue, ethnodrama has been mobilized in various disciplines as an embodied performance way of knowing. Its roots lie in clinical mental-health care inquiry and topics such as uncovering the experience of schizophrenia and psychosis through detailed ethnographic and phenomenological research, used in ethnodrama for instance in the pioneering work of Jim Mienczakowski and Stephen Morgan in 1993.[21] It further developed in health and education studies to explore questions related to race and gender, positionality, alcohol dependency and detoxification, and knowledge transfer.[22] For example, Peggy Warren, following a Black feminist and postcolonial approach, centers and privileges Black women working in the UK National Health Service. The participating women, practicing performative autoethnography, "transition through the research process, unearthing, examining and unapologetically speaking their 'truths'," making

21 Mienczakowski and Morgan, "Ethnodrama"; Mienczakowski, "Ethnodrama."
22 On health, see Taylor, et al., "Beyond the Page"; on education studies, see Dell'Angelo, "Down the Rabbit Hole"; Malhotra and Hotton, "Contemplating Positionalities"; Petersen, "Resistance and Enrolment"; on race and gender, see Ward Randolph and Weems, "Speak Truth and Shame the Devil"; Devereaux, "Breaking the Fourth Wall"; on positionality, see Malhotra and Hotton, "Contemplating Positionalities"; on alcohol dependency, see Glynn, *Speaking Data*; on knowledge transfer, see Warren, *Black Women's Narratives*.

visible their embodied knowledges and seeking professional emancipation.[23] Criminologist Martin Glynn, on the other hand, uses ethnodrama to research together with Black male youth on marginalized perspectives in crime and justice and to discuss the importance of data verbalization.[24] "The implications of such performances is far from symbolic, as their realisation is what informs research," Jim Mienczakowski points out, highlighting the mutuality and transresistivity in the making of drama and critical social theory in ethnodramatic inquiry.[25]

Despite social scientists' influential work on performance texts and multiple examples of studies mobilizing performance ethnography as a methodological avenue across various disciplines,[26] performance *ways of knowing* have been neglected in urban and landscape academic scholarship. Innumerable approaches have tied theatrical praxis to the *production* of urban space, both conceptually and analytically: as a space;[27] as a practice;[28] as a metaphor for the exploration of urban politics,[29] urban spectacularization,[30] and the emergence of urban social movements;[31] and as as a means for plural urban historiography.[32] Especially in Greece, and in particular in the streets of Athens of the recent decades, performance practices have been employed extensively as a key means of political urban resistance during the years of the crisis and onwards,[33] for instance the *Revolted Opera* (Εξεγερμένη Λυρική, 2008), the *Open Orchestra* (Ανοιχτή Ορχήστρα, since 2022), or *Vrisoules* (Βρυσούλες) on ecological struggles (since 2018). Nevertheless, examples of urban ethnotheatrical inquiry are scarce in the field, while the literature on the potential of the performative turn in urban studies is almost inexistent.

Urban studies: ambivalent textualities and the possibility of a performative exploration of the "periphery"

Researchers in landscape and urban studies rely closely on ethnographic methods developed in social sciences for the exploration of urbanization processes in contemporary landscapes. These entail the use of qualitative research methodologies and a series of

---

23 Warren, *Black Women's Narratives*, 29.
24 Glynn, *Speaking Data*.
25 Mienczakowski, "Ethnodrama," 468.
26 See, for instance, Barone and Eisner, *Arts Based Research*; Conquergood, "Beyond the Text"; Mienczakowski, "Ethnodrama"; Saldaña "Ethnodrama and Ethnotheatre"; Barone, "From Genre Blurring to Audience Blending"; Goldstein "Hong Kong, Canada"; Vanover & Saldaña "Chalkboard Concerto."
27 See McKinnie, *City Stages*.
28 See "Street Theater and Urban Space."
29 See Stavridis, *Από την Πόλη Οθόνη*.
30 See Antimiichuk, "Contemporary City."
31 See Shepard, "Urban Spaces as Living Theater."
32 See Kockelkorn, "Uncanny Theater."
33 See Kanellopoulou, "Space in Common."

ethnographic tools—such as interviews, participant observations, and visual methods—for the investigation of contemporary urban phenomena. While many sensorial tools have been introduced in the research apparatus of the disciplines, textualization remains at the heart of the urban ethnographic enterprise, both in academia and during fieldwork and both in producing and in representing knowledge: "Fieldwork is synonymous with the activity of inscribing diverse contexts of oral discourse through field notes and recordings,"[34] while the communication of the results is shaped and restrained within academic textuality. An immediate example of this contradiction is the present text that *I am now writing* in this book, *for you to read later*.

In recent years, a "peripheral turn" is observable in urban studies, obliging us to rethink our ways of conducting research. According to Xuefei Ren, this turn is characterized by a deliberate spatial, social, political, and analytical shift away from centers of knowledge and power.[35] Urban scholars have shifted their analytical lenses from privileged centers to multiply inscribed peripheries and to the Global South more generally. In Latin America, a rich scholarship in "writing urban history from the margins" has been deployed, with prominent voices including the Peruvian sociologists Aníbal Quijano and John Friedmann and anthropologists Teresa Caldeira and James Holston,[36] while researchers such as AbdouMaliq Simone reveal the periphery as a space of "anticipatory urban politics" and subversive ways of being.[37]

This turn calls for a radical rethinking of dominant concepts and methodologies used in urban landscape research. In 2021, *Engaging the Urban from the Periphery*, a special issue of the *South Asian Multidisciplinary Academic Journal* by Shubhra Gururani, Loraine Kennedy, and Ashima Sood focusing on India's urbanizing agrarian and rural rhythms, points to the need for methodological and theoretical openings to explore such territories.[38] Similarly, the recent publications *Beyond the Megacity* by Nadine Reis and Michael Lukas and *After Suburbia* by Roger Keil and Fulong Wu call for a reconceptualization of existing concepts and methodologies to address the emerging

34 Marcus, "Afterword," 263.
35 Ren, "Peripheral Turn."
36 See, for instance, Quijano, *Los Movimientos Campesinos Contemporáneos*; Friedmann, "The Future of Urbanization in Latin America"; Caldeira, "Peripheral Urbanization"; Holston, "Insurgent Citizenship."
37 Simone, "People as Infrastructure."
38 Gururani, Kennedy, and Sood, *Engaging the Urban*.

urban peripheries at a planetary scale.[39] As urban research increasingly extends into non-city peripheral territories—the mountain peaks of the Swiss Alps, the transnational hinterlands of Singapore, less accessible and sparsely populated areas, depopulating mountainous and archipelagic regions, emptying forests and diminishing seas[40]—a series of urgent questions occur: How do we approach their actors and subjectivities marginalized for a long time? Are the existing tools of qualitative ethnographic urban inquiry enough to include and represent their subjugated voices and knowledge? With and for whom are we conducting this research?

In the light of these questions, performance ways of knowing and the embodiment and orality entailed in ethnotheatrical methodologies percolate as an exciting new potential for urban studies to approach the "periphery" and "peripheral knowledges." Theater has often been used to counter dominant ways of storytelling, and performance has opened up a medium for transdisciplinary encounters and the collective and multivocal production and reproduction of knowledge. Below, I will narrate how such questions of agency and right to knowledge production emerged during my fieldwork in the peripheral mountainous landscapes of Arcadia, Greece,[41] and how my encounter with the UrbanDig Project performance collective reframed my research experience. "It seemed to me so sensible, so natural, to employ the medium of theatre to tell these non-fictional stories about real people," as Jonny Saldaña once pointed out.[42]

Part II

To put my methodological position into practice I narrate my research process in the format of an enacted, embodied performance. What I do here is present an autoethnographic analysis of my own research-making through an ethnodramatic script that follows the different stages of this research: from the field to the stage and to the public dialogue it triggered. The script starts with a "prelude" that sets the general stage of this research. This is followed by three "research acts" that describe three

39 Reis and Lukas, *Beyond the Megacity*; Keil and Wu, *After Suburbia*.
40 See Diener, et al., *Switzerland*; Topalovic, "Hinterland"; Couling, "Formats."
41 Markaki, "Expropriation and Extended Citizenship."
42 Saldaña, "Ethnotheatre," 16.

Metaxia Markaki

distinct research stages: first, the individual fieldwork for my doctoral dissertation in Arcadia (Act I: The Field); second, my creative encounter with the UrbanDig collective and the making of the performance *Who owns the land?* (Act II: The Stage); third, the public dialogue that emerged (Act III: More Voices). The theatrical praxis is only the second of the three acts, a mediating instance in a larger process of a performance way of knowing that takes continuous shape. The script concludes with an "exodus," which helps the audience and readers to exit the convention of the theatrical sphere and reflect on the broader meaning and impact of such research.

Following through the acts, the reader will encounter a researcher—this is me involved in the different stages of this research. You will also encounter the voices of informants that I met during the fieldwork I conducted for in Arcadia from 2019 to 2021 (Act I), the voices of the UrbanDig collective artists who shaped the performance *Who owns the land?*," and of the performers who enacted it on stage (Act II). You will then hear the voices of the speakers invited to present an open, public series of lectures that was organized as part of the performance (Act III) and the thoughts of the audience, finally exiting the scene back to the city (exodus). Some voices are often assembled together, echoing the way the chorus functions in classical drama. Other voices are attributed to distinct speakers and presented in dialogue format. Speech is complemented with stage comments that shed light on the materiality of the imaginary "stage set" and geographies within which this research performs. Stage directions and scene descriptions are provided in square brackets. Analytical and descriptive parts (in normal paragraph font) intertwine with and enrich the script, guiding the reader through an analytical layer of this work. Before concluding with the "exodus," the script is interrupted, complemented by a main analytical section on research poetics. The reader may imagine me reading all the analytical parts.

Who Owns the Land?

The hybrid multivocal textuality that follows, composed of dialogues and analytical passages, gives an auto-ethnographic account of my research process, unveiling the complex process of research-making through a performance way of seeing. The notional borders of words as "actors," "acts," and "acting" blur as one transcends from the peripheral landscapes of the fieldwork site to the theater space and to the public sphere of the centralized urbanity of Athens. It makes things hard to separate: Where does performance stop and where does social practice begin? The following section stays with this ambiguity and narrates the continuities, mutuality, and research constellations that this generates.

Who owns the land? A performative narration of the research process

PRELUDE
[Peripheral landscapes. Mountains and islands. Depopulating sceneries. Abandoned agricultural fields, rewilding productive grounds, touristified idyllic outsides, exhausted farmlands.]

> Researcher speaks to the audience
> These are all places that have been systematically peripheralized in Greece over the last decades, as state policies and legislative reforms have promoted centralization and concentration around a few major cities, mostly the capital, Athens. In the last few decades, peripheral landscapes have also experienced the results of austerity policies and the Greek economic crisis, along with the impact of the climate and energy crises which have further pushed their peripheralization. Uncontrollable wildfires, socio-ecological disruptions, and new speculation interest in large-scale "green" operations in peripheral lands are now putting their fragile socio-ecologies, forests, and cultivation under pressure. Dispossessions, enclosures, privatizations unfold there under the frozen image of a static rural world, while their inhabitants, their voices and knowledge, remain "peripheral," unseen and un-recounted.

Metaxia Markaki

Voices
Who owns this land?
Who speaks for it and who governs it?
Who claims it, and what is there left to defend and
    to care for?

Researcher
I invite you to imaginatively engage with these questions in the sensory worlds of the performance script that follows.

ACT I   THE FIELD
[A young female researcher with a notebook, a voice recorder, a camera, and some maps, drives down the slopes of Mount Mainalon. She is conducting her fieldwork.]

Researcher notes in her diary
November 2021. Tripotamia. The area is located at the intersection of the rivers Alfeios and Erymanthos, in the semi-mountainous region of Arcadia. This is a landscape of olive groves and grazing lands; small villages scarcely connected and scarcely populated. The few permanent inhabitants feel neglected, as an unbridgeable distance seem to divide them from any center and from the Greek capital city. I collect their stories: oral histories about the progressive emptying of the area and everyday narrations about their land, which is now changing.

[Kapelitsa village, surrounded by olive groves. We are at Kafeneio, where a few old Greek men and Albanian workers are sitting around a table talking.]

→ Figure 1

Men talking to the researcher
Are you looking for a groom? We have
    no women here. They all left for
    the city.
Are you a journalist? We have complaints to the
    government. They've forgotten us.
Are you a public servant? A few days ago an Athenian
    from the ministry popped up. He asked to see
    the borders of our olive properties. Holding a bunch
    of satellite views, he wanted the plot lines, the
    proofs of our land ownership.

Who Owns the Land?

We had no maps here, no cadastre, we told him. We
    didn't need to measure the fields. We knew
    that from this root to this root it belonged to my
    grandfather. From the stream to the big tree,
    it belonged to somebody else.
Our fields are fragmented, but in this fragmentation,
    they narrate family trees, dowries, and heritages:
    the histories of those who migrated and those who
    stayed behind to care for their land.
Buckets of olive oil leave every year to Tripolis, to
    Athens, abroad: to sons, daughters, grand-
    children. How far do they go? And for how long
    can they go on?

Researcher notes in her diary
Uncharted land, chaotic at first glance, as scattered
and dispersed as the community that harvests it. One
here is the landowner, the other is the one who
tends it. The "absurdity" of this land does not allow
someone who comes from far to understand it, to
govern and rationalize it, to manage it, to buy, to sell,
to tax it. In a strange way, this "irrationality" seems
to protect it. Remaining in undefinition and periph-
erality has delayed this land from being modern-
ized, valorized, commercialized.

[Pirris village. A fire recently damaged the olive groves.
Black earth, black trees. A smell of burnt wood.]

Local pastoralists walking their herd
Huge fires ripped through our fields this summer.
    We lost everything: trees, roots, and animals.
We've been abandoned. Too far from the capital, no
    one listens.
A Spanish company wants to buy the burnt land to in-
    stall a photovoltaic park. They pay ten times the
    value. Some of us are disappointed, we might sell.

[Arvitsa. Alpine pastures.]

An 80-year old woman practicing transhumance
We've always grazed these meadows. They used to be
    public land, commons, accessible to everyone.
    Now we've become "illegal." We've been expelled.

Metaxia Markaki

A private wind-turbine park is planned to be installed on the mountaintops.

Researcher notes in her diary
Farmers and shepherds, olives and grazing lands, peripheral ecologies—all are unwillingly entangled in questions of energy transition and are confronted by much larger interests of international companies and investors. A radical land transition is occurring silently in the periphery, while local socio-ecological knowledge remains neglected. The "official story" is written far from the periphery, without its inhabitants. But at this moment of climatic socio-ecological emergency, isn't this a story that concerns us all in terms of earthly survival? Is it enough to academically report these findings, extracting the local experience and struggle, to generate textual institutional knowledge that will remain within an elite community of scholars? For whom would I, alone, write this academic report, and who would listen? What kind of knowledge does this need to be? Who are the authors and who the audience for this research to be meaningful? The responsibility of carrying these voices in my recorder is immense, and the need to share and collectively process this lived experience is urgent.

ACT II   THE STAGE
[The researcher meets with the Athenian performance collective, the UrbanDig Project. The collective has a historical script from 1855, and in dialogue with the researcher's current ethnographic material they stage a theatrical performance about the Greek "periphery."]

→ Figure 2

UrbanDig Collective
The script narrates a story about land, history, and origins of the land question in Greek periphery. It is located in nineteenth-century *Trives* (meaning "frictions" in Greek, an imaginary village positioned by the author at the intersection of the rivers Alfeios and Erymanthos) …

Researcher
… precisely there where I've been doing my fieldwork. They match each other!

Who Owns the Land?

UrbanDig Collective

The script was written in 1855 by the Greek politician Pavlos Calligas. Set in the historical moment of national independence, it narrates the long and complex processes of land distribution in post-Ottoman Greece, together with their profound socio-political ramifications. Following the play's protagonist Thanos Vlekas, a landless farmer, in his futile endeavor to root himself and cultivate a piece of land, we witness the formation of a state and of a whole society where justice and penalty; taxation and governance; corruption, power, and class; the agrarian question all stem from a specific and conflictual relation to its land. Due to its striking relevance to contemporary Greece and the urgent questions it raises about land, state, and governance, we have decided to put the play on stage for the first time since it was written. We want to open up a dialogue between the historic script and the contemporary ethnographic material collected from the same area in order to explore what this act of bringing them together will reveal.

[A playwright (Panayiota Pantazi), a choreographer (Irini Alexiou), a theater director (Giorgos Sachinis), a stage designer (Anna Magoulioti), an urban scholar (Irini Ilioupoli), and me (the urban researcher on site) get into an intense exchange, beginning an unfamiliar transdisciplinary dialogue.]

> Voices in dialogue
> What story do these stories tell together?
> What knowledge can they reveal if they're performatively combined?
> How can our different tools form a dialogic stage and how will performance mediate the production and reproduction of democratic knowledge, open and accessible to more people?

The UrbanDig Project is an Athenian performance group engaged in exploring contemporary urban matters. It was created by director Giorgos Sachinis and choreographer Irini Alexiou, with a transdisciplinary team from various fields of art and science.[43] The UrbanDig Project defines itself as a meeting point between art and space within the culture of an

Metaxia Markaki

urban environment: "It produces art as a continuous report from the front of the imaginary, the unmeasurable, the unspoken. It is a statement for the production and the reproduction of space as a continuous process of realizing social relations. Theatre and dance transcend predefined spaces and forms, engaging with urban space ... as the group aims at building imaginary bridges in the urban mosaic."[44] The group had previously usually performed in non-theatrical city spaces—Athenian squares, roof terraces, in neighborhoods undergoing gentrification and workers' districts—inviting a collective reimagination and reappropriation of the city's urban realm.[45] Yet it has become clear that urban matters extend beyond the city scale. Emerging ways of thinking in urban studies, the "peripheral" turn, and climatic discourse, both in academia and beyond, point to peripheral landscapes and their marginalized ecologies as the site of the most crucial socio-ecological urban struggles of our times. As part of this turn, the UrbanDig collective took an interest in the Greek countryside, and for the first time extended its performative way of urban exploration to reach out and engage with the complexity of peripheral landscapes.

[43] Institutionally, the UrbanDig Project was created by Ohi Pezoume, an urban non-profit theater organisation, in 2004. The team created the UrbanDig Project as an action axis, with performances held in non-theatrical urban spaces, including participatory actions and community art-based projects. See https://www.urbandigproject.org/home.

[44] UrbanDig Project, "About," https://www.urbandigproject.org/copy-of-about-1 (accessed March 23, 2023).

[45] See Zontou and Sachinis, "UrbanDig Project."

Researcher
January 2022. Athens downtown. I step on stage. Transplanted here from my familiar academic context, I speak to the public, introducing the story of Thanos Vlekas in a historical narration intertwined with contemporary oral histories from the field.

[Three men, professional actors (Yannis Askaroglou, Grigoris Ballas, Yorgos Fritzilas) go on stage and act. They move. They transfigure. They enact the nineteenth-century villagers: the authorities, the judges, the farmers who lost their land. Then they tell the stories of Tripotamia.]

Performers
We lost our fields in the fire.
A Spanish company has come to buy our land.
We had no maps here.
Uncharted land, chaotic at first glance, its
    "irrationality" seems to protect it.

Who Owns the Land?

[The stage set is crafted as a blow-up from the researcher's notebook, a hand-drawn map of the area where the ethnographic visual and oral material surrounds the performers. Statistical diagrams, movement pendulums, hand-sketches and interview quotes overlap on the map with the names of the villages: Pirris, Kapelitsa, Arvitsa. They reveal the peripheral landscapes of Tripotamia as a multi-layered script, a palimpsest inviting attentive readings and interpretations.]

→ Figure 3

Researcher notes in her diary
The researcher is transplanted onto a theater stage. And the histories of the periphery are transplanted to the center of the capital. Both transfigured, they become part of a performance storytelling and a performance inquiry. Reembodied, reenacted, the same stories sound different. How are the *villagers* represented? How do historic power structures and the immense complexity of the periphery reflect in the performers' postures (the landowner, the landless workers, the corrupted public servants)? How do the workers' bodies come together when united, and how do they isolate when in conflict? How differently do *women* move? What is the sound they make? Does the history sound different or does it have a continuity with the contemporary testimonies? As I watch the three male performers' bodies transcending through all roles and all temporalities, many questions and an immense density of layers of interpretation and meaning come across. "Can you send me the video and sound recordings of your fieldwork interviews? And your historic sources?" Askaroglou asked me while researching the ways to shape his performance. "Texts of critical urban theory were influential to me when putting this together" the director Sachinis reported. The scriptwriter Pantazi assembled invaluable historical resources to support the script, while the choreographer Alexiou delved into to inquiries about embodiment. Gathered, decomposed, and recomposed through the critical, sensory, and cultural lenses of all the artists (researchers) involved, the movements, sounds, and details of bodies and postures from the field become significant. A perfor-

Metaxia Markaki

mance way of inquiring cares and can encompass far more elements, including all those that would usually evade traditional academic textuality. In this collective process of fermentation, the research reshapes. Knowledge emerges as in a kaleidoscope. Plural-, trans-, or counter-disciplinary, entailing ruptures, it does not stand alone. It requires the gaze and critical reflection of a viewer to be meaningfully seen. As the performance builds trans-temporal and translocal links, bringing fragments and narratives into the present moment, the urban audience laughs, nods, falls silent, or disapproves. A relation of coexistence, visibility, and consensus is built, reshaping once again the inquiry. Knowledge is not delivered here as a scientific statement but as an ongoing, multi-authored process.

ACT III   MORE VOICES
[A public lecture series takes place every evening before the play. Selected specialized speakers are invited to discuss the same question of "Who owns the land?"⁴⁶]

→ Figure 4

    Historian Panayotis Tournikiotis
    We don't own the land; the land owns us. Nomads, we move on top of it, and in the end we definitely return to it. Land is always there, and we just walk over [it].

    Activists Eleni Tzirtzilaki and Support Earth
    Land is our commons taken from us.

    Artist Ludwig Berger⁴⁷
    Land is ecology, the sound of the melting glaciers.

    Academic Marija Maric
    Land is a commodity, let's talk about real-estate poetry.

    Collective Boulouki
    Land is a community, roots, and family bonds, the trees of my grandmother.

46 The "Who owns the land?" lecture series was organised by Metaxia Markaki and Irini Iliopoulou at the Theatro Simeion in Athens from Dec. 2021 to Feb. 2022. Recordings of the lectures can be found at https://www.youtube.com/playlist?list=PLxvvDiomHi_KU-OHeymvvS_CIPqWctJhq.

47 See also Berger's contribution in this volume.

Journalist Vasiliki Grammatikogianni
Who owns the land? Who owns
   the Moon?

Every evening before the play, invited artists, academics and activists respond to the same question "Who owns the land?" from their own unique perspective in a parallel lecture series. They bring together academic knowledge and historical perspectives on topics such as Greek national lands or the Greek agrarian question. They combine with reports on contemporary struggles from other peripheral landscapes: the ongoing gold mining operations at Skouries, the dam on the Acheloos River, stories of nature protection on the Prespes Lakes, ecological movements against wind-turbine park on mountain peaks, a manifesto for the fragile island ecologies drained and exhausted by over-touristification and commodification. The public questions, adds, responds to the arguments raised by the performing academics.

> Researcher notes in her diary
> The usual academic format of a lecture series is transplanted within the theatrical forum, intertwining with the theatrical performance and its public. It brings another layer of theory, scientific knowledge, and a multitude of perspectives, which contribute to a multivocal epistemic landscape. They amplify and constantly reframe the performative historic and ethnographic narration of the stage. Together, these formats shape a frame for the question of land to be asked within, extending it to further dimensions and relating it to more landscapes and contemporary struggles. With the emergence of this instant discursive community of the theatrical forum, *an amplified way of storytelling and an extended way of inquiry become possible.*

Research poetics

Poetics is distinguished from hermeneutics by the focus not on the meaning of a text but rather on understanding how different elements come together, explains Stein Olsen.[48] *Who owns the land?* is precisely this, namely a place where a multitude of elements

Metaxia Markaki

came poetically together, generating research relations and shaping a construction site for knowledge production to perform within.

The UrbanDig Project understands its performative research practice as "a methodology in the shape of a triangle … where qualitative research, artistic interventions and community actions materialise interconnected … a manner of place-making from the bottom."[49] This reflects, in the way set out above, three research "acts," respectively representing these research dimensions: first, *the field*, where qualitative inquiry happens; second, *the stage*, where the artistic intervention occurs; and third, *the voices*, where a multifaceted community was shaped and intervened. Similar to the Lefebvrian triadic production of space in lived, perceived, and conceived dimensions, within this methodological research triangle a new space emerges—it is a place where the research question re-contours itself, *it shapes itself a land to be asked within*.[50] This land is not a "thing," but rather an unraveling, moving process: a construction site, inhabited by a multiplicity of performing actors which act, dialogically relate, and poetically co-construct the ecology for knowledge to be produced within. It is therefore important to unpack the three dimensions that form this site.

First, this is a site of acting and of action. For the UrbanDig collective "the philosophy of action" is found in the core of the relation between art, space, and society. "Action creates new relations and therefore new space, new geographies, and new artistic imprints. It extends, reattributes, and transcends them"; as such, acting manifests as "the origin and the site of all concepts," states Henri Lefebvre.[51] From there, we can then analyze how in this particular piece of performative research, acting was not the end goal but rather the beginning of a generative, embodied process of knowledge production.

Second, this is a site of dialogue, where dialectical thought and relations become possible. For this, fragments are important—historic fragments, ethnographic fragments, oral histories, auto-ethnographies, stories from elsewhere. We gather fragments, we act in fragments. We narrate fragments.[52] A

49 UrbanDig Project, "Our Philosophy," https://www.urbandigproject.org/our-philosophy (accessed March 23, 2023).
50 See Chatziefstathiou, Iliopoulou, and Magkou, "UrbanDig Project."
51 Quoted in Schmid, *Henri Lefebvre*, 97.
52 See also McFarlane, *Fragments of the City*.

→ Figure 5

Who Owns the Land?

fragmented way of telling a story is a way to talk about relations; about the possibilities of them coming together; of us bringing them together; of all the possible relations that can potentially occur. To bring (fragments) together is a subversive act; it takes a poetic gesture. It is an act of *poiesis*.

Third, this is a site of *poiesis*. *Poiesis* means poetry, but it also means the making or to make, to create; to imbue shape, life, meaning; to bring into being something that did not exist before. In the Lefebvrian universe, *poiesis* is the third element of a dialectical triad. Lefebvre places *poiesis* alongside the praxis of Marx and the dialectical thought of Hegel to generate a dialectical relation between the three.[53] In this triad, *poiesis is* revolutionary, as it transcends and raises both act and thought to a "higher, poetic or poietic level. … Unleashing fantasy, the poetic exploration of the impossible, makes possible that which lies beyond the possible," Lefebvre asserts.[54] Centring imagination at the heart of creation, *poiesis* ultimately speaks of the possibility of becoming.

Ever since Aristotle's primary definition of poetics and differentiation from other forms of mimesis, poetics has been bound to enactment.[55] According to Lefebvre, "Only an active, poietic (creative) thought, a form of energy that is practical and based on a praxis, can cross the point at which differences, contraries, oppositions, contradictions, confront one another and rigidify in an endless confrontation."[56] It is in this regard that poetics is perceived as entailing the unique potential to sublate contradictions in both knowledge production and in power structures. For French philosopher Gaston Bachelard, poetics entails the power to transcend "epistemological obstacles," opening new, imaginative ways for knowledge production.[57] He argues that "scientific" thinking is not a linear and objective process, and highlights the dynamics between imagination, intuition, and reason in the formation of knowledge. For Martinican poet philosopher Édouard Glissant, poetics contains a decolonial potential in sublating historic ruptures and in crafting relations:

> Thinking thought usually amounts to withdrawing into a dimensionless place in which the idea

[53] Lefebvre, *Metaphilosophy*.
[54] Lefebvre, *Metaphilosophy*, 86.
[55] Aristotle, *Poetics*.
[56] Lefebvre, *Metaphilosophy*, 46.
[57] Bachelard, *Formation de l'esprit scientifique*.

Metaxia Markaki

of thought alone persists. But thought in reality spaces itself out into the world. It informs the imaginary of peoples, their varied poetics, which it then transforms, meaning, in them its risk becomes realized.[58]

For Glissant, relations are poetic, relating is the process of changing mentality, imagining the force that drives it, constituting a transformative mode of history.

The entanglement of the three dimensions mentioned above allows us then to imagine a construction site of knowledge in which poetics play a core role. In my own case, inquiring into the research question "Who owns the land?" within such a site left me with the lived experience of how and what kind of knowledge this space can produce.

First, it allowed for many perspectives, interpretations, and ways of making knowledge to percolate. Qualitative ethnographic material and oral testimonies, together with analytical observations and abstract theoretical accounts of the researcher, were deinstitutionalized and shared. The ethnodramatic textuality of a script enabled a collaborative transdisciplinary process of critical interpretation and became the subject of a collective imaginative transfiguration. It was reembodied and reenacted, involving innumerable bodily interpretations, subtextual meaning-making and storytelling, mediated by the sensorial and perceptual sensitivities of all the artists involved. In the artistic process, unexpected elements came together, generating meaning and concepts. Body and the enactment—the doing was central to the process of deinstitutionalization, whereby bodies became the carriers of knowledge and "their living flesh and breath," the mediator for it to transfer further.

Second, in this process "dialogue" replaced the traditional researcher's monologue and established a discursive, multivocal way of reporting and a dialectic manner of inquiry. This consisted of partial, plural, incomplete, and contingent understandings, different from the analytic distance of detachment that marks textual and positivist paradigms. Instead of assertive claims and a concrete outcome, the audience and participants were presented with various

[58] Glissant, *Poetics of Relation*, 1.

findings translocated from their sites and brought together on a stage. For instance, voices from other landscapes and an audio piece of melting glaciers were coupled with historical accounts and ethnographic oral testimonies from the Greek periphery, staged together in the temporality of central Athens. Audience and participants were invited to make an interpretation through their experience, revealing unexpected continuities and relations, not only between the city center and periphery but also liking to broader socio-ecological struggles. "This is my father's village," "I recognize this fragmented land, we harvest it too," "the green investors came to our village, too." This revealed a latent community of shared experiences, relations, and links, and a subversive geography that then centered the lived experience of the Greek periphery to a collective ground and a struggle to be further explored.

Last, the way the question of land was asked transpired links between different groups. It generated the beginning of a web of knowledge relations, exchange, and sharing. Activists forged links between local struggles and possibilities of synergies. Academic researchers, including myself, figured future research paths and collaborations. Involved artists shaped new coalitions. For example, learning from the soundscapes of Ludwig Berger, together with him UrbanDig ventured to artistically explore drought in the ecology of the Greek island of Sifnos in the upcoming project "Thirst of the Land."[59]

My own impression is that the employed research tools will not remain static. They will continue to develop, and out of them new research constellations will emerge—ultimately to enable exploration of a research poetics in which many ways of knowledge production become possible. In this, knowledge making emerges as differently unique depending on each research constellation, and knowledge outlines as a social craft. Against the singularity of a universal truth, this signifies a pluriversality, emerging from the innumerous possibilities of creatively coming together. Poetics is bound to a trajectory of creation and "incomparable pleasures," which is shared, Lefebvre highlights, emphasizing it as an act done in togetherness.[60]

Metaxia Markaki

[59] See https://www.urbandigproject.org/single-post/_δίψα (accessed Dec. 12, 2023).

[60] "Yet the poet finds help and support—from musicians, dancers, actors, who share the same frightening path, for which they are compensated with 'incomparable pleasures'." Lefebvre, *Production of Space*, 181.

In this respect, the concept of *sympoiesis* emerges as relevant for the kind of research poetics I argue for here. The term finds its roots in Greek etymology, where *sym-* means "together" or "with," and *poiesis* translates to "making." When combined, it conveys the idea of collaborative or collective creation. Sympoiesis is a concept rooted in ecological thought, notably introduced by the philosopher and biologist Donna Haraway.[61] It embodies the collaborative and interconnected nature of living systems. Unlike the more traditional notion of *autopoiesis*, which emphasizes self-creation and self-maintenance within an individual (biological or social) entity, sympoiesis extends this understanding to highlight the mutual relationships and interdependencies between diverse entities and species in a symphony of co-creation. Organisms and elements coalesce, exchanging resources, information, and energy to collectively shape and sustain complex ecosystems. This perspective emphasizes the intricate dance of interactions where the actions of one entity ripple through the network, influencing and responding to the behaviors of others. The concept of sympoiesis invites us to perceive the natural world as a dynamic and ever-evolving ensemble of contributors, composing a harmonious narrative of life's continuous emergence and adaptation.

Learning from ecological thought, we can imagine knowledge-making as an ecology of sympoiesis, an episteme with a poetic potential of a pluriversal word-making of learning with, doing, with and imaging with. In such a view, questions of agency and right to knowledge production brutally emerge. *Who owns the land?* employed performance ethnography and performance ways of knowing to make a place where a multitude of elements and actors came poetically together, generating a research ecology of relations, interactions, and co-making. Nevertheless, this way of researching entails the potential to extend further, embracing margins and more-than-human dimensions. Research poetics ultimately speaks to the possibility of another way of researching

61 See Haraway, "Symbiogenesis."

> Research poetics ultimately speaks to the possibility of another way of researching and knowledge-making, imaginative and synthetic, and of a creative enactment of critique and analysis in subversive manners.

Who Owns the Land?

and knowledge-making, imaginative and synthetic, and of a creative enactment of critique and analysis in subversive manners. Nonetheless it remains incomplete until a radical reshaping occurs of the socio-ecological communities in which knowledge is produced, shared, and reproduced.

Exodus

[Whispers, discussions. The performance has ended. Some of the audience stay to discuss together. Others leave the room, heading back to the city. The theatrical convention is a safe place, a heterotopia. Things can happen here, convincingly belonging to the sphere of fantasy and art. What happens later, outside? On the street, people hover around.]

Voices
Who owns the land?
None of us. Or everyone …
Speaking of which, ownership of land is anyway
     absurd. Absurd and ridiculous.

Researcher notes in her diary
How will this evolve? The material is by now out of the researchers' and performers' hands and authorship, open to develop further, to be appropriated and explored. The transportation and reembodiment of peripheral struggles and histories to the city center of Athens has reached the urban audience. Unexpected continuities and links emerged, activating people's own experiences and pointing to a latent geography beyond the center/periphery binary, one with subversive potential.
    Yet I still recall the variegated reactions of the village residents who came as part of the audience. Some recognized their familiar stories voiced-out. They felt empowered by the centrality their stories acquired and the power of the medium to report their struggles to a wider audience. They informally filmed parts of the performance and proudly uploaded them on the social media of their local communities. Others remained puzzled. The well-educated mayor judged it a great but too intellectual endeavor. "Villagers will not find it fun." He was expecting more of a parody of their village life. P., one of my key informants, did

Metaxia Markaki

not come—"I know the story, it's my life, no need to see it"—leaving me deeply perplexed. Who was the play for? And for whom was the knowledge produced? Can one ever truly represent the story of another? And how deeply are embodied power—knowledge relations rooted?

"I am located in the margin," writes bell hooks. "Not the marginality which is imposed by oppressive structures but that marginality one chooses as site of resistance. … We are transformed, individually, collectively, as we make radical creative space which affirms and sustains our subjectivity, which gives us a new location from which to articulate our sense of the world."[62] In her words, I found some answer—and the meaning of creatively exploring ways of knowing as a space of resistance.

[62] hooks, "Choosing the Margin," 23.

ACKNOWLEDGMENTS

I would like to extend thanks to all the anonymous participants for their oral testimonies, and to all and each single member of the UrbanDig team for embracing me so kindly in this creative learning journey—Giorgos Sachinis, Eirini Alexiou, Panayota Pantazi, Anna Magouliti, Eirini Iliopoulou, the talented actors Giannis Askaroglou, Gregoris Fritzilas, and Grigiris Giwrgos Fritzilas, and all guests speakers in the "Who owns the land?" lecture series for sharing resources with us. I would also like to thank Jan Silberberger for his review, the editor of this book, Nitin Bathla, for the productive feedback, the editor from gta Verlag, Jennifer Bartmess, for her invaluable contribution and engagement with this text, as well as Julien Lafontaine Carboni and Maria Chassioti for their insightful discussion and generous resources.

Who Owns the Land?

Figure 1   "Field": the olive harvest around the village of Kapelitsa, November 2019

Figure 2   "Stage": three bodies perform, transcending through all roles and all temporalities during the UrbanDig Project performance *Who owns the land?* Athens, 2021–2022

Metaxia Markaki

Figure 3 Stage set, performing in the researcher's notebook, designed by Anna Magoulioti and Nadia Sokou for the UrbanDig Project performance *Who owns the land?*

Figure 4 "More Voices": the researcher on stage introducing the public open-lecture series to the audience, flanking the UrbanDig Project performance *Who owns the land?*

Who Owns the Land?

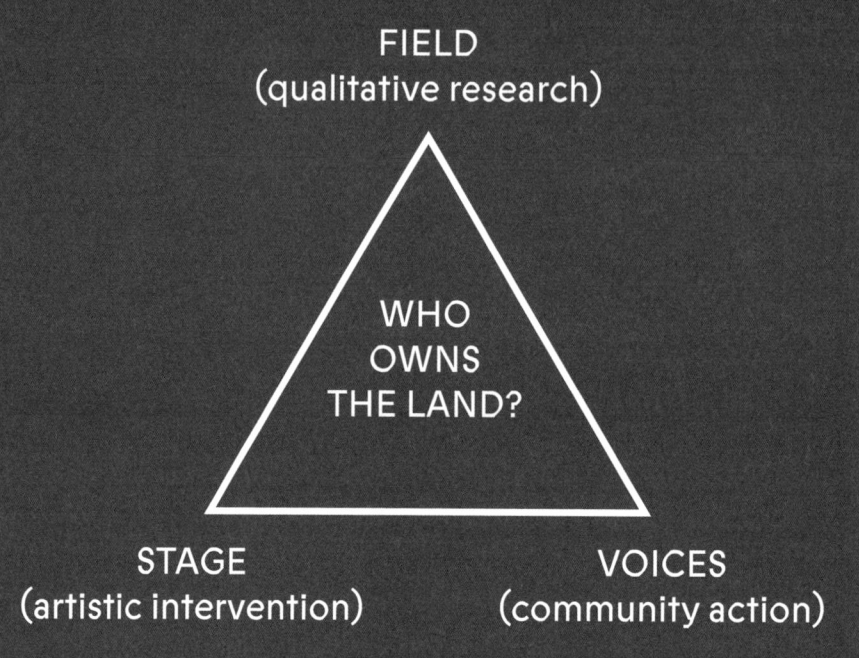

Figure 5   A methodological research triangle: The three research acts produce a space for a question to be asked.

Metaxia Markaki

BIBLIOGRAPHY

A

Antimiichuk, Roman. "The Contemporary City as Theater." LinkedIn, July 30, 2019. https://www.linkedin.com/pulse/contemporary-city-theater-roman-antimiichuk/ (accessed February 16, 2023).

Aristotle. *Poetics*, translated by Anthony Kenny. Oxford: Oxford University Press, 2013.

B

Bachelard, Gaston. *La formation de l'esprit scientifique: Contribution à une psychanalyse de la connaissance*. Paris: Vrin, 1993.

Barone, Tom. "From Genre Blurring to Audience Blending: Reflections on the Field Emanating from an Ethnodrama." *Anthropology & Education Quarterly* 33, no. 2 (2002): 255–267.

Barone, Tom, and Elliot W. Eisner. *Arts Based Research*. Los Angeles: Sage, 2012.

Boal, Augusto. *Theatre of the Oppressed*, translated by Charles A. McBride, Maria-Odilia Leal McBride, and Emily Fryer. London: Pluto Press, 2000.

C

Caldeira, Teresa PR. "Peripheral Urbanization: Autoconstruction, Transversal Logics, and Politics in Cities of the Global South." *Environment and Planning D: Society and Space* 35, no. 1 (2017): 3–20.

Chatziefstathiou, D., E. Iliopoulou, and M. Magkou. "UrbanDig Project: Sport Practices and Artistic Interventions for Co-Creating Urban Space." *Sport in Society* 22, no. 5 (2019): 871–84. https://doi.org/10.1080/17430437.2018.1430485.

Conquergood, Dwight. "Beyond the Text: Toward a Performative Cultural Politics." In *The Future of Performance Studies: Visions and Revisions*, edited by Sheron J. Dailey, 25–36. Annandale, VA: National Communication Association, 1998.

Couling, Nancy. "Formats of Extended Urbanisation in Ocean Space." In *Emerging Urban Spaces: A Planetary Perspective*, edited by Philipp Horn, Paola Alfaro d'Alencon, and Ana Claudia Duarte Cardoso, 149–76. Cham: Springer International, 2018. https://doi.org/10.1007/978-3-319-57816-3_8.

D

Dell'Angelo, Tabitha. "Down the Rabbit Hole: An Ethnodrama to Explore a Fantastical First Year of Teaching." *Qualitative Inquiry* 27, no. 1 (2021): 77–84. https://doi.org/10.1177/1077800419879192.

Denzin, Norman K. "The Call to Performance." *Symbolic Interaction* 26, no. 1 (2003): 187–207. https://doi.org/10.1525/si.2003.26.1.187.

Denzin, Norman K., and Yvonna S. Lincoln, eds. *The SAGE Handbook of Qualitative Research*. 4th edition. Thousand Oaks, CA: Sage, 2011.

Devereaux, Cathryn A. "Breaking the Fourth Wall: An Ethnodrama of Blackgirls' Life Notes on Urban Schooling." EdD, Teachers College, Columbia University ProQuest Dissertations Publishing, 2021.

Diener, Roger, Jacques Herzog, Marcel Meili, Pierre de Meuron, and Christian Schmid. *Switzerland: An Urban Portrait*. 3 volumes. Edited by ETH Studio Basel, Contemporary City Institute. Basel: Birkhäuser, 2006.

F

Foucault, Michel. *The History of Sexuality*. Vol. 1: *An Introduction*, translated by Robert Hurley. New York: Pantheon, 1978.

Foucault, Michel. "What is Enlightenment?" In *The Foucault Reader*, edited by Paul Rabinow, 32–50. New York: Pantheon Books, 1984.

G

Glissant, Édouard. *Poetics of Relation*. Michigan: University of Michigan Press, 1997.

Glynn, Martin. *Speaking Data and Telling Stories: Data Verbalization for Researchers*. New York: Routledge, 2019.

Goldberg, RoseLee. "Performance—Art for All?" *Art Journal* 40, no. 1/2 (1980): 369–76. https://doi.org/10.2307/776603.

Goldstein, Tara. "Hong Kong, Canada: Playwriting as Critical Ethnography." *Qualitative Inquiry* 7, no. 3 (2001): 279–303.

Gururani, Shubhra, Loraine Kennedy, and Ashima Sood, eds. *Engaging the Urban from the Periphery*. SAMAJ: South Asia Multidisciplinary Academic Journal 26 (2021).

H

Halberstam, Judith, *The Queer Art of Failure*. Durham, NC, and London: Duke University Press, 2011.

Haraway, Donna. "Symbiogenesis, Sympoiesis, and Art Science Activisms for Staying with the Trouble." In *Arts of Living on a Damaged Planet: Ghosts and Monsters of the Anthropocene*, edited by Anna Lowenhaupt Tsing, Heather Anne Swanson, Elaine Gan, and Nils Bubandt, M25–M50. Minneapolis: University of Minnesota Press, 2017.

Holston, James. "Insurgent Citizenship in an Era of Global Urban Peripheries." *City & Society* 21, no. 2 (2009): 245–267.

hooks, bell. "Choosing the Margin as a Space of Radical Openness." *Framework: The Journal of Cinema and Media* 36 (1989): 15–23.

K

Kanellopoulou, Charis. "Space in Common: Socially Engaged Art in the Athens of Crisis." *Journal of Greek Media & Culture* 5, no. 2 (October 2019): 211–30. https://doi.org/10.1386/jgmc.5.2.211_1.

Keil, Roger, and Fulong Wu, eds. *After Suburbia: Urbanization in the Twenty-First Century*. Toronto: University of Toronto Press, 2022.

Knowles, J. Gary, and Ardra L. Cole, eds. *Handbook of the Arts in Qualitative Research: Perspectives, Methodologies, Examples, and Issues*. Los Angeles: Sage, 2008.

Kockelkorn, Anne. "Uncanny Theater: A Postmodernist Housing Play in Paris's Banlieues, 1972–1992." In *Productive Universals—Specific Situations: Critical Engagements in Art, Architecture, and Urbanism*, edited by Anne Kockelkorn and Nina Zschocke, 336–381. London: Sternberg Press, 2019.

L

Leavy, Patricia, ed. *Handbook of Arts-Based Research*. New York: Guilford Publications, 2017.

Lefebvre, Henri. *Metaphilosophy*, edited by Stuart Elden, translated by David Fernbach. London and New York: Verso Books, 2016.

Lefebvre, Henri. *The Production of Space*, translated by Donald Nicholson-Smith. Oxford and Cambridge, MA: Blackwell, 1991.

M

Malhotra, Neera, and Veronica Hotton. "Contemplating Positionalities: An Ethnodrama." *Journal of General Education* 67, no. 1–2 (January 2018): 152–71. https://doi.org/10.5325/jgeneeduc.67.1-2.0152.

Marcus, George E. "Afterword: Ethnographic Writing and Anthropological Careers." In *Writing Culture: The Poetics and Politics of Ethnography*, edited by J. Clifford and G. Marcus, 262–66. Berkeley: University of California Press, 1986.

Markaki, Metaxia. "Expropriation and Extended Citizenship: The Peripheralisation of Arcadia." In *Extended Urbanisation: Tracing Planetary Struggles*, edited by Christian Schmid and Milica Topalović, 197–234. Basel: Birkhäuser, 2023.

McFarlane, Colin. *Fragments of the City: Making and Remaking Urban Worlds*. Oakland, CA: University of California Press, 2021

McKinnie, Michael. *City Stages: Theatre and Urban Space in a Global City*. Toronto, Buffalo, and London: University of Toronto Press, 2007.

McNiff, Shaun. "Philosophical and Practical Foundations of Artistic Inquiry: Creating Paradigms, Methods, and Presentations Based in Art." In *Handbook of Arts-Based Research*, edited by Patricia Levy, 22–36. New York: Guilford Publications, 2017.

Mienczakowski, Jim. "Ethnodrama: Performed Research—Limitations and Potential." In *Handbook of Ethnography*, edited by Paul Atkinson, Amanda Coffey, Sara Delamont, John Lofland, and Lyn Lofland, 469–475. London: Sage, 2001.

Mienczakowski, Jim, and Stephen Morgan, "Ethnodrama: Constructing Participatory, Experiential and Compelling Research through Performance." In *Handbook of Action Research*, edited by Peter Reason and Hilary Bradbury, 219–226. Concise edition. London, Thousand Oaks, CA, and New Delhi: Sage, 2006.

O

Olsen, Stein Haugom. "What Is Poetics?" *The Philosophical Quarterly* 26, no. 105 (October 1976): 338–51. https://doi.org/10.2307/2218864.

P

Petersen, Eva Bendix. "Resistance and Enrolment in the Enterprise University: An Ethnodrama in Three Acts, with Appended Reading." *Journal of Education Policy* 24, no. 4 (2009): 409–22. https://doi.org/10.1080/02680930802669953.

R

Reis, Nadine, and Michael Lukas. *Beyond the Megacity: New Dimensions of Peripheral Urbanization in Latin America*. Toronto: University of Toronto Press, 2022.

Ren, Xuefei. "The Peripheral Turn in Global Urban Studies: Theory, Evidence, Sites." *SAMAJ: South Asia Multidisciplinary Academic Journal* 26 (2021), 1–7. https://doi.org/10.4000/samaj.7413.

S

Saldaña, Johnny, ed. *Ethnodrama: An Anthology of Reality Theatre*. Vol. 5 of *Crossroads in Qualitative Inquiry*, series editors Norman K. Denzin, and Yvonna S. Lincoln. Thousand Oaks, CA: AltaMira, 2005.

Saldaña, Johnny. "Ethnodrama and Ethnotheatre." In *Handbook of the Arts in Qualitative Research*, edited by J. Gary Knowles and Ardra L. Cole, 195–207. Los Angeles: Sage, 2008.

Saldaña, Johnny. *Ethnotheatre: Research from Page to Stage*. London and New York: Routledge, 2016.

Salvatore, Joe. "Ethnodrama and Ethnotheatre." In *Handbook of Arts-Based Research*, edited by Patricia Levy, 267–87. New York: Guilford Publications, 2017.

Schmid, Christian. *Henri Lefebvre and the Theory of Production of Space*, translated by Zachary Murphy King. London and Brooklyn: Verso, 2022.

Shepard, Benjamin. "Urban Spaces as Living Theater: Toward a Public Space Party for Play, Poetry, and Naked Bike Rides (New York City, 2010–2015)." *Revue française d'études américaines* 146, no. 1 (2016): 107–24. https://doi.org/10.3917/rfea.146.0107.

Simone, A. M. (Abdou Maliqalim). "People as Infrastructure: Intersecting Fragments in Johannesburg." *Public Culture* 16, no. 3 (2004): 407–29.

Stavridis, Stavros. Από την Πόλη Οθόνη στην Πόλη Σκηνή [From the City Screen to the City Stage]. Ελληνικά Γράμματα [Ellinika Grammata]: Athens, 2009.

T

Taylor, Diana. *Performance*. Durham, NC: Duke University Press, 2016.

Taylor, Jamilah, Emily Namey, Annette Carrington Johnson, and Greg Guest. "Beyond the Page: A Process Review of Using Ethnodrama to Disseminate Research Findings." *Journal of Health Communication* 22, no. 6 (2017): 532–44. https://doi.org/10.1080/10810730.2017.1317303.

Topalović, Milica. "Hinterland: Singapore and Urbanisms beyond the Border." *Kerb: Journal of Landscape Architecture* 24 (2016): 98–99.

V

Vanover, Charles, and Johnny Saldaña. "Chalkboard Concerto: Growing Up as a Teacher in the Chicago Public Schools." In *Ethnodrama: An Anthology of Reality Theater*, edited by Johnny Saldaña, n.p. Walnut Creek, CA: AltaMira, 2005.

W

Ward Randolph, Adah, and Mary E. Weems. "Speak Truth and Shame the Devil: An Ethnodrama in Response to Racism in the Academy." *Qualitative Inquiry* 16, no. 5 (2010): 310–13. https://doi.org/10.1177/1077800409358864.

Warren, Peggy P. *Black Women's Narratives of NHS Work-Based Learning: An Ethnodrama—The Difference Between Rhetoric and Lived Experience*. Berlin: Peter Lang, 2019.

Z

Zontou, Zoe, and George Sachinis "UrbanDig Project: Theatre of Neighbourhoods." Chapter 3 in *Redefining Theatre Communities*, edited by Marco Galea and Szabolcs Musca, n.p. Bristol: Intellect Books, 2019.

IMAGE CREDITS

Figure 1: Metaxia Markaki
Figure 2: Alekos & Christos Bourelias. ©*UrbanDig Project*
Figure 3a: Set Design: Anna Magoulioti, Nadia Sokou; Photo: Alekos & Christos Bourelias. ©*UrbanDig Project*
Figure 3b: Set Design: Anna Magoulioti, Nadia Sokou; Photo: Metaxia Markaki
Figure 4: Pavlina Zika
Figure 5: Metaxia Markaki, based on the UrbanDig Project's methodology. Redrawn by Offshore

---

Markaki, Metaxia. "Who Owns the Land? On Research Poetics and Performance as Ways of Knowing." In Nitin Bathla, ed., *Researching Otherwise: Pluriversal Methodologies for Landscape and Urban Studies*. Zurich: gta Verlag, 2024, 97–129. https://doi.org/10.54872/gta/4692-3.

Sensory Methods

Ludwig Berger

Knowing a Place by Ear: Approaches to the Sonic Research of Landscapes

Sound is a key factor in our everyday experience of the environment.[1] Sound and acoustics of a place not only give us orientation and a sense of space but also impact our health and quality of life. Apart from the negative impact of noise, the sonic characteristics of a place influences, for example, whether we feel belonging or exclusion, tranquility or anxiousness, intimacy or alienation.[2] Furthermore, our identity and perception of our living environment is shaped by the sonic relationship between natural elements, different living beings, mechanical sounds, and cultural sound signals.[3] It is also an important indicator for the social and ecological state of a site.[4]

A variety of scientific disciplines, as well as artistic research practices, have developed promising approaches for sound-oriented analysis.[5] Through the emergence of soundscape studies in the late 1970s and sound studies in the early 2000s, the importance of sound as a dimension of landscapes has been highlighted. A broad variety of disciplines are increasingly engaging with the sonic dimension of places, leading to the emergence of a number of sub-disciplines, such as soundscape ecology, archaeoacoustics, or sound ethnography. In parallel, the branch of sound art has developed many compositional, installation-based, and performative approaches to reveal sonic characteristics of places. Yet a broad consideration of the sonic dimension of places is still missing in landscape and urban studies. In the teaching and practice of (landscape) architecture, the role of sound is often reduced to noise protection, which is pursued through quantitative acoustic measurements. The multi-layered cultural and sociopolitical factors in the perception of sonic landscapes are often disregarded.

At the Chair of Landscape Architecture of Christophe Girot at ETH Zurich we have been studying soundscapes for over a decade. Through numerous courses and workshops, as well as publications and dissertations, exhibitions, and symposia, we have been analyzing the sonic dimension of landscapes and

[1] See Augoyard and Torgue, *Sonic Experience*; Samuels, et al., "Soundscapes"; Kang and Schulte-Fortkamp, *Soundscape*.
[2] On exclusion, see Kato, "Soundscape"; on tranquility and anxiousness, see Watts, et al., "Influence of Soundscape"; on intimacy or alienation, see Aletta, et al., "Monitoring Sound Levels."
[3] See Feld, "Sound Structure."
[4] See LaBelle, *Acoustic Territories*; Qi, et al., "Soundscape Characteristics."
[5] See Bull and Cobussen, *Handbook of Sonic Methodologies*.

Ludwig Berger

their design possibilities through means of experimental audiovisual fieldwork and composition.[6] My teaching and research activities at the chair overlap with my own artistic practice as a sound artist. To explore landscapes with the ears, I use various strategies and techniques that have proven very useful for experiencing, examining, and reimagining landscapes. They may serve as starting points for a multi-sensorial landscape and urban research that incorporates the sonic dimension of a place.

Listening and responding

Building upon the rich tradition of Pauline Oliveros's "Deep Listening,"[7] as well as contemporary composition and sound art, I use listening exercises to develop an embodied knowledge for the sound of a place. A simple exercise that I use at the beginning of my courses and workshops is what I call "soundscape contour drawing." As a part of this exercise, participants sit down in a place, close their eyes, and hold a pencil over a piece of paper. On cue, they begin to trace their auditory experience in gestures with their drawing hand. As a rule, the pen always remains in contact with the paper and never stands still. The direction, intensity and speed of the drawing are translated directly from the ear to the hand in an intuitive way. The resultant drawing on paper is not the product or goal of the exercise, but the listening experience itself. The exercise helps bring an utmost concentration to listening and to strengthen the presence in the moment. As hearing always remains in motion, in flow, the constant change of the soundscape with its finest nuances becomes comprehensible. In my own experience, I remember places and moments I have listened to in this way for a very long time. The gesture of drawing inscribes the sounds firmly in memory. Exercises like these form the basis for differentiated precise hearing that is deeply rooted in one's own body. The exercise also shows that there is no such thing as neutrally listening to a place, but instead that our concentration, the choice of our focus, our physical state, and our interpretation of the sounds are an inseparable part of what is commonly called "soundscape."

6 Camera Obscura Auditiva in 2010, Melting Landscapes in 2018, Sonic Topologies in 2022. See also Girot, et al., *Sampling Kyoto Gardens*; Nadine Schütz, "Cultivating Sound"; Berger, et al., *Bodies of Water*.

7 See Oliveros, *Deep Listening*.

Collective improvisations on site can in turn bring these different ways of listening into communication with each other. During a seminar trip in the volcanic landscape of Etna in Sicily we followed this simple score to investigate different types of landscapes:

→ Figure 1

— Spread out in the field but stay close enough to hear the others.
— Listen to the present and potential sounds in the landscape: its textures, tones, rhythms, silences, gestures, and acoustics.
— Gently start creating sounds with the silent objects around you. Play them as they would play themselves. Don't force anything. Practice attention instead of intention.
— Let your movements be guided by all your sensations: sight, smell, touch, temperature, movement of air, the perceived atmosphere.
— Keep your attention broad, continuously listening to the whole field of sound.

In the interplay of the various human and nonhuman bodies in the landscape, a non-verbal discourse emerges about the qualities and potentiality of place. This form of discourse between listening and responding can also be practiced on a smaller scale. The instructions for the listening game "Babbling" encourage participants to modify the sound of a stream by taking turns and paying close attention to the sonic role of the various objects in the landscape, such as stones, sticks, and leaves in the water:

→ Video 1

Babbling, performance piece documentation
doi.org/mjh2

— A stone or another thing in or close to the water emits a call to the human player.
— The human player places, replaces, or removes the thing into, within, or out of the running water.
— The water responds to the action by changing its sonic expression.

All these exercises aim to develop a sense of the often subtle differences in sounds between different locations, as well as within the same location at different times or configurations. In the process, an intimate and embodied knowledge is produced that is a prerequisite for further engagement with the sounds of a place.

Ludwig Berger

Multiperspectival field recording

In accordance with the methods of active listening and responding described above, I understand field recording as a performative practice in which the bodies of the recorder and the technical devices interact with other bodies in the landscape. Among the decisive factors are the choice of microphones, their position or trajectory, the activity of the person recording, as well as the moment of recording. By having a variety of recordists with different interests and microphones spread out, a site can be unfolded into a complex set of audio recordings.

In a series of courses taught over different seasons of the year, we visited a dam and electricity power plant in the Grisons Alps. Together with assistants from the ETH Department of Architecture, sixteen students took analog photos, laser scans, as well as recording sounds at different zones of the landscape.[8] A wide variety of equipment was used for the sound recordings: surround microphones, binaural microphones, contact microphones, hydrophones, geophones, electromagnetic sensors, and laser Doppler vibrometers. In this way we made sounds audible that were hidden or barely audible to the human ear and took acoustic perspectives of a wide variety of objects in the landscape. For example, in the same room inside the dam we could hear the reverberation of the place in surround sound, the impact of water drops on concrete at close range, the electromagnetic waves of the cables hidden in the walls, and our voices echoing inside the pendulum wire that stretches the entire height of the wall.

For *Melting Landscapes* in the *Bodies of Water* trilogy, we studied the tongue of the Morteratsch Glacier over several years and over different seasons.[9] In winter we pressed underwater microphones into the ice using snow as an adhesive mass. Once the microphones made contact with the glacial ice they acted like stethoscopes on a body, revealing the complex sounds taking place inside the glacier. In the summer we dropped hydrophones into the glacier puddles and crevasses. Each entry point offers a unique and unpredictable spectrum of sounds. In this process, sounds became audible that were not perceivable from

[8] Berger et al., *Bodies of Water*. The trilogy includes *Melting Landscapes* (described below), *Dammed Landscapes* (described here), and *Buried Landscapes*.

[9] Berger et al., *Bodies of Water*.

→ Audio 1

Excerpts from *Dammed Landscapes*
doi.org/mjh3

→ Figure 2

the outside with the human ear: melodic squeaking, clicking and rattling, gargling and gurgling, hissing and fizzing, deep droning. Numerous sounds of microscopic melting processes, repeatedly interrupted by large ice blocks moving or breaking off. What looks like a solid mass from the outside, sounds like a living body from the inside.

We made our recordings available to the public as a three-record set with a photo book (*Bodies of Water,* gta Verlag 2022), and also as spatial sound installations, as a concert series in dialogue with musicians, and in sonic lectures.[10] The presentations opened a sensory access to glaciers and the climate crisis for the listeners, and thus the possibility of an "intimacy without proximity."[11] The comparative images of today's glaciers to their past are well known, as is data on ice loss and the predictions concerning their future. Sound, however, offers a different temporal perspective: not the before and after, but the continuous time in which the glacier is melting. The sounds also allow access to another spatial scale. On a visual level, one perceives mostly the events of a glacier on a large scale, like the collapse of ice blocks. In sound one can experience the small scale in which the global climate catastrophe also takes its course. Every change in the temperature of a glacier is immediately audible in sound because of increased melting activity. Not only do the sounds of the ice itself became audible, but also sounds from the outside reaching into the interior of the ice: wind, snow, flowing meltwater, and our footsteps and voices resonated in the glacier. The microphones embedded in the glacier enable a perceptual shift through which we listen to the world and ourselves from a nonhuman perspective.

In the 2020 film *Fieldworking*, artist Laura Harrington documents how such an interaction can look and sound in a bog. In the Pennine Moors in the north of England, we buried hydrophones in the peat and recorded our movements on the vegetation, mainly consisting of *Sphagnum* moss. If a microphone is buried within the peat of a bog, that bog not only becomes a responsive membrane but a resonant body of sorts. Listening through the bog, we forget which is body or activator, namely our own breathing or that

[10] Exhibitions at *CLIMATE CARE* Vienna Biennale for Change 2021 (MAK Museum Vienna, Austria), *Spazio Materia* (Prato, Italy) 2021, *Cima Norma Art Festival* (Dangio, Switzerland) 2022, etc. Concerts of the Chuchchepati Orchestra (with Patrick Kessler, Dieb13 and Julian Sartorius).

[11] See Metcalf, "Intimacy without Proximity."

Ludwig Berger

of the moss compressing and decompressing, and which voice belongs to the wind, ourselves, or another. The peat is porous enough to allow us to listen deep yet coherent enough to answer in its own resonant voice. Every action has far-reaching consequences. Each momentary footstep upon the moss or peaty ground leaves a trace—it triggers a release that may last a week, an impression that may last for months or even years. As the bog recovers, the duration and level of the microscopic sounds correspond to the energy of that impact. By responding so clearly, it calls for responsibility. The idea is that we not only listen to the bog, but that the bog—as well as the glacier and other phenomena—might open new perspectives on landscapes.

Sonic mapping

But how can multiple sound recordings of a location be organized? One popular method is that of "sound maps," where sound recordings are arranged on a visual map, often with satellite imagery. What is often underexplored in such sound maps is the dimension of time: although the geolocated sound recordings are only snapshots of a specific moment, they are treated as fixed representations of places. Working with a field recording, I tried to develop an approach in which a place can be experienced specifically through its changes over time. In a village in Alsace, France, I mounted a microphone under a roof for a year, recording the sounds of the surrounding gardens, meadows, and backyards (listen via the link to Audio 2).[12] Every full hour, I automatically recorded one minute of sound. Then I assembled representative recordings from four times of day (morning, noon, evening, night) into four time-compression sequences through the year. The sonic landscape is composed of birds, sporadic cars, church bells, dogs, distant human activity, insects, wind. Arriving at an arbitrary moment there, it could seem like a silent place. Yet what we call silence is just a slowness of development—a density that forms over time, rather than in space. Especially a place with a high biodiversity and lack of constant and dominant sounds is a constantly shifting field of possibilities, in which the effects but also the actors

[12] Berger, *A Year's Hours*.

→ Audio 2
Excerpts from *A Year's Hours behind My Father's House*
doi.org/mjh4

change all the time—from hour to hour, day to day, season to season. The sun and the rain make the birds sing or fall silent. When the wind blows from a certain direction, the church bells are heard from a village in the distance. The grasshoppers in August stridulate from a different position every evening. The leaves rustle differently in spring than in autumn. Youngsters race through the village on newly tuned mopeds. Every year the territory of the resident species shifts. Some disappear, others arrive. This process is destructively accelerated by climate change and ongoing mass species extinction. Now the soundscape does not only change cyclically from season to season but also irretrievably from year to year. The landscape of the place has not visibly changed in the past thirty years. Yet sonically the extinction of 80 percent of the insect population is strongly perceivable. The acoustic identity of a place is much more fragile and dynamic than the visual identity of a place, and thus asks for a greater attention.

> The acoustic identity of a place is much more fragile and dynamic than the visual identity of a place, and thus asks for a greater attention.

As for spatially arranged sound maps, I propose a performative and bodily approach. For the ETH Zurich /EPF Lausanne Summer School "Tentacular Writing,"[13] organized in the Swiss mountain village of Tschlin, this took the form of a "Tentacular Sound Map." In the workshop, eight groups of participants with recording devices started their recording devices simultaneously in a hall located in the center of the village. After a synchronization clap, they swarmed out into the eight cardinal directions. The group became a large collective body with extended ears, reaching into the distant alleys and paths for sounds. During the silent walk, the groups listened to the sounds in the landscape on their headphones and explored different acoustic perspectives with their recorders. They were invited to make silent materials or spaces audible using their voice and hands, but always aiming for attention instead of intention. After fifteen minutes they were asked to find a place with an interesting acoustic perspective and record it for another fifteen minutes. While sitting still, they wrote down short observations of the sounds and their way

[13] Organized by Metaxia Markaki, Johanna Just, and Sila Karataş.

Ludwig Berger

of perceiving them, indicating the minutes of the recorder with each note. Finally they walked back to their initial meeting place and stopped the recording. In the hall they found eight loudspeakers arranged in the same cardinal directions, through which the eight recordings were played synchronously. In the hall emerged an acoustic miniature of the environment as recorded by the different groups. The dense village in the north and the wide valley in the south became clearly tangible as larger acoustic structures. Larger sonic events, such as passing cars, connected the distant recording locations, creating spatial sound gestures in the hall. The listeners could hear the entirety of the sounds in the center or get close to individual speakers. When the static recording portion was reached, participants read their timed notes aloud, adding context and personal interpretations of the sounds. In this way a polyphonic spatial portrait of the village unfolded on a morning in September 2022.

While in this case a larger spatial structure was translated into a smaller scale, the work *Bien* takes the opposite approach. For this sound installation, a miniature of a shed was reconstructed on a scale of 1:8, placed next to the original shed and settled with a bee colony. In each of the rows of honeycombs, a contact microphone was embedded in the wax to pick up the bees' vibrations. The signals from the microphones were transmitted in real time into the large shed, where the sounds were transmitted into the wood via vibration transducers. The transducers were arranged in the shed correspondingly to the microphones in the miniature. In this way the small scale of the beehive became tangible on a human scale. Thus the shed became an enlarged acoustic model of the beehive on a scale of 8:1. The continuous live installation allowed returning visitors to hear how the activity of the bees in the beehive changes depending on the time of day and the weather.

→ Figure 3

→ Video 2

Bien, installation documentation
doi.org/mjh5

Sonic thinking

In the academic world, knowledge is accepted primarily in linguistic, literary, as well as numerical and visual forms. Recently, promising sonic research has approached sound not only as content but also as a medium of knowledge production. Frameworks such as "acoustemology,"[14] "sonic ways of knowing,"[15] and the recent development of presentation formats such as "audio papers"[16] call for discourses through sonic media, rather than exclusively through spoken or written language. In the same spirit we organized a "Sonic Symposium" in June 2022 within the festival *Sonic Topologies,* organized by the Chair of Professor Christophe Girot. The symposium took place in the Old Botanical Garden in Zurich and brought together actors from design, theory, science, and art who are concerned with the sonic dimension of landscape and architecture.

The participants were invited to investigate the site and its environment from the perspective of their respective practices. These included historical and socio-political analyses of the site, the sonification of plant and animal habitats, and the practice of landscape architectural design by means of sound compositions. Five days prior to the public presentation, the participants were able to work on site, allowing for the development of a site-specific contribution. On the public weekend, a multichannel loudspeaker system was installed, through which the participants presented their sonic lectures and performances. The forms of presentation had a strong focus on sonic media, such as field recordings, sonification of data, or acoustic signals. The speaker system allowed the participants to play back existing recordings from the site, amplify sounds live or diffuse new sounds into the site.

By encouraging non-verbal forms of presentation, the discursive potential of spatialized sound became apparent. The compositional montage of different sounds offers a syntax from which an argument can emerge. Furthermore, the sounds played mingled with the other sounds of the place and its surroundings, commenting, contradicting, or blending each other. In their performance *Blood on the Fruits and Blood at the Root*, Nathalie Anguezomo Mba Bikoro and Gilles Aubry connected the airplanes flying over the botanical garden with the record collection of the adjacent Ethnological Museum. There, the artists selected records from the countries with which

14 See Feld, "Acoustemology."
15 See Henriques, *Sonic Bodies*.
16 See Krogh Groth and Samson, "Audio Papers."

→ Figure 4

Ludwig Berger

Switzerland has questionable CO_2 compensation agreements: Georgia, Peru, Senegal, and Ghana.[17] In a live performance during the festival, Aubry played one of these vinyl records on the top of the Old Botanical Garden each time an airplane was departing or landing at Zurich airport. By linking the sounds of the local soundscape with its climate-damaging air traffic, the colonial collection of the museum, and the neocolonial national politics ("CO_2lonialism"), a non-verbal discourse on translocal power structures emerged. Thus even simple sonic setups can reveal complex entanglements. As an equal element alongside language, different perspectives and themes can be related in a meaningful way.

These described methods of active listening, recording, and composing have a great potential to generate and communicate new knowledge about places and to critically negotiate relationships taking place in them—performatively, situated and embodied.

[17] "In recent years, Switzerland has reached agreements with Georgia, Peru, Senegal and Ghana to support the implementation of 'low-hanging fruit' climate change mitigation. In return, the countries will transfer the mitigation outcomes to Switzerland to help it meet its national target under the Paris Agreement. These agreements send no signal for decarbonisation in Switzerland and make it more difficult for the host countries to meet their own climate target" (artist text).

ACKNOWLEDGMENTS
I wish to express my sincere appreciation to Christophe Girot for his invaluable support and trust throughout my sonic research endeavor at ETH Zurich. Grateful acknowledgment is extended to my esteemed colleagues at the MediaLab (Laura Endres, Fabian Gutscher, Dennis Häusler, Johannes Rebsamen, Matthias Vollmer), all my other colleagues at the the Chair of Christophe Girot, and last but not least the dedicated architecture students at ETH Zurich, whose collaborative efforts enriched the scholarly exploration. Furthermore, special thanks are extended to the participating artists and collaborators of "Sonic Topologies," as well as to the diverse group of artists with whom I have had the privilege to engage in meaningful collaboration.

Knowing a Place by Ear

Ludwig Berger

Figure 1   Collective listening and responding, Etna, Sicily

Knowing a Place by Ear

Figure 2 Students recording the Morteratsch Glacier in Grissons, Switzerland

Figure 3 "Bien," installation by Ludwig Berger, Klang Moor Schopfe Festival, Gais, Switzerland, 2019

Ludwig Berger

Figure 4　"Sonic Topologies" symposium, Old Botanical Garden Zurich, 2022

Knowing a Place by Ear

BIBLIOGRAPHY

A

Aletta, Francesco, Dick Botteldooren, Pieter Thomas, Tara Vander Mynsbrugge, Patricia De Vriendt, Dominique Van de Velde, and Paul Devos. "Monitoring Sound Levels and Soundscape Quality in the Living Rooms of Nursing Homes: A Case Study in Flanders (Belgium)." *Applied Sciences* 7, no. 9 (2017), 874. https://doi.org/10.3390/app7090874.

Augoyard, Jean-François, and Henry Torgue. *Sonic Experience: A Guide to Everyday Sounds*. Montreal: McGill-Queen's University Press, 2005. https://doi.org/10.1515/9780773576919.

B

Berger, Ludwig. *A Year's Hours behind My Father's House*. Impulsive Habitat, 2014.

Berger, Ludwig, Christophe Girot, Fabian Gutscher, Dennis Häusler, Johannes Rebsamen, and Matthias Vollmer, eds. *Bodies of Water: A Swiss Landscape Trilogy*. Zurich: gta Verlag, 2022.

Bull, Michael, and Marcel Cobussen, eds. *The Bloomsbury Handbook of Sonic Methodologies*. New York: Bloomsbury, 2020. https://doi.org/10.5040/9781501338786.

F

Feld, Steven. "Acoustemology." In *Keywords in Sound*, edited by David Novak and Matt Sakakeeny, 12–21. Durham, NC, and London: Duke University Press. https://doi.org/10.1215/9780822375494-002.

Feld, Steven. "Sound Structure as Social Structure." *Ethnomusicology* 28, no. 3 (1984), 383–409. https://doi.org/10.2307/851232.

G

Girot, Christophe, Ludwig Berger, Lara Mehling, Nadine Schütz, Matthias Vollmer, eds. *Pamphlet 21: Sampling Kyoto Gardens*. Zurich: gta Verlag, 2017.

H

Henriques, Julian. *Sonic Bodies: Reggae Sound Systems, Performance Techniques, and Ways of Knowing*. New York: Continuum/Bloomsbury, 2011. https://doi.org/10.12801/1947-5403.2015.07.02.07.

K

Kang, Jian, and Brigitte Schulte-Fortkamp, eds. *Soundscape and the Built Environment*. Boca Raton: CRC Press, 2018. https://doi.org/10.1201/b19145.

Kato, Kumi. "Soundscape, Cultural Landscape and Connectivity." *Sites: A Journal of Social Anthropology and Cultural Studies* 6, no. 2 (2009), 80–91. https://doi.org/10.11157/sites-vol6iss2id123.

Krogh Groth, Sanne, and Kristine Samson. "Audio Papers—A Manifesto." *Seismograf* (August 2016). https://doi.org/10.48233/seismograf1601.

L

LaBelle, Brandon. *Acoustic Territories: Sound Culture and Everyday Life*. New York: Continuum/Bloomsbury, 2010. https://doi.org/10.5040/9781501336225.

M

Metcalf, Jacob. "Intimacy without Proximity: Encountering Grizzlies as a Companion Species." *Environmental Philosophy* 5, no. 2 (Fall 2008), 99–128. https://doi.org/10.5840/envirophil20085212.

O

Oliveros, Pauline. *Deep Listening: A Composer's Sound Practice*. New York: iUniverse, 2005.

Q

Qi, Jiaguo, Stuart Gage, Wooyeong Joo, Brian Napoletano, and S Biswas. "Soundscape Characteristics of an Environment: A New Ecological Indicator of Ecosystem Health." In *Wetland and Water Resource Modeling and Assessment: A Watershed Perspective*, edited by Wei Ji, 201–11. Boca Raton: CRC Press, 2008. https://doi.org/10.1201/9781420064155.

S

Samuels, David W., Louise Meintjes, Ana Maria Ochoa, and Thomas Porcello. "Soundscapes: Toward a Sounded Anthropology." *Annual Review of Anthropology* 39 (2010), 329–45. https://doi.org/10.1146/annurev-anthro-022510-132230.

Schütz, Nadine. "Cultivating Sound: The Acoustic Dimension of Landscape Architecture." Doctoral Thesis, ETH Zurich, 2017.

W

Watts, Greg, Amir Khan, and Rob Pheasant. "Influence of Soundscape and Interior Design on Anxiety and Perceived Tranquillity of Patients in a Healthcare Setting." *Applied Acoustics* 104 (2015), 135–41. https://doi.org/10.1016/j.apacoust.2015.11.007.

IMAGE CREDITS

Figures 1–3: Ludwig Berger
Figure 4: Johannes Berger

Ludwig Berger

Berger, Ludwig. "Knowing a Place by Ear: Approaches to the
Sonic Research of Landscapes." In Nitin Bathla, ed., *Researching Otherwise:
Pluriversal Methodologies for Landscape and Urban Studies*.
Zurich: gta Verlag, 2024, 133–149. https://doi.org/10.54872/gta/4692-4.

Knowing a Place by Ear

Nancy Couling

Sensing Ocean Space

Researching Otherwise
Nitin Bathla, ed.

To conduct spatial research on the ocean is to attempt to gain access to a world where we do not belong. While Rachel Carson reminds us that the evidence of our oceanic origins runs through our very system—that the sodium, potassium and calcium constituents of plasma, the watery part of the blood, are similar to the proportions in seawater—she also points out that, having left the sea, our species can no longer physically re-enter it for prolonged periods without mechanical assistance.[1]

In the case of the world ocean,[2] researching otherwise is inextricably connected to researching *elsewhere*. The effort to gain a deeper understanding of both the inherent properties of oceanic space and the exploitative urbanization processes lodged within these spaces poses new research challenges in urban studies and calls for an expanded repertoire of investigative methods.

Habitual urban research methods are ill equipped to capture the fluidity and temporal specificities of ocean space—a profoundly three-dimensional volume deeper than the highest geographical features on land and made up of differentiated seascapes and moving water masses with specific saline and temperature properties that form habitats and meet at fronts or clines.[3] I argue that this space has long ceased to be "natural," and rather has been transformed into an urbanized realm of oil, communications, and transport infrastructure, as well as of large-scale enclosures defining exclusive economic zones, exploration areas, offshore wind production areas, and marine protection zones.[4]

The ocean is an archive of planetary environmental change, containing knowledge about deep time and space. It takes around one thousand years for water to complete one thermohaline circuit around the globe, otherwise referred to as the Great Ocean Conveyor Belt. Seas and other bodies of water also carry crucial intrinsic, embodied sociocultural histories that are communicated otherwise—for example verbally—through generations.[5] Indigenous societies in particular conceive of little separation between a body of water and a human body, between the rights of nature and human rights, an aspect explicitly exemplified

1 Carson and Levinton, *Sea Around Us*, 15.
2 The world ocean is today frequently referred to in the singular to emphasize that the world seas and oceans are interconnected, creating one world ocean. See, for example, UNESCO, "One Ocean Summit."
3 The oceanographic term "cline" is a thin horizontal layer within a fluid with greatly varying properties over a short vertical distance. For example, a cline with a strong vertical salinity gradient within the body of water is called a halocline.
4 See Couling and Hein, *Urbanisation of the Sea*.
5 See Couling, d'Alençon, and Altiok, "Narrative Cartography."

Nancy Couling

by the awarding of legal rights to the Whanganui River in Aotearoa/New Zealand.[6]

The ocean engages multiple human senses. It commands respect and awe and is full of things we do not *know* solely intellectually. The record for underwater free diving is currently just over twenty-four minutes.[7] This limits most direct, unaided human experience of the ocean space to the surface, making it a literally superficial cognitive understanding. However, in this chapter I aim to demonstrate how a fuller spatial understanding can be gained through explorative, immersive research methods that engage a range of senses—in particular sound—in addition to intellectual logic and reason.

Why would such research methods be important for landscape and urban scholars? The overriding reason is that, so far, techno-scientific approaches to ocean management have failed to improve the degraded ecological condition of the world ocean. Instead these approaches have produced abstract, operationalized seas, laid out for marine industries and energy production, and alienated from everyday societal interaction.[8] To date, the "tsunami" of specialized marine data produced has not served to enable a deep human understanding of the issues at stake.[9] My own research on the Baltic,[10] Barents,[11] and North[12] Seas has revealed the degree to which pressure exerted on vital, delicate marine ecosystems through human activities is unrelenting. Holistic, imaginative, and critical research is required that disseminates knowledge, stimulates emotion, and describes potential new human–oceanic relations. In this context, researching otherwise becomes an urgent critical agenda, requiring an expanded range of conceptual and methodological approaches that open new ways of sensing not only liquid environments.

The methods discussed in this chapter link spatial research to both the arts and natural science, whereby results from my explorative design studios carried out with architecture students exemplify different forms of synthesis between these domains.[13] I argue that using the design process as a way of mediating ephemeral spatial phenomena in the ocean is itself a form of researching otherwise. These methods draw

[6] See Argyrou and Hummels, "Legal Personality."
[7] Budimir Šobat (Croatia) is listed in the *The Guinness Book of Records* as holding the underwater (breathing) record at 24 minutes, 37.36 seconds, achieved on March 27, 2021.
[8] See Couling, "Losing Sea."
[9] See Brett, et al., "Ocean Data."
[10] Couling, "Nine Principles."
[11] Couling, "Urbanization of the Ocean."
[12] Couling and Hein, *Urbanisation of the Sea*.
[13] The author leads the master's design course "Explorations in Ocean Space" at Bergen School of Architecture, Norway. See https://explorationsinoceanspace.cargo.site.

Sensing Ocean Space

on critical artistic work that tells stories about the sea, presenting less explored modes of knowing, conversing, and exchanging in an open process inspired by the sea itself as a medium, a place, and an agent with its own history.

Oceanographers' knowledge gives them a detailed understanding across spatial and temporal scales within specialized areas. As an architect carrying out spatial research, the objective is to decipher critical societal connections to the sea, to communicate the emerging phenomena of an urbanized sea, and to consider how other types of knowledge can decolonize and inform our oceanic understanding.

Rather than presenting a complete scientific picture, I explore shifting fragments that raise important questions within a holistic view of a sea's specific spatial system. As Nitin Bathla states in the introduction to this volume, imagination, as an active mode of experience and perception, can help account for what is forgotten, disappeared, hidden, and lost (see p. 21). Large voids remain, but while voids around unanswered questions are the *raison d'être* of research itself, such voids perhaps enable the mystery of the ocean to be carried and maintained, rather than to be submerged, erased, or too roughly explained by scientific facts.[14] Voids—certainly as vital habitats for nonhuman inhabitants—acknowledge a space for other types of intelligence. Hence the very nature of oceanic space affords us the opportunity to reflect and explore otherwise, embracing precisely the realm of the imagination outlined by uncertainty.

14 The idea of "carrying the mystery" comes from artist and professor Tom Chamberlain, expressed in a studio review at Bergen School of Architecture in 2021.

> But while voids around unanswered questions are the *raison d'être* of research itself, such voids perhaps enable the mystery of the ocean to be carried and maintained, rather than to be submerged, erased, or too roughly explained by scientific facts.

Other types of knowledge

Technology mediates our Western relationship with the sea. More than being simply materialized through breathing or navigational devices, the application of technology is the outcome of complex scientific, political, economic, and cultural liaisons, and therefore is never neutral. As Melvin Kranzberg and Carroll Pursell claim: "Technology may be ambivalent, but it does not exist in the abstract; it exists in society."[15] In the case of glaciers in Antarctica and Greenland, ice cores are used by scientists to study the planet's condition thousands of years ago and how it has been modified by anthropogenic change. The oldest ice core records date to 130,000 and 800,000 years ago for Greenland and Antarctica respectively. Then, tracing ice in its liquid form, a new tool from The National Aeronautics and Space Administration (NASA) Jet Propulsion Lab can trace which specific water sources contribute to sea level rise in which parts of the world, thus helping visualize what the researchers involved in this project call "hydrological globalization."[16]

Drawing on this science, anthropologists Cymene Howe and Dominc Boyer try to make sense of these dramatic events from a societal perspective, addressing a conceptual void that I argue is also echoed in architectural and urban debates.[17] In addition to making the short film *Not Ok* about the first major glacier to disappear in Iceland, Howe and Boyer organized the Un-glacier Tour to the glacier's former site, and worked together with local collaborators to make and install a bronze memorial plaque to Okjökul.[18] International news coverage of the plaque's installation ceremony is testimony to the societal impact of such methods of research and dissemination.[19] Contributing an artist's sensibility to these questions, Susan Schuppli explores how different knowledge practices engage with situated materials, for example ice core science and glaciology, indigenous traditions, local observations, activism, policy, and law in the project "Learning from Ice."[20]

The accumulation of global ocean knowledge, while lagging behind space exploration, also relies heavily on the application of techno-science. In 2017 only 6 percent of the global seabed had been mapped to modern standards; five years later this figure stands at 20 percent. UNESCO aims to have 80 percent of the seabed mapped by the end of the 2020s.[21] One of the objectives of the UN Decade of Ocean Science for Sustainable Development, 2021–2030, is to create a digital twin of the world ocean, an incredible investment that requires the mobilization and coordination of a vast number of

15 Kranzberg and Pursell, "Technology's Challenge," 706.
16 Watkins et al., "Improved Methods for Observing Earth's Time Variable Mass Distribution."
17 Howe and Boyer, "Redistributions."
18 *Not Ok*, a 2018 Mingomena film. Trailer available at https://www.notokmovie.com (accessed Dec. 7, 2023).
19 Engel, "Scientists Unveil Memorial to Iceland's 'First' Dead Glacier."
20 "Learning from Ice" is summarized on the artist's website: https://susanschuppli.com/LEARNING-FROM-ICE-1 (accessed Nov. 14, 2023).
21 UNESCO, "One Ocean Summit."

scientists in both public and private institutions. The Decade of Ocean Science initiative has been launched out of urgent concern for the ecological condition of the world ocean and has formulated ten challenges aimed at "collective impact," albeit with the subtext for Challenge 8 being to create a digital representation of the ocean in order to "better understand and protect our ocean's blue wealth."[22]

The world ocean, according to the Decade of Ocean Science's introductory video, is also "set to become the world's seventh largest economy by 2030."[23] The rewards of new ocean knowledge, therefore, are not only more accurate predictions of tsunamis and clearer identification of areas needing environmental protection, but also potential new frontiers of exploitation to feed the "Blue Economy."

But can such a scientific endeavor help prevent rising sea levels, increasing oceanic acidity, or the lesser-known slowing of thermohaline circulation? The latter is a cycle driven by temperature (thermo) and salt content (haline) where warm, wind-driven surface currents, such as the Gulf Stream, sink when they cool in the North Atlantic, forming dense deep-water currents that flow towards the Southern Ocean. This cycle drives world climate. Scientists have observed it slowing—it is currently at is weakest since the whole of the last millennium.[24] Possible consequences, in addition to rising sea levels, are increasingly *colder* temperatures in certain regions, although the potential effects are yet to be fully comprehended.[25]

Waning belief in techno-science signals an urgent need to develop new methods, to produce other narratives and practices. In particular in relation to indigenous knowledge, as articulated by indigenous artist and filmmaker Alanis Obomsawin, "the children have to hear another story."[26] The work of Sámi artist Máret Ánne Sara is driven by her interest in sensual power as a parallel form of intelligence. Working for example with reindeer stomachs at the 2022 Venice Art Biennale, she refers to the enteric nervous system—"a thin layer of millions of nerve cells that line the stomach and intestines and which operate as a communication highway back and

[22] UN Decade of Ocean Science for Sustainable Development (2021–2030), video for "Challenge 8" at https://www.youtube.com/watch?v=bE8uFffqeIE (accessed Nov. 14, 2023).
[23] UNESCO Intergovernmental Oceanographic Commission, "10 Challenges."
[24] See Caesar, et al., "Current Atlantic Meridional."
[25] See Mooney, "Global Warming."
[26] Hill and Peleg, "Introduction," 7.

Nancy Couling

forth to the brain via the vagus nerve," and hence, literally "gut" feelings.[27] A second work in the exhibition communicates through the sense of smell—a sense directly linked to memory and emotion, which Sara advocates as a form of non-verbal communication that has been heavily overridden by colonial practices and the Western dominance of the visual.[28]

Despite the fact that our native human faculties are limited in gaining access to oceanic knowledge, the nonhuman oceanic world reveals sophisticated sensory mechanisms that assist in navigating this space—ones far superior to human sensory systems. The most complex eyes in the animal kingdom are owned by the mantis shrimp and have twelve to fourteen types of photoreceptors.[29]

Polynesian navigation is one example of a complex matrix of interconnected human knowledge, combining astronomy, observation of wave movement, currents, bird flight paths, as well as directly sensing the physical movement of the boat in the water. Hawaiian navigator Nainoa Thompson describes how on dark nights at sea, when it is impossible to read visual signs such as star constellations or wave patterns, his teacher would lie down in the hull of the canoe and feel the pattern of the waves on the canoe, thereby able to determine the boat's direction.[30]

A further astonishing tradition is that of *dulam*— of "feeling" sound in the sea, as practiced by Muslim fishing communities along the southern coast of the Gulf of Thailand and Malaysia.[31] Fish listeners use their hands, skull, and bones underwater to sense the presence of fish through vibrations, and to relay this information to fishers. Such multisensory understandings are being acknowledged and explored in an ongoing artistic project led by the Thyssen-Bornemisza Art Contemporary Academy (TBA21) in collaboration with marine scientists.[32] The project aims to ask new questions and use multiple sensory registers to revitalize the way humans engage with the ocean, in particular regarding equity and justice. The spatiality of the ocean is a vital aspect of this research. In the exhibition "Oceans in Transformation," architects Territorial Agency consider the world ocean itself a sensorium—a body that senses

27 García-Antón and Brissach, "When the Red Calves Arrive," 91.
28 García-Antón and Brissach, "When the Red Calves Arrive."
29 See Bode and Yarina, "Thick Representations."
30 Thompson, "Star Compass."
31 See McCormick-Goodhart, "Underwater (Un)Sound."
32 The TBA21 Academy works "as an incubator for collaborative inquiry, artistic production, and environmental advocacy." See https://tba21.org/about, accessed Nov. 14, 2023.

Sensing Ocean Space

and registers the effects of human exploitation.³³ Seven selected trajectories trace transformations to the world ocean through, for example, intensification of maritime transport, overfishing, depletion of coastal ecosystems, deep-sea mining, seafloor trawling, oil exploration, extraction, migration, changing ocean circulations, militarization, and melting ice. Importantly, these transformations were previously fragmented sections of knowledge, unseen in such complex spatial totality and in such clarity in terms of their impact. They have been presented within the artistic context of the TBA21 Academy in order to reach a wider public audience, and as such avoid the dominant silos of research and inquiry that have largely prevented a sensorial understanding of current ecological urgencies.³⁴

My own research on the space of the sea investigates the ways in which considering the sea as simply a surface space, with an open horizon, is also inherently problematic, even visually. We can observe interactions, such as periodic shipping movements, only partially, since on the open sea the curvature of the Earth can already be felt at a distance of just under 5 kilometers, beyond which objects disappear behind the horizon. The expert Viking sailors were well aware of this phenomenon. When approaching land, and counting on the element of surprise to conduct a raid, or to find minimal resistance, they pulled down the sails at a certain point of approach, so remaining hidden behind the horizon as long as possible.³⁵ I have argued elsewhere that it is partly due to this phenomenon that the public at large is unaware of the heavy industrial use of, for example, the North Sea, and the vast spatial impact of activities being carried out there.³⁶

At the same time, the visual impression of the open sea is celebrated as a quality of ocean space to be preserved through planning processes. For example in Germany, offshore wind turbines have been kept at least 32 kilometers from the coast, with visible hub heights limited to 125 meters in order to preserve the visually open seascape.³⁷ My own North Sea research revealed that as industrial processes have intensified and their spaces proliferated, Western civic society

33 The exhibition "Territorial Agency: Oceans in Transformation," curated by Daniela Zyman, and commissioned by TBA21–Academy, was held at Ocean Space in Venice from Aug. 27, 2020, to Aug. 29, 2021.
34 Zyman, *Oceans Rising*.
35 See Pye, *Edge of the World*, 70.
36 Couling, "Formats of Extended Urbanisation."
37 Bundesamt für Seeschifffahrt und Hydrographie (BSH) "Anlage zur Verordnung."

Nancy Couling

has effectively withdrawn from the sea.[38] This withdrawal is accompanied by an institutionalized nostalgia for the open horizon, and the artificially "natural" space it continues to represent for society at large. Spatial research that investigates different ways of "sensing" the sea can contribute to shifting this distanced perspective, potentially offering a way for Western society to reconnect to seas that have been "lost" to industrial activities organized by state governments in collaboration with the marine, energy, and mining industries.

Forms of immersion

Kimberley Peters and Jon Anderson offer potential openings as to how we can advance from understanding the ocean not as a space that is *known* but to a space that is *experienced*, thereby potentially reducing the effect of the withdrawal outlined above. They discuss the growing recognition of "embodied experiences of the world" in the social sciences and argue for the increasing relevance of "fluid ontology" in a world that is in flux, processual, and always becoming.[39]

Drawing examples from student research in architecture, the following section discusses how forms of immersion can be simulated—not in order to provide solutions or describe objects, but rather to illustrate processes, interdependencies, and ecologies, and to draw attention to critical conditions.

A hydrophone is a simple tool that is dropped into the water and attached to earphones and a recording device, facilitating human access to the acoustic space below the water surface. Video 1 includes simultaneous footage of a serene Sunday urban harborscape and a disturbingly penetrating soundtrack of underwater recordings taken at the same site. Nothing seems to be moving or generating noise. Sounds of vessels, or human activities that do not appear in the field of vision, make the extended reach of underwater sound-transfer immediately palpable. In this way, we too can gain partial access to the sensory apparatus of marine animals and "see" something with our ears. The stark contrast communicates a counterintuitive understanding that the idea of the quiet visual ocean is mostly fake.

[38] Couling, "Losing Sea."
[39] Anderson and Peters, "A Perfect and Absolute Blank."

→ Video 1

Der Har Vi Det Som Fisken i Vannet, underwater hydrophone audio with above-water video by Lena Winderen
doi.org/mjh6

Sensing Ocean Space

Sound travels almost five times faster in water than in air. The actual speed of sound in water depends on temperature, pressure, and salinity, producing a complex oceanic soundscape. The layer where the surface ocean meets the deep ocean, a place of rapid temperature change, acts as a channel for sound. In what is called the SOFAR (sound fixing and ranging) channel, at depths of 800 to 1000 m, depending on temperature and salinity, low frequency sounds can travel long distances without losing energy to absorption. Some animals use this channel for long-distance navigation. Above this layer, sound tends to bounce back up to the surface, and below bounces back down into the deep.

Light at that depth is limited, and many forms of marine life have organs for hearing that are much more sensitive than their organs for sight, making sound the ocean's primary language. Fish, for example, have a swim-bladder organ connected to the inner ear, which regulates their depth but also senses vibrations and pressure. Through passive use of sound, marine animals detect predators and prey, navigate the sonar landscape, perceive the proximity of co-species in a school or colony, and perceive changes in their environment, such as tides, currents, and seismic movement. Their active use of sound involves creating sound for communication and guidance of others in their species, for territorial and social relations, for echolocation, and for stunning and apprehending prey.[40]

But today's oceans are full of other noises. Ongoing construction and repowering of wind parks in the North Sea is an increasing acoustic disturbance, and on Norway's continental shelf the research project "Mareano" uses echo sounders to gain information about the seabed.[41] The sonic pulse in this case is a burst of sound issued by an echo-sounder that can provide detailed information about the seabed features, such as coral reefs, ripple marks, and also about the water column. In the oil industry, surveying for hydrocarbons is undertaken by seismic surveys, which involve letting off small explosions and sending powerful shockwaves to the subsurface, called seismic "shooting" by fishers, resulting in a negative impact on fish populations whereby adult fish leave the area,

40 See Morrissey, "Artistic Research, Jana Winderen."
41 See https://www.mareano.no/en/ (accessed Nov. 14, 2023).

→ Figure 1

Nancy Couling

and fish larvae at close range are destroyed.[42] In addition, such noises interfere with the oceanic soundscape, making navigation, communication and orientation difficult for many species, in particular whales and dolphins.

In order to gain closer insight into the levels of oceanic noise pollution, simulation is required, since the human ear cannot perceive noise in the same way as marine life. Julia Morrissey, author of the unpublished acoustic project "Moving Zone of Silence," first fully researched the frequencies of different types of marine soundwaves—both from living creatures and operations such as shipping and wind-park construction—and then developed a library of her own recordings and self-constructed sound based on this knowledge. In a third stage, she incorporated such imagined recordings from the future into the design of a five hundred-year North Sea soundscape. The result is an immersive experience, telling the plausible story of a moving "sound park" over a long period of time and directly demonstrating the acoustic effect of proposed interventions in the North Sea. Presenting the project with a listening space around which speakers were placed in the four positions of North, South, East, and West, the work also simulated the geographic location of sound. Morrissey takes the listener on a journey through North Sea space and time, using the timescale of one second per year, showing that as oil exploration began to cease and maritime transport switched to quiet technology, more abundant sea life could slowly be heard.

Sound experienced in this way is highly spatial. Morrissey was inspired by the fact that sound is a pollutant that leaves no trace—as soon as the source is eliminated, sounds cease to exist. To accompany the recording, she developed an original hand-drawn score comparable to a music score, where the listeners could read the pathways and acoustic character of the design. Such a score of oceanic sound over five hundred years is without precedent. This original sensory representation offers new forms of ocean literacy that do not rely solely on scientific knowledge, but rather communicate directly to the spatial imagination through bodily vibrations within a context of acoustic immersion.

42   The Norwegian Petroleum Directorate carries out continuous seismic surveys and has accumulated large amounts of publicly accessible data, available at https://www.npd.no/en/about-us/open-data/ (accessed Nov. 14, 2023).

Surfing, canoeing, diving, and sailing are further ways humans can experience ocean space more directly. In the case of surfing, Jon Anderson discusses ways of knowing space through situations of "ontological instability" and the phenomenon of convergence, which he calls "merging with the medium."[43] Sailing is a quiet mode of maritime transport, involving the negotiation of wind, waves, and currents in a constant process of adaptation to changing conditions. On an architectural fieldtrip to the Lofoten archipelago, four architecture students who chose sailing as both a means of transport and a research tool to engage more closely with the sea and these conditions from the Norwegian coast experienced direct encounters with pods of both fin and killer whales very close to the boat.[44] This thrilling but also potentially dangerous experience deeply influenced their spatial understanding and modes of architectural research.

Suddenly a long, sleek, dark shape slipped above the surface and under again, 5 meters from the boat. And another, and another. One turned and looked me in the eye. Are we dangerous (it thought)? Will we capsize (we thought)? We are sharing this space with creatures that are very large, extremely agile, and highly intelligent. They have let us in. We maneuver through the same range, dependent on wind, currents, and ongoing permission, exploring ocean space through physical engagement—a personal meeting.[45]

Drawing on this form of oceanic immersion, Magnus Gjesdal's project at the Bergen School of Architecture, the video *The Whale's Council* proposes an alternative order through which we can begin to decipher a whale's urgent message. Taking the perspective of a fin whale, the work centered around a call to council by Hafgufa—the ancient mythological whale-god—where the fin whale-protagonist must report on the last five hundred years of intensifying maritime industries and exploitation since Hafgufa himself retreated to the North Pole to escape the whaling industry. In a multi-layered thirteen-minute video, incorporating both hand and computer-aided drawings, the fin whale describes the different historical epochs of technological advancement and their accompanying effects in his ocean. Over time,

[43] Anderson, "Merging with the Medium?" 80.
[44] The fieldtrip was held in September 2021 as part of the master's in architecture course "Explorations in Ocean Space: A Choreography for Norskehavet" at Bergen School of Architecture.
[45] Description of the event compiled by the author in consultation with Magnus Gjesdal, Nora Håskjold, Vilje Valland, and Martin Janssen.

→ Video 2

The Whale's Council by Magnus Gjesdal, doi.org/mjh7

the whale observes new eighteenth-century vessels loaded with cannons, increasingly larger and louder vessels, and the construction of offshore oilrigs.

Talking to me? the whale asks of these new intense sounds. Shortly afterwards it releases another series of pulses ... *I feel lost.*

As wind farms crowd the waters alongside oilrigs, the whale sends out the message: *I can't navigate in these waters.*

In consultation with marine biologist Marianna Anichini, Gjesdal's video soundtrack was carefully conceived and composed by combining underwater recordings with a simulation of fin whale communication in deep, low-frequency staccato sounds. As the whale council comes together, other whale voices are heard, including that of Hafgufa himself. The whales express their desperation about the unbearable levels of sonar interference in the ocean—something the video listener had also been directly exposed to.

Together these two projects can be understood as a kind of "counter-mapping" that challenges dominant power structures and ways of reading place.[46] Particularly within indigenous contexts, counter-mapping has been used to open up possibilities for decolonial representations of space. We argue that the oceans have also been colonized. In addition to indigenous communities who have been dispossessed and whose access to traditional fishing grounds is increasingly being impeded, indigenous inhabitants of the ocean include whale populations and thousands of other species. This type of mapping takes the listener to an unaccustomed standpoint, from which the perception of a simulated fin whale message or of seismic surveys is made possible. Rather than having the difficult and intangible problem of sound interference described, the resulting blends of science and imagination become directly sensual. New cognitive understandings are transmitted by sound vibrations through the body itself. I argue that this embodied method of gaining knowledge is more powerful; leaves a deeper, more lasting impression; and, most importantly, transmits a completely new perspective on the not only scientific but also sociocultural problem of understanding the urgent condition of the world ocean.

46 Comment made by guest reviewer Christophe Barlieb, Dec. 2021, referring also to Peluso, "Whose Woods Are These?"

→ Figure 2 (a–f)

Conclusion

How relevant are such results? They are much less far-fetched than we may think. Human arrogance supposes the superior levels of our own intelligence. Curator Chus Martínez relates the story of researchers about to crack the code of whale and dolphin language, including the fact that they seemed to be "chatting and joking" at specific times and places. *What are they saying about us?* she speculated.[47]

Truly innovative research is capable of capsizing inherited assumptions and opening up new avenues of thought. Other scholars have reflected on the extent to which artistic research can pass the gatekeepers of research as a whole and be admitted into the sacred halls of traditional science. The *Manifesto of Artistic Research* claims that the term "artistic" coupled with "research" (the latter dominated by academic methodology and defined by the Bologna reform) can only fall short and "squander its original potential":[48]

> The arts do not proceed according to a strict method (*met'hodos*) along a predetermined trajectory, but rather in the form of leaps, digressions, and detours which continually generate new and unexpected counter-expressions, and do not set a goal for their nonlinear "experiments," but instead trigger irritations and thus daring revelations.[49]

If, as according to Paul Feyerabend, science is essentially an anarchic enterprise, is perhaps this distinction between artistic and scientific research in itself artificial and approaching the end of its usefulness?[50] A full discussion on this point exceeds the capacity of this chapter. However, in an epoch of accelerating climate change and complex "wicked" environmental problems for which the scientific world cannot have a straightforward answer, it is becoming ever more essential to train ourselves in sensing these tendencies in more embodied ways— to listen to what the ocean has to tell us.

47 Martínez, "Dear Care, ... ," presentation at Bergen School of Architecture, Sep. 1, 2021.
48 Henke, et al., *Manifesto of Artistic Research*, 6.
49 Henke, et al., *Manifesto of Artistic Research*, 13.
50 Feyerabend *Wissenschaft als Kunst*.

ACKNOWLEDGMENTS

To my students and colleagues for their generosity, creativity, insight, and support in the ongoing explorations of ocean space. Thank you to Julia Morrissey, Magnus Gjesdal and Lena Winderen for making their work available for this publication, and to Tom Chamberlain and Marianna Anichini for their invaluable inputs. Thank you also to Nitin Bathla for his dedication and for inviting me to contribute to this volume.

Nancy Couling

Figure 1 Julia Morrissey (left) demonstrating the use of hydrophones at Bergen School of Architecture, 2021

Sensing Ocean Space

Nancy Couling

Figure 2a–2f   Stills from *The Whale's Council*, a film by Magnus Gjesdal that narrates the story of a fin whale reporting to the mythical whale god Hafgufa about the last five hundred years of human activities in ocean space.

Sensing Ocean Space

BIBLIOGRAPHY

A

Anderson, Jon. "Merging with the Medium? Knowing the Place of the Surfed Wave." In *Water Worlds: Human Geographies of the Ocean*, edited by Jon Anderson and Kimberley Peters, 73–88. Farnham: Ashgate, 2014.

Anderson, Jon, and Kimberley Peters. "'A Perfect and Absolute Blank': Human Geographies of Water Worlds." In *Water Worlds: Human Geographies of the Ocean*, edited by Jon Anderson and Kimberley Peters, 3–19 Farnham: Ashgate, 2014.

Argyrou, Aikaterini, and Harry Hummels. "Legal Personality and Economic Livelihood of the Whanganui River: A Call for Community Entrepreneurship." *Water International* 44, no. 6–7 (October 3, 2019): 752–68. https://doi.org/10.1080/02508060.2019.1643525.

B

Bode, Claudia, and Lizzie Yarina. "Thick Representations for Ocean Space." In *The Urbanisation of the Sea: From Concepts and Analysis to Design*, edited by Nancy Couling and Carola Hein, 189–203. Rotterdam: nai010, 2020.

Brett, Annie, Jim Leape, Mark Abbott, Hide Sakaguchi, Ling Cao, Kevin Chand, Yimnang Golbuu, Tara J. Martin, Juan Mayorga, and Mari S. Myksvoll. "Ocean Data Need a Sea Change to Help Navigate the Warming World." *Nature* 582, no. 7811 (June 2020): 181–83. https://doi.org/10.1038/d41586-020-01668-z.

Bundesamt für Seeschifffahrt und Hydrographie (BSH). "Anlage Zur Verordnung über die Raumordnung in der deutschen Ausschließlichen Wirtschaftszone in der Nordsee (AWZ Nordsee-ROV) vom 21. September 2009." Bundesanzeiger Verlag GmbH, September 21, 2009. https://www.bsh.de/DE/THEMEN/Offshore/Meeresraumplanung/Raumordnungsplaene_2009/_Anlagen/Downloads/Raumordnung_2009/Raumordungsplan_Textteil_Nordsee.pdf?__blob=publicationFile&v=5 (accessed December 8, 2023).

C

Caesar, Levke, Gerard Daniel McCarthy, David J. R. Thornalley, Niamh Cahill, and Stefan Rahmstorf. "Current Atlantic Meridional Overturning Circulation Weakest in Last Millennium." *Nature Geoscience* 14, no. 3 (March 2021): 118–20. https://doi.org/10.1038/s41561-021-00699-z.

Carson, Rachel, and Jeffrey S. Levinton. *The Sea Around Us*. New York: Oxford University Press, 1991.

Couling, Nancy. "Formats of Extended Urbanisation in Ocean Space." In *Emerging Urban Spaces: A Planetary Perspective*, edited by Philipp Horn, Paola Alfaro d'Alençon, and Ana Claudia Duarte Carduso, 149–76. Cham: Springer International, 2018.

Couling, Nancy. "Losing Sea. Abstraction and Loss of the Commons in the North Sea." In *Extended Urbanisation. Tracing Planetary Struggles*, edited by Christian Schmid and Milica Topalović, 159–196. Basel: Birkhäuser, 2023.

Couling, Nancy. "Nine Principles of Ocean Urbanization in the Baltic Sea." In *The Baltic Atlas*, edited by Jennifer Boyd, 172–79. Berlin: Sternberg Press, 2016.

Couling, Nancy. "Urbanization of the Ocean; Extractive Geometries in the Barents Sea." In *Infrastructure Space*, edited by Ilka and Andreas Ruby, 238–249. Berlin: Ruby Press, 2016.

Couling, Nancy, Paola Alfaro d'Alençon, and Medine Altiok. "Narrative Cartography: Capturing a Holistic Perspective on Waterscapes." *European Journal of Creative Practices in Cities and Landscapes* 2, no. 1 (2019): 11–36. https://doi.org/10.6092/issn.2612-0496/8808.

Couling, Nancy, and Carola Hein, eds. *The Urbanisation of the Sea: From Concepts and Analysis to Design*. Rotterdam: nai010, 2020.

E

Engel, Currie. "Scientists Unveil Memorial to Iceland's 'First' Dead Glacier." *Time*, July 22, 2019. https://time.com/5631599/iceland-glacier-climate-change/.

F

Feyerabend, Paul. *Wissenschaft als Kunst*. Frankfurt am Main: Suhrkamp, 1984.

G

García-Antón, Katya, and Liv Brissach. "When the Red Calves Arrive, the Hope Returns: Sámi Healing and Sensate Sovereignty in Máret Ánne Sara's Practice." In *Čatnosat: The Sámi Pavilion, Indigenous Art, Knowledge and Sovereignty*, edited by Liisa-Rávná Finbog, Katya García-Antón, and Beaska Niillas. 84–113. Oslo/Amsterdam: Office for Contemporary Art Norway (OCA)/Valiz, 2022.

H

Henke, Silvia, Dieter Mersch, Thomas Strässle, Jörg Wiesel, and Nicolaj van der Meulen. *Manifesto of Artistic Research: A Defense Against Its Advocates*. THINK ART. Zurich: Diaphanes, 2020.

Hill, Richard, William, and Hila Peleg. "Introduction: The Children Have to Hear Another Story." In *Alanis Obomsawin: Lifework*, edited by Richard Hill William, Hila Peleg, and HKW. Berlin: HKW Prestel, 2022.

Howe, Cymene, and Dominic Boyer. "Redistributions: From Atmospheric Carbon to Melting Cryospheres to the World Ocean." *E-Flux Architecture*. https://www.e-flux.com/architecture/accumulation/212496/redistributions/ (accessed October 27, 2022).

Nancy Couling

K

Kranzberg, Melvin, and Carroll W. Pursell. "Technology's Challenge." In *Technology in Western Civilization*, vol. II: *Technology in the 20th Century*, edited by Melvin Kranzberg and Carroll W. Pursell, New York, London, and Toronto: Oxford University Press, 1967.

M

McCormick-Goodhart, Emma. "Underwater (Un)Sound." *E-Flux Architecture*, August 2020. https://www.e-flux.com/architecture/oceans/341778/underwater-un-sound/ (accessed August 28, 2023).

Mooney, Chris. "Global Warming Is Now Slowing Down the Circulation of the Oceans—with Potentially Dire Consequences." *Washington Post*, October 27, 2021. https://www.washingtonpost.com/news/energy-environment/wp/2015/03/23/global-warming-is-now-slowing-down-the-circulation-of-the-oceans-with-potentially-dire-consequences/.

Morrissey, Julia. "Artistic Research, Jana Winderen." Blog for the BAS Master Course "Explorations in Ocean Space," 2019., 2019. https://explorationsin.wixsite.com/oceanspace/copy-of-aliki-jos-by-saara-palmujok-2 (accessed December 8, 2023).

P

Peluso, Nancy Lee. "Whose Woods Are These? Counter-Mapping Forest Territories in Kalimantan, Indonesia." *Antipode* 27, no. 4 (1995): 383–406. https://doi.org/10.1111/j.1467-8330.1995.tb00286.x.

Pye, Michael. *The Edge of the World: How the North Sea Made Us Who We Are*. London: Penguin Books, 2015.

T

Thompson, Nainoa. "The Star Compass." Hōkūleʻa/Polynesian Voyaging Society. https://hokulea.com/the-star-compass-by-nainoa-thompson/ (accessed October 28, 2022).

U

UN Decade of Ocean Science for Sustainable Development (2021–2030). *Ocean Decade Challenge 8: Create a Digital Representation of the Ocean*, 2021. https://oceandecade.org/challenges/ (accessed November 14, 2023).

UNESCO. "One Ocean Summit: UNESCO Pledges to Have at Least 80% of the Seabed Mapped by 2030 | UNESCO." UNESCO. https://www.unesco.org/en/articles/one-ocean-summit-unesco-pledges-have-least-80-seabed-mapped-2030 (accessed November 18, 2022).

UNESCO Intergovernmental Oceanographic Commission. "10 Challenges: Ocean Decade Challenges for Collective Impact." Ocean Decade. https://www.oceandecade.org/challenges/ (accessed July 27, 2022).

W

Watkins, Michael M., David Wiese, Dah-Ning Yuan, Carmen Boening, and Felix W. Landerer. "Improved Methods for Observing Earth's Time Variable Mass Distribution with GRACE Using Spherical Cap Mascons." *Journal of Geophysical Research: Solid Earth* 120, no. 4 (2015): 2648–71. https://doi.org/10.1002/2014JB011547.

Z

Zyman, Daniela, ed. *Oceans Rising: A Companion to Territorial Agency—Oceans in Transformation*. Berlin: Sternberg Press, 2021.

IMAGE CREDITS

Figure 1: Bergen School of Architecture
Figure 2: Magnus Gjesdal

Couling, Nancy. "Sensing Ocean Space." In Nitin Bathla, ed., *Researching Otherwise: Pluriversal Methodologies for Landscape and Urban Studies*. Zurich: gta Verlag, 2024, 151–169. https://doi.org/10.54872/gta/4692-5.

Sensing Ocean Space

Klearjos Eduardo Papanicolaou

Mirror Images: Cinematic and Sensory Ethnography for Landscape and Urban Studies

Researching Otherwise
Nitin Bathla, ed.

"With the invention of the camera everything changed," the art historian John Berger tells us in the first episode of his 1972 television program *Ways of Seeing*[1] (later released as a book by the same name). He refers to the transformation in perspective that the camera offered at its outset, which, unlike paintings (until that point, only ever to be seen at one place, at one time), allowed us to "see things that were not there in front of us." The relationship with our understanding of the world initiated by the advent of the camera, however, is more epistemologically complex than that: as much as photographic images gather astonishing amounts of information about a subject through visual means, they also conceal and distort information.[2] Indeed, the camera presents a conundrum: How can something as multidimensional and complex as "reality" be depicted within its framed, two-dimensional image? Moreover, does the act of operating the camera (in other words, the relation between the person holding the camera, the subject, and the camera itself[3]) not also further complicate the question of what kind of "reality" the camera's image captures? While Berger notes that we could "see things that were not there in front of us,"[4] it remains unclear exactly what it is that we are seeing (and perceiving) beyond what is depicted by the photographic image.

The contemporary ubiquity of photography and filmmaking makes understanding the discrepancy between what we see, what we think we see, and the complexity of what is actually there, all the more important. Precisely because cameras offer such a powerful set of tools for understanding the world, it is imperative that those who use them devise strategies and epistemologies for reflecting on what it is that they actually capture. While this is generally important for anyone whose work is highly visual, it is of particular relevance for visual and audiovisual researchers engaging in fieldwork. Reflecting on these conundrums may provide pathways to articulate the thick and epistemologically complex layers of space and time in the field[5]—dimensions specifically meaningful to researchers within landscape and urban studies.

[1] Berger, *Ways of Seeing*.
[2] See Sontag, *On Photography*.
[3] See Baudry and Williams, "Ideological Effects."
[4] Berger, *Ways of Seeing*, episode 1 (1972), 01:52–01:54, viewable at https://www.youtube.com/watch?v=opDE4VX_9Kk&t=170s (accessed Dec. 14, 2023).
[5] See Geertz, *Interpretation of Cultures*.

→ Figure 1

Klearjos Eduardo Papanicolaou

This chapter, drawing from my experiences as a practicing filmmaker, researcher, and educator within landscape and urban studies, has three main purposes. First, to define principles that are sensitive to the challenges and opportunities of using cameras as tools for spatial research through filmmaking. In doing this, it will explore the history of audiovisual ethnography in understanding how it addresses various epistemological challenges through its embrace of "sensory" approaches, suggesting that it may be a useful model for "expanding the repertoire of both seeing and image production" in landscape and urban studies.[6] Second, to offer examples of such principles in practice through reflections on filmmaking and the teaching of filmmaking to students of architecture, landscape, and urban studies. In doing so, it will also reflect on the forms of knowledge that such research results in, emphasizing the importance of physical experience and affectivity as the basis for syncretic knowledge models that align with the arts, among other fields. Third, to recognize that such research and knowledge production does not exist outside of physical space but is rather filtered by it. This point underlines the integral importance of the physical spaces in which we watch films for the entire cycle of research, filmmaking, and knowledge production. The chapter will therefore reflect on "cinema" spaces in order to understand how certain architectural and urban conditions may facilitate this knowledge cycle through their design. What the chapter will not offer, however, is practical filmmaking advice. Rather, its focus is to define key principles that may aid aspiring audiovisual researchers within landscape and urban studies to define their overall *position* vis-à-vis audiovisual practices.

Ultimately, the questions brought up here circle around our relationship with emerging technologies of representation and the ways they enable us to experience and think about the world in new and different ways. With this in mind, it is clear that the same concerns can be applied to newly emerging technologies, such as virtual reality and AI-generated imagery, as well as to the massive rollout of existing technologies, as in the proliferation of cameras across

6   Truniger, *Landscript 2*, 17.

Mirror Images

urban areas and even around the Earth's orbit in the form of remote sensing and Earth observation. It is thus incumbent upon us to remain critical about our relationship with such developments and the epistemologies that they produce. We might imagine, if John Berger were still alive today, that he might think not only that "everything changed" but also that everything continues to change again and again.

A lie through which we tell the truth

If we were to try to trace the trajectories of "documentary" and "cinema" through history, we would soon find that rather than tracing two lines we would have to trace an ever-growing number of blurry, intersecting lines. Forms like docudrama, ethnofiction, and mockumentary, among many others (themselves building on previous forms, such as cinema verité and direct cinema), blur the boundaries between the aesthetics of fiction in "cinema" and the aesthetics of non-fiction in "documentary." For researchers interested in the use of audiovisual methods, it may thus be helpful to begin by thinking not about form or aesthetics in filmmaking, which are typically the end result of a filmmaking process, but about the mechanical ways in which cameras work in the first place, as a way of clarifying the material relations that emerge in photographic processes. In doing so, potential filmmaking traditions from which to draw inspiration may come into view.

What does the camera, rather the cameraperson, actually "see" in the creation of photographs and films? To consider this discrepancy, one may turn to Étienne-Jules Marey, the French scientist whose "chronophotography" methods—early forms of moving images—foreshadowed the development of cinematography. In 1878 he wrote of his innovations: "when the eye ceases to see, the ear to hear, the touch to feel, or indeed when our senses give deceptive appearances, these instruments are like new senses of astonishing precision."[7] In 1923 the Soviet filmmaker Dziga Vertov echoed similar ideas, donning the perspective of the camera itself, writing: "I am an eye. A mechanical eye. I, the machine, show you a world the way only I can see it. I free myself for today

7 Marey, *La méthode graphique*, 108.

→ Figure 2

Klearjos Eduardo Papanicolaou

and forever from human immobility. My way leads towards the creation of a fresh perception of the world. Thus, I explain in a new way the world unknown to you."⁸ Both Marey and Vertov remind us that photographic and film images do not necessarily represent the perspective of the person operating the camera, but rather produce their own realities, through technological means. These "mechanical" perspectives, however—framed, two-dimensional, and dependent on the operator to be placed, engaged, and disengaged—are evidently fragmentary. It is the work of the human operator to meaningfully order them in the production of a new meaning through the filmmaking process—a process which is itself determined by the multiplicity of *types* of cameras, lenses, and other equipment. To characterize this relationship between camera and filmmaker through an analogy with writing: where one uses writing tools, surfaces, and scripts to translate what are otherwise shapes into words and sentences in texts, we use cameras to translate audiovisual fragments of "reality" into representation and meaning in films, inevitably leaving an imprint of ourselves along with it.

It is through this self-conscious negotiation between the perspective of the filmmaker and the perspective of the camera, from cinematography to editing, that one may overcome certain limitations of the camera by "going beyond the frame,"⁹ creating meaning beyond the limits of the mechanical representation of the photographic and film image. This notion holds a key for audiovisual researchers—especially those in landscape and urban studies who are challenged by the sheer scale and diffuseness of their subjects—in developing complex portraits of space.¹⁰ Indeed, the tangible vastness of landscape and urban subjects speaks of their intangible vastness as well (and of the potential for interior vastness in any subject, in fact). Addressing this condition, landscape and film theorist Fred Truniger suggests the term "dynamic landscape" to define landscape itself as a field beyond topography—a "cultural construction" produced by the "perceiving, interpreting human being"¹¹ (a definition that also creates space for the urban within a dynamic frame). The capacity of

8   Vertov, "Kino-Eye Manifesto," 17–18.
9   See Favero, "Learning to Look."
10 See Bathla and Papanicolaou, "Reframing the Contested City."
11 Truniger, *Landscript* 2, 15.

Mirror Images

"going beyond the frame" in filmmaking thus renders it an equally dynamic tool for interacting with such dynamic notions of landscape and urban studies.

A conscious relationship with our research instruments only gets us halfway, however—we must also consider this relationship socially and politically. The focus on the construction of meaning through filmmaking provides a clue of how this may be done, recalling a view about fiction familiar in literature studies[12] that fiction is a lie through which we tell the truth, a notion popularly attributed to Albert Camus. As the work of the researcher requires, how does one contextualize and reconcile forms of fiction or construction back into the realm of "reality"? Such a question, political as it is philosophical, brings another: could ideology—in terms of the "social role" played by our position in the production of images[13]—be a pathway for the researcher to seek filmmaking traditions coherent with their work?

Consulting ideological bifurcations in the early days of cinema may help in this search for a tradition—the contrasts between early Hollywood and early Soviet cinema are indicative examples. While both forms experimented with editing techniques (with Soviet cinema pioneering "Montage Theory"[14]), the Soviet model, by the 1930s, began to mandate a style of top-down "socialist realism," a "cinema for the millions."[15] Hollywood films, instead, typically focused on ways to invite commercial audiences more familiar with visiting the theater to transition into going to the movies, such as by borrowing principles of scenography involving sets and actors always facing the audience.[16] Contrasting the two, it is clear that not only the aesthetics but also the social imperatives within the ideological models of each tradition orient practices of meaning-making through filmmaking in different directions.

The history of ethnographic filmmaking points to a tradition influenced less by economic and political motivations, and more by concerns that would eventually be called reflexivity. Indeed, despite

12 See Lamarque and Olsen, *Truth, Fiction, and Literature*.
13 See Green, "Ideology and Ambiguity in Cinema."
14 See Bordwell, "Idea of Montage."
15 See Kepley, "Pudovkin."
16 See Sannah, "Characteristic Features."

> A conscious relationship with our research instruments only gets us halfway, however—we must also consider this relationship socially and politically.

Klearjos Eduardo Papanicolaou

their highly suspect "othering" of the non-white, non-Western "savage," the early anthropologists behind the first ethnographic films shifted their attention (and that of their cameras) from glorification to observation, recalibrating the ideological calculus behind their photographic and film images, if only slightly.[17] As if in response to Camus, the question of "whose truth?" begins, blurrily, to appear. Key examples of such filmmakers are Margaret Mead and Gregory Bateson, active in the 1930s, whose experiments in filmmaking inaugurated a trajectory towards situated, reflective filmmaking, beyond Vertov's Soviet reflection of triumphalism. Their film, *Trance and Dance in Bali* (filmed in 1937 and released in 1951), exemplifies both the shortcomings and the promise of their approach.[18] In it, they point their camera at their (non-white, non-Western) subjects and apply themselves to decipher what is going on around them. Mead's voice can be heard matter-of-factly describing a ceremonial dance that she and Bateson observe. The heavy camera turns its attention, left and right, following the local Balinese dancers into trance states unknown to the gazes of Mead and Bateson. One cannot help but wonder what a person depicted in the film might think of Mead's New England tone of voice, describing their trances. It would be decades, however, until anthropology as a discipline, let alone the ethnographic film form, would critique its own colonial roots. By the early 2000s, Michel-Rolph Trouillot and others would argue that the "other" is actually everywhere and everyone.[19]

The redefinition of what is meant by the "other" in anthropology and its associated disciplines speaks to a broader set of ideological redefinitions, resulting in contemporary ethnographic practices today. Over the decades, ethnographers began to articulate more sophisticated and self-conscious practices through concepts like "thick description,"[20] which extended the observation of the researcher not only to what people do and say but to the whole set of relations in a time and place that produce those behaviors. Elsewhere, Glaser and Strauss codified the notion that a hypothesis should follow experience in the field, rather than be tested in the field, with the concept of

[17] See Trouillot, "Anthropology and the Savage Slot."
[18] Mead and Bateson, *Trance and Dance*.
[19] Trouillot, "Anthropology and the Savage Slot."
[20] Geertz, *Interpretation of Cultures*.

grounded theory.[21] By the time Trouillot and others signaled the reorientation of the anthropological gaze towards everywhere and everyone in the 1980s and 1990s, camera technology, itself growing equally more sophisticated, was on its way to enabling newer generations of ethnographic filmmakers to merge these ideas with new forms of practice.

In parallel, countless film works from a variety of ideological positions preceded and paved the way for the groundbreaking epistemological film experiments that would appear in the mid-2000s. Notably, works like William Greaves's 1968 *Symbiopsychotaxiplasm: Take One* pushed the notion of reflexivity to almost absurd levels.[22] In the film, three separate film crews—one filming a fiction film, another documenting the fiction film crew at work in documentary style, and a third documenting the relations between the two—are left to make sense of their respective gazes and positions, while the director of the entire project oversees their shifts in perspective. Other works, like Robert Gardner's 1986 *Forest of Bliss*, set a standard for audiovisual storytelling guided by visual atmosphere and sound design rather than narrative voiceover, joining with the conventions of cinematic fiction.[23] Gardner's characterization of the nuances of Varanasi, India are thus made as much by *not* pointing his camera at places and people, as by pointing it at them. Both films form part of a broader evolution in the concept of the cinematic, itself slowly becoming a category of film production specifically geared towards embodied affectivity that produce moments that "lodge themselves under the skin of the spectator."[24]

By 2012, films like *Leviathan* from Lucien Castaing-Taylor and Véréna Paravel at the Harvard Sensory Ethnography Lab heralded a substantial step in the development of ethnographic film.[25] Borrowing from Greave's radical reflexivity and Gardner's sense-cinematic, atmospheric attention, while also shifting the gaze of the camera from the human to the non-human, their work contributed to the emergence of a film form called audiovisual sensory ethnography.[26] *Leviathan* combined these elements through the innovative use of GoPros—easy-to-use, durable cameras that can be mounted almost anywhere, which were new

21 Glaser and Strauss, *Discovery of Grounded Theory*.
22 Greaves, *Symbiopsychotaxiplasm*.
23 Gardner, *Forest of Bliss*.
24 Rutherford, "Cinema and Embodied Affect."
25 Castaing-Taylor and Paravel, *Leviathan*.
26 See Pink, *Doing Sensory Ethnography*.

Klearjos Eduardo Papanicolaou

technologies at the time—placed at various locations on a large fishing vessel, thereby allowing them to co-create the unfolding action. These technologies and camera types did not revolutionize ethnographic filmmaking as much as they facilitated the shift in perspective that offers new research possibilities today.

Perhaps one of the most significant contributions of this "sensory" turn is the potential for interdisciplinarity in research, creating common ground for various modes of investigation that focus on embodied affectivity as a means to generate knowledge. Beyond cinematic and sensory approaches, "visceral methods,"[27] "body mapping,"[28] and, more generally, "non-representational theory"[29] in geography are only a few examples of such contemporary approaches. Through various forms of "sensing," rather than merely depicting and explaining, interlocutors from a multitude of backgrounds may find a common intelligibility and shared purpose in the research—one that views the entire body as part of the thinking organ.

Although certain sensory approaches are not without criticism,[30] they are still specifically useful for landscape and urban studies researchers interested in contemporary audiovisual methods for fieldwork. After all, what distinguishes the contemporary sensory or cinematic ethnographic film today is not that it necessarily looks different from other types of film forms between documentary and fiction, but rather that it typically emerges from ideological, aesthetic, and methodological commitments to reflexivity, situatedness, grounded theory, and thick description. It establishes the body as a sensory apparatus—a conscious camera controlling the unconscious camera—in collapsing the discrepancy between the gaze of the camera and the gaze of the human by placing both within the affective, rather than rational, register of meaning-making "beyond the frame."

The field and the classroom

For a number of years, the principles of cinematic or sensory ethnography have influenced my own work as a filmmaker in landscape and urban studies. Together with various collaborators, we have produced numerous films distinguished by approaches of

[27] See Hayes-Conroy, "Critical Visceral Methods."
[28] See Sweet and Escalante, *Bringing Bodies into Planning*.
[29] See Thrift, *Spatial Formations*.
[30] See Henley, *Beyond Observation*.

co-creation that encompass the camera and subjects as essential co-creators of our work, resulting in unique aesthetics and ideological profiles. Exploring these projects may help to illustrate how some of the sensibilities described above can serve audiovisual researchers to conduct themselves more effectively in the development of their film work, both in the field and during the editing and post-production processes.

Unlike other forms of filmmaking, which may begin with scripts and the definition of style and aesthetics in the form of a mood board, audiovisual ethnography typically begins in the field site. This does not ignore that audiovisual ethnographers, as anyone else, come to the field with their own biases and styles. Following ethnographic practices like grounded theory, the researcher in the field typically begins by negotiating and reflecting on these biases and styles, finding ways to articulate, rather than impose them.[31] This is much in the same way as one negotiates and reflects on their relationship with the camera and the subjects that appear to them. It is from this that an aesthetics emerge, later, through iterative repetition in the filming and editing phases.

To use one example, in *The Seven Sisters Indoor Market*, made with Marios Kleftakis in 2016, we tested these approaches in developing a portrait of a migrant community threatened by the "regeneration" of their neighborhood in north London.[32] The project elaborates on an earlier non-audiovisual ethnographic study of the same market,[33] which we returned to with the intent to make an ethnographic film in order to deepen our understanding of this site in ways that only film can do. We sought the potential for lingering silences, liminal patterns, ephemeral shapes and sounds that can uniquely be conveyed through cinematic and sensory ethnography. Thus, over several weeks and months, we would return to this field site as participant observers, slowly putting together a picture of a community in crisis, not by merely describing what the camera saw but through iterative editing, taking place after every day of filming, and also by giving a sense of the hidden lifeworlds of the people living and working there.

Klearjos Eduardo Papanicolaou

31 See Hemmersley and Atkinson, *Ethnography*.
32 Papanicolaou and Kleftakis, *The Seven Sisters Indoor Market*. See more about the film at https://www.sevensistersmarketfilm.com (accessed Nov. 14, 2023).
33 Papanicolaou, "Living With Difference."

→ Video 1

Excerpt from
The Seven Sisters Indoor Market
doi.org/mjh8

A haven for migrants since the mid-twentieth century, the Seven Sisters area in Tottenham, north London, created a safe, urban environment for economic migrants, political refugees, and subjects of the former British Empire to navigate their changing fortunes through migration. The subject of our film, *The Seven Sisters Indoor Market*, which formed over decades in a derelict Edwardian building by the name of Wards Corner, provided commercial space functioning outside the radar of the neoliberal logic of London's urban fabric[34]—traders at the market subdivided their spaces in flexible frameworks that facilitate living with low incomes and changing conditions of life, as working migrants in a big city do. A key motivation for the film project followed news that this space would be demolished, as the "regeneration" (and, one might assume, gentrification) of London moved northward from the city center. Thus the bias that brought us to this site in the first place took the form of a question: What intangible characteristics of the community frequenting this market will be lost if the market disappears?

By casting the camera as yet another protagonist in the portrayal of this community, the resulting film captured not only what was in front of the camera but also the details of how people reacted to both myself as an interlocutor and the camera as a recording device —another interlocutor.[35] Revealing the totality of such encounters through reflexivity and situatedness, the film captures details impossible to anticipate. A scene in which a Jamaican barber is cutting the hair of a Brazilian customer illustrates the point. A three-way conversation begins, despite the fact that neither I, behind the camera, nor the barber, speaks Portuguese, the only language spoken fluently by the customer. While a series of comical misunderstandings make it clear that much is lost in the conversation, the camera articulates many other processes occurring in the background. Besides the fact that a commercial transaction is seamlessly taking place, there is an understanding, through body language and the senses, of the way that the bodies of the three people involved react to each other and to the camera. Countless further associations may be made by reading into the

34 Hill, "Regeneration."
35 See MacDougall, *Looking Machine*.

→ Figure 3

complex visual composition that is rendered by these bodies moving in the small space of a barbershop.

Particular about this mode of registering thick description are the "haptically visual" representations of physical experience and affectivity that film allows—ones based on multisensorial memories of touch.[36] The resulting epistemologies (as well as aesthetics) align these practices with the arts, giving the audiovisual work a role, identity, and ideology in the space in which artistic production and knowledge production overlap. This occurs through various mechanisms, as articulated by the American philosopher and pedagogue John Dewey.[37] For him, art has a unique pedagogical potential in that, unlike in rationalist modes of explication, art is *experiential*. Indeed, it is this experiential and affective quality in which cinematic and sensory ethnography share that audiovisual ethnography is able to produce the extra-linguistic meaning and knowledge for which it is unique.[38]

Recalling the notion that in carrying out such work the audiovisual researcher must negotiate with the camera in order to develop a common reality further underlines that the affective knowledge produced through these approaches must also be understood through the filter of machines. In the sense that affective knowledge is made of a hybrid set of inputs, and thus acknowledges a hybrid set of more-than-human conditions in processing those inputs, these approaches align themselves with techno-feminist concepts, such as those emerging from Donna Haraway's 1985 "Cyborg Manifesto."[39] They concur in the rejection of rigid boundaries both in the composition of actors—the human and the camera—and in the makeup of ethnographic filmmaking, while also suggesting that the resulting knowledge of such work does not fit into clear boundaries. Instead it is experienced as an amalgam, spanning the rational, experiential, and affective, among other modes of understanding.

As the production of knowledge is necessarily connected to pedagogy, it is also important to evaluate

36 See Marks, *The Skin of Film*.
37 Dewey, *Art as Experience*.
38 See Plantinga, "Affective Power of Movies."
39 Haraway, "Cyborg Manifesto."

> Particular about this mode of registering thick description are the "haptically visual" representations of physical experience and affectivity that film allows—ones based on multisensorial memories of touch.

Klearjos Eduardo Papanicolaou

the ways in which it feeds back into established educational frameworks. Teaching audiovisual ethnography to architecture, landscape, and urban design students at ETH Zurich with the Chair of Architecture and Urban Design for a number of years has allowed me to filter the ways in which these approaches and the forms of knowledge that they produce may be of use to students in these fields. A key finding in carrying out this teaching is that, while the importance of visual methods in architecture, landscape, and urban studies means that the skills of the audiovisual ethnographer are highly sought after, experiential and affective forms of knowledge are less familiar and thus harder to grasp for many students.

A struggle for students such as my own, as with the general population, is to reflect on their relationship with cameras before setting out to work on their film projects. Throughout the semester-long courses that we carry out, students, many of whom have never been involved in film "projects" before, are asked to use their phones to carry out experiments in basic audiovisual ethnography around a variety of themes (from informality to urban play, among many others). The word "projects" is in quotation marks to differentiate from the fact that almost every student uses the camera function on their phone every day. Thus instruction takes the form of conscious unlearning of certain principles in the use of the phone camera in order, once again to quote John Berger, to learn new "ways of seeing"—ones that might permit them to "go beyond the frame" in the perception of a presence bigger than the sum of the parts that they may record. Similarly, students are asked to edit their films iteratively after each day of filming to reflect on what they see, finding the patterns that will eventually lead them to a concept for their films. Subsequent assessment is made not in terms of the length, scope, and aesthetic of their finished works, but rather in terms of their process: How well did they manage to reflect on their relationship with the instruments they used and the environments that they depicted?

Indeed, many fields seek the representational power that audiovisual methods offer, but it is less common that these fields engage with the deeper

→ Figure 4

questions inherent to the use of cameras, as those that this chapter attempts to shine a light on. The first step towards teaching these methods to students such as my own is to give them the opportunity to comprehend films not as either representations of an overarching "reality" in the form of documentaries or wholly fictitious works in the form of "cinema," but rather as a large set of potential practices that focus on embodiment, materiality, and process. Through the senses, they may also offer knowledge in terms of physical experience and affectivity. For this, however, it is important to also consider that films themselves entail a physicality not only in how they are made but also in how they are watched and felt.

40 Barthes, "Leaving the Movie Theatre," 418.

The spaces of cinema

Reflecting once again on the materiality of cameras —on the mechanisms with which they produce their gaze—brings us back to the topic of physical space. Indeed, even the *trompe d'oeil* sometimes achieved by cameras is a trick situated in physical space. Any new "reality" divined by cameras is one that uses, as raw materials, its physical surroundings. Is it not then curious that, for many filmmakers, the only film-watching spaces that matter after their films are completed are those of prominent cinema halls that may cement the prestige of their work? As affective and experiential theories of knowledge suggest, is there not also an importance in the materiality of our viewing of films (as in our reading of books)? As with the discrepancy between the "reality" *within* images and the "reality" of the *material* of images, so is there a discrepancy between the "reality" *within* films and the "reality" of *our bodies* both watching and also discussing and negotiating their meaning afterwards.

→ Figure 5

The literary theorist and semiotician Roland Barthes shines light on this discrepancy in his 1975 essay "Leaving a Movie Theatre." He recounts that upon doing just that he "walks in silence ... a little dazed, wrapped up in himself, feeling the cold ... he's sleepy... his body has become ... soft, limp, and he feels a little disjointed ... In other words," he says, he is "coming out of a hypnosis."[40] While the scene may be familiar to those who go to cinema halls to watch

Klearjos Eduardo Papanicolaou

films, the association of hypnosis, emphasizing the physiological and psychological quality of the experience, may not be.

The somatic experience of the cinema in both senses (as a work and as a space) has been discussed by numerous scholars, such as Elsaesser and Hagener;[41] the use of color, light, rhythm, sound, and silence, among many other tools, are deployed to have physiological effects on the viewer, resulting in an audiovisual grammar legible not only by our brains as ideas but also by our bodies as sensory experiences. A loud noise surprises us, triggering a rush of blood; an excess of light causes the eyelids to retract; an image shown for a long duration induces a sense of reflection, inviting our thoughts back into the sensory realm in conversation with the unfolding physical reaction. Specifically in terms of landscape and urban studies, Fred Truniger writes of the "the capacity of the cinema to connect memories to experience, through which a real landscape experience can be approximated for the moviegoer in their seat."[42] Indeed, the conundrum in Barthes' anecdote—How can a space in which people are prompted not to move be so physically demanding?—underlines how the sensory mechanisms of the body work in response to such stimuli.

Yet it is ironic that "cinema"—a word derived from the Greek, *kinema*, meaning movement—is a space in which people congregate in order to sit still. Quite in contrast to movement, for many cinemagoers even small movements, sounds, or smells—any type of disturbance of the sensory field—is considered an aberration of the cinematic experience. Norms regarding what to do and how to behave in a "cinema" space did not emerge from the outset of film, however. Apocryphal anecdotes of early cinemas in Japan told of audiences that sat not exactly in front of the screen, but rather, obliquely, in order to also contemplate the relationship between the projector and the screen.[43] The German expression *Kopfkino*—head cinema in English—is meant to denote a simple fantasy, perhaps speaking to potential formlessness and plasticity within the concept of the cinema as a space. As if to illustrate this potential

41 Elsaesser and Hagener, *Film Theory*.
42 Truniger, *Landscript* 2, 64.
43 Chapman, *Cinemas of the World*.

for anarchic creativity in the application of the term cinema, while reminding us of its physicality, in the late 1960s the Austrian artist Valie Export performed what she called the *Tapp- und Tastkino* (touch and tap cinema) by wearing a box shaped like a small cinema, inviting passersby to place their hands inside the box where, behind the curtain, was the performer's nude torso.[44]

To approach a definition relevant for research and knowledge production, one may inquire, as with filmmaking practice, how the definition of "cinema" spaces corresponds to the ideologies and epistemologies of the films that are shown there. If one determines that the cine-plex corresponds to the films emerging from the commercial film industry, what are the spaces, then, for filmmakers working in the mode of cinematic and sensory ethnography, who are ideologically committed to affective and experiential forms of knowledge? Asking this question is not a matter of insisting that traditional cinema spaces, dark and quiet, are the only appropriate spaces within which to experience the full potential as cinema—this would be tantamount to insisting that one should only read books in libraries. Rather, the critical element is to consider how certain films convey their meaning in order to ascertain the physical conditions that allow for that meaning to be conveyed. Obviously, there is variation among different people in terms of this—sensory organs are not uniform—but it is easy to understand why for many people (to continue the metaphor of books) reading might be hard in loud places or where there is too much or too little light.

The design and urban condition of such spaces thus becomes important, as it determines the physical characteristics that will define the experiences that will be had there. This applies to the multitude of possible "home cinema" experiences or the possibility of watching films on a mobile phone practically anywhere. The bottom line is that spaces that inhibit the "hypnosis" Barthes describes typically diminish the cinematic and sensory qualities of a film. How should one deal with daylight and ambient light in such spaces? What about sound? If they are not commercial spaces, what kind of economic models can allow

[44] Export, *Tapp- und Tastkino*.

Klearjos Eduardo Papanicolaou

them to sustainably carry out these activities? What kinds of access should they establish with different members of society? Should such spaces be independent or exist within institutions like those of higher education? These are questions of architectural and urban design.

Certain spaces that respond to these questions may be found in most urban centers, some of them in the form of public experiences. "Third spaces" of various kinds, in the form of community centers and independently organized political spaces, to name a few, provide examples for this.[45] University spaces, while themselves beholden to ideologies closely tied to the state and market economies, also have the potential to produce such spaces, especially in those contexts where students have freedoms in the self-organization of activities and spaces. Exhibitions and public experiments of various kinds also point to ephemeral cinema spaces designed to address new audiences.

→ Figure 6

An ongoing experiment in the design of such spaces is the Studio Mobile project, emerging from the Chair of Architecture and Urban Design at ETH Zurich. Consisting of a mobile pavilion designed to host exhibitions, workshops, community meetings, and show films, it was originally devised for the Vienna Biennale 2021 and deployed across various locations in the city over a series of months. Recalling, perhaps, the experiments of Valie Export both in location and in terms of collapsing established notions of where cinema should be seen, film screenings that took place in the space of the Studio Mobile de facto invited any passersby to join, turning the street into a cinema space and its volumes into furniture. While elements like street noise naturally inhibited certain sensory elements in the experience of watcing films, the physicality and sociability of the experience created conditions conducive for sharing. In this sense, while an imperfect experiment as a cinema space, the Studio Mobile points to ways in which we might continue to consider film production and consumption as part of a cycle ordered by the production and sharing of experiential and affective forms of knowledge.

[45] See Soja, *Thirdspace*.

The success of these spaces rests on their ability to reconnect films with their materiality, and the experience of watching films with their physicality. Such spaces would align their ideological commitment with those of the filmmaker concerned: not primarily with aesthetics but with the production of forms of knowledge that are accessible and open towards new audiences, as those discussed in the previous section.

Ways of living (and researching)

Andrei Tarkovski's 1975 film *Mirror* depicts experiences derived from the life of the director in an explicitly fragmented manner, eschewing conventions of cinematic continuity and offering instead an associative, dream-like passage through the story.[46] While enigmatic for many, the intent of the film hides in plain sight: the "mirror" is Tarkovski's camera, which he uses to look at himself, in the endless disparate ways in which one can do so. It would seem that Tarkovski took Marey and Vertov's pronouncements seriously, using the camera to sculpt a "reality" based on his encounters with the world—a "dynamic landscape" of his life.

In an acute manner, Tarkovski's *Mirror* points to techniques instructive to anyone interested in making a serious commitment to filmmaking as a method to articulate the complexities of the "reality" that surrounds us—landscape, urban, or otherwise. These techniques do not hide the artifice of the camera in that process; on the contrary, they emphasize its presence. In the same vein, filmmakers working within the mode of sensory ethnography use their tools not to hide the materiality of the camera or the physicality of their presence but to emphasize them to provide a richer account of what it is that they experience.

Researchers interested in audiovisual methods such as cinematic and sensory ethnography as a means of articulating extra-linguistic nuances in their work may be interested in reflecting on their relationship not only with the technologies discussed in this chapter—namely the camera—but with any other technological means of conveying an idea. In doing so, they may find that the knowledge that

46   Tarkovsky, *Mirror*.

Klearjos Eduardo Papanicolaou

they produce is not without context but is instead firmly rooted in various epistemological commitments and ideological "social roles." Within (but not limited to) landscape and urban studies, embracing these points may be a pathway for audiovisual fieldwork to be understood as both affective and experiential. If these approaches are furthermore fed back into physical spaces where they may be discussed and negotiated—as in "third" cinema spaces, in the case of films—then a cycle of knowledge production and sharing may develop, strengthening both research and output. For researcher-filmmakers, such spaces may be thought of as the critical element that reach the knowledge that their films themselves promise.

While it is often technology that drives changes in perception of realities around us, perhaps a renewed focus on our overall physical experiences, as well as the physical experiences of those technologies, can help drive a broader understanding of these transitions. As if in recognition of this point, towards the end of his life John Berger's contributions as an art historian shifted from writing books and presenting television programs to tending to his homestead in rural France, where he lived with his family. While there are fewer books written about his contributions to intellectual life from this time, what one may perhaps see is that he understood that beyond our ways of seeing the world it is also important to devise "ways of living" that prioritize our physical experiences in it.[47]

47 See Sperling, "Ways of Living."

ACKNOWLEDGMENTS
This text would not have been possible without the sustained encouragement and support of Nitin Bathla. The same applies, especially in terms of filmmaking practice, to Marios Kleftakis, and in terms of daily inspiration, to Claudia Sinatra. I would also like to thank Ludwig Berger, Ileana Apostol, Philip Cartelli, Angelos Papanicolaou and my colleagues at the Chair of Architecture and Urban Design, especially Prof. Hubert Klumpner.

Mirror Images

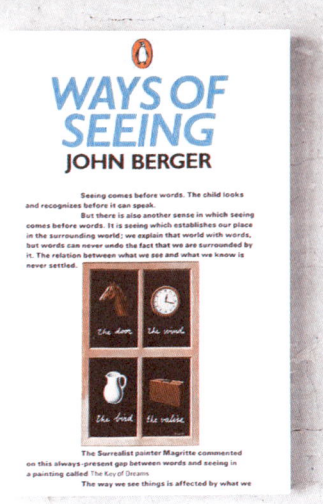

Figure 1   *Ways of Seeing* by John Berger, 1972

Klearjos Eduardo Papanicolaou

Figure 2 — Phases of movement of a man jumping a hurdle. Sequence captured using a chronophotographic gun. Étienne-Jules Marey, ca. 1892

Mirror Images

Figure 3   Still from *The Seven Sisters Indoor Market* by Klearjos Eduardo Papanicolaou and Marios Kleftakis, 2016

Figure 4   Autumn 2018 poster for an ethnographic filmmaking course at ETH Zurich

Klearjos Eduardo Papanicolaou

Figure 5   "Ein Drama ist auch ein Raum" (a drama is also a space), sign outside Kino Arthouse Le Paris in 2023

Figure 6   Studio Mobile film screening at Viktor-Adler-Markt in Vienna, June 2021

Mirror Images

BIBLIOGRAPHY

B

Barthes, Roland, "Leaving the Movie Theater." In *The Art of the Personal Essay: An Anthology from the Classical Era to the Present*, edited by Phillip Lopate, 418–422. New York: Anchor Books, 1995.

Bathla, Nitin, and Klearjos E. Papanicolaou. "Reframing the Contested City through Ethnographic Film: Beyond the Expository on Housing and the Urban." *International Journal of Housing Policy* 22, no. 3 (2022): 351–70. https://doi.org/10.1080/19491247.2021.1886028.

Baudry, Jean-Louis, and Alan Williams. "Ideological Effects of the Basic Cinematographic Apparatus." *Film Quarterly* 28, no. 2 (1974): 39–47. https://doi.org/10.2307/1211632.

Berger, John, director. *Ways of Seeing*. Episode 1. 1972.

Berger, John. *Ways of Seeing*. London: Penguin Classics, 2008.

Bordwell, David. "The Idea of Montage in Soviet Art and Film." *Cinema Journal* 11, no. 2 (1972): 9–17. https://doi.org/10.2307/1225046.

C

Chair of Architecture and Urban Design, ETH Zurich. *Studio Mobile*. 2021–2023. https://klumpner.arch.ethz.ch/researching/exhibitions/studio-mobile-venice-sarajevo-2023 (accessed April 24, 2023).

Chapman, James. *Cinemas of the World: Film and Society from 1895 to the Present*. London: Reaktion Books, 2003.

D

Dewey, John. *Art as Experience*. New York: Perigee Books, 1934.

E

Elsaesser, Thomas, and Malte Hagener. *Film Theory: An Introduction through the Senses*, 2nd edition, New York and Abindon, Oxon: Routledge, 2015. https://doi.org/10.4324/9781315740768.

Export, Valie, director. *Tapp- und Tastkino*. 1968.

F

Favero, Paolo. "Learning to Look beyond the Frame: Reflections on the Changing Meaning of Images in the Age of Digital Media Practices." *Visual Studies* 29, no. 2 (2014): 166–79. https://doi.org/10.1080/1472586X.2014.887269.

G

Geertz, Clifford. *The Interpretation of Cultures: Selected Essays*. New York: Basic Books, 1973.

Glaser, Barney G., and Anselm, L. Strauss, *The Discovery of Grounded Theory: Strategies for Qualitative Research*. Chicago: Aldine Publishing, 1967.

Green, Philip. "Ideology and Ambiguity in Cinema." *The Massachusetts Review* 34, no. 1 (Spring 1993): 102–26.

H

Hammersley, Martyn, and Paul Atkinson. *Ethnography: Principles in Practice*. 4th edition. London: Routledge, 2019. https://doi.org/10.4324/9781315146027.

Haraway, Donna. "Manifesto for Cyborgs: Science, Technology, and Socialist Feminism in the 1980s." In *Socialist Review* no. 80 (1985): 65–108.

Hayes-Conroy, Allison. "Critical Visceral Methods and Methodologies: Debate Title: Better than Text? Critical Reflections on the Practices of Visceral Methodologies in Human Geography." *Geoforum* 82 (June 2017): 51–52. https://doi.org/10.1016/j.geoforum.2017.03.017.

Henley, Paul. *Beyond Observation: A History of Authorship in Ethnographic Film*. Manchester: Manchester University Press, 2020.

Hill, Dave. "Regeneration—Or Pushing Out the Poor? Labour Divides in Bitter Housing Battle." *The Guardian*, October 29, 2017. https://www.theguardian.com/society/2017/oct/29/gentrification-pushing-out-the-poor-haringey-council-housing-battle-corbyn-labour (accessed April 21, 2023).

K

Kepley, Vance, Jr. "Pudovkin, Socialist Realism, and the Classical Hollywood Style." *Journal of Film and Video* 47, no. 4 (1995): 3–16.

L

Lamarque, Peter, and Stein Haugom Olsen. *Truth, Fiction, and Literature: A Philosophical Perspective*. Oxford: Oxford University Press, 1994.

M

MacDougall, David. *The Looking Machine: Essays on Cinema, Anthropology and Documentary Filmmaking*. Manchester: Manchester University Press, 2019.

Marey, Étienne-Jules. *La méthode graphique dans les sciences expérimentales et principalement en physiologie et en médecine*. Paris: G. Masson, 1878.

Marks, Laura U. *The Skin of the Film: Intercultural Cinema, Embodiment, and the Senses*. Durham, NC: Duke University Press: 2019.

Mead, Margaret, and Gregory Bateson, directors. *Trance and Dance in Bali*. 1951. Foerstel (Lenora) Collection (The Library of Congress) 2425201. https://www.loc.gov/item/mbrs02425201/.

P

Papanicolaou, Klearjos E. "Living With Difference: The Right to the (Cosmopolitan) City." MSc dissertation, London School of Economics and Political Science, 2014.

Pink, Sarah. *Doing Sensory Ethnography*. 2nd edition. London: SAGE Publications, 2015.

Plantinga, Carl. 2013. "The Affective Power of Movies." In *Psychocinematics: Exploring Cognition at the Movies*, edited by Arthur P. Shimamura, 94–111. Oxford: Oxford University Press. 2013. https://doi.org/10.1093/acprof:oso/9780199862139.003.0005.

R

Rutherford, Anne. "Cinema and Embodied Affect." *Senses of Cinema*, issue 25, March 2003. https://www.sensesofcinema.com/2003/feature-articles/embodied_affect/#16. (accessed August 17, 2023).

S

Sannah, Bassim. "The Characteristic Features of Hollywood's Scenographical Stylization (1930–1939)." PhD dissertation, Ruhr University, 2004.

Soja, Edward W. *Thirdspace: Journeys to Los Angeles and Other Real-and-Imagined Places*. Oxford: Basil Blackwell, 1996.

Sontag, Susan. *On Photography*. New York: Farrar, Straus, Giroux, 1977.

Sperling, Joshua. "Ways of Living." *AON*, December 3, 2019. https://aeon.co/essays/john-bergers-ways-of-seeing-and-his-search-for-home (accessed April 21, 2023).

Sweet, Elizabeth L., and Sara O. Escalante. *Bringing Bodies into Planning: Visceral Methods, Fear and Gender Violence*. London: SAGE, 2015.

T

Tarkovsky, Andrei, director. *Mirror*. Mosfilm, 1975.

Thrift, Nigel. *Spatial Formations*. London, Thousand Oaks, CA: SAGE, 1996.

Trouillot, Michel-Rolph. 2003. "Anthropology and the Savage Slot: The Poetics and Politics of Otherness." In *Global Transformations: Anthropology and the Modern World*, 7–28. New York: Palgrave Macmillan, 2003. https://doi.org/10.1007/978-1-137-04144-9_2.

Truniger, Fred. *Landscript 2: Filmic Mapping—Documentary Film and the Visual Culture of Landscape Architecture*. Berlin: Jovis Verlag, 2013.

V

Vertov, Dziga. "Kino-Eye Manifesto." In *Kino-Eye: The Writings of Dziga Vertov*, edited by Annette Michelson, translated by Kevin O'Brien, 17–18. Los Angeles: University of California Press, 1984.

IMAGE CREDITS

Figure 1: Wikimedia Commons
Figure 2: © The Board of Trustees of the Science Museum, London
Figure 3: Klearjos Eduardo Papanicolaou and Marios Kleftakis
Figure 4: Chair of Architecture and Urban Design, ETHZ / Klearjos Eduardo Papanicolaou
Figure 5: Klearjos Eduardo Papanicolaou
Figure 6: Chair of Architecture and Urban Design, ETH Zurich / Klearjos Eduardo Papanicolaou

Restitutive Methods

Ludo Groen

Investigating Subterranean Swiss Banking with Open-Source Intelligence Tools

Researching Otherwise
Nitin Bathla, ed.

As we scroll through the village of Amsteg, slowly climbing the street to the Gotthard Pass, our eye is caught by a concrete retaining wall, standing next to a nondescript garage door. If we had delegated this investigation to an image recognition algorithm, it would have recognized the dry-stone wall from an archival photograph of the K8 Federal Council bunker. Indeed, we are standing face-to-face with the place where Switzerland's highest governmental officials would have sought shelter if Nazi Germany had invaded their country. The enemy never came, but the Swiss National Bank keenly used their specially designated room between 1942 and 1945 to store banknotes.[1] Even though the bunker was decommissioned by the end of last century, its archival documentation remains classified, and the existence of Alpine bank vaults largely limited to the realms of fiction. Only a few archival photographs survive from this enigmatic period of Swiss banking history. The location where they were taken can be identified or geolocated through a "reverse image search" in an engine such as Yandex, Bing, or Google.[2] Over the past decade, open-source intelligence tools like these have become common practice in journalism but are still relatively little adopted by researchers in the fields of architecture, landscape, and urban studies. Expanding on the research methodologies of radical cartography and forensics unpacked in the introduction to this volume, this chapter will offer a glimpse into the potential of these methodologies in overcoming gaps in institutional archives. As such, buildings and infrastructures serve as a lens through which to investigate the contested conduct of financial institutions, even if they are designed to remain illegible.

Amsteg, August 25, 1948. A cloudless day at a flight altitude of 3,050 meters. Every monochrome pixel of the aerial photograph covers half a meter on the ground, making visible the evidential elements of the landscape. The same site was also captured before the Second World War, twelve years earlier, as part of a landscape survey. Comparing both images, substantial alterations can be noticed in the roads and topography of the mountain spur along the Gotthardstrasse. A built structure seems to have been added

1   A letter dated Mar. 6, 1951, discusses the technical requirements for a new bunker and refers to the exact dates that the K8 bunker in Amsteg was in use by the National Bank, namely from Dec. 3, 1942, to Sep. 5, 1945, to store banknotes in boxes and bags. The minutes of a secret meeting of the bank's directors from Aug. 25, 1960, report that between 1941 and 1945 the room in Amsteg was used for the storage of gold bars, coins, and banknotes. Swiss National Bank Archive, box no. 1000970, 1950–1970.
2   See Toler, "Guide to Using Reverse Image Search."

→ Figure 1+2

Ludo Groen

at the location that we encountered in the Street View discussed above (evidence 1 in figure 3). If this is indeed the entrance to a bunker built around 1941, there might be an egress on the other side of the mountain. Such an entrance would be situated where the topography of the valley suddenly slopes to become a rock wall. A geometric lesson of significance here is that if trees stand on a mountainous terrain, they cast longer shadows than the same trees in a flat valley. The dark, long shadows of the forest ridge could indicate such a shift in topography and would therefore be a logical site for an entrance into the mountain (evidence 2). Our suspicion is strengthened by the new access that has been paved over (evidence 3).

In 1943 the road's ostentatiousness was also noticed by a colonel, who grumbled in a letter to the army command that "the access road to the facility is so wonderful that it must immediately jump into the eyes of every airman."[3] He was so concerned because the site of the Federal Council bunker was stamped as top secret. In July 1940, under the threat of an invasion by the Axis powers, the Swiss army's General Henri Guisan unfolded his *Reduit* strategy to retreat the military to the Alps, to fortifications that were yet to be built and extended. Switzerland's head of state, the Federal Council, was expected to follow their example. In February 1941, when finally reaching consensus on the most appropriate site, they wrote to Guisan:

> General, the Federal Council has reconsidered the question of the seat of government in the event of an evacuation and has designated Amsteg as its location. [...] I ask you to make the following preparations: 1. The village of Amsteg is to be entirely reserved for the Federal Council. 2. The army will provide the necessary garrison and air defense. 3. To build a bomb-proof living and working quarters in the rock, with the necessary installations (working, living and sleeping quarters, catering storage, kitchen, sanitary facilities, rooms for guards, couriers and kitchen staff, ventilation, gas protection, heating, lighting, and a garage for the cars).[4]

Unlike the other military bunkers that were built at the time by the army's in-house engineers, for this

3   Cited in Auf der Mauer, *Die Schweiz unter Tag*, 39.
    In his book, the journalist Jost Auf der Mauer reports from various underground sites across Switzerland, including the Federal Council bunker in Amsteg, based on oral histories taken from villagers and archival research in the Swiss Federal Archives.

4   Cited in Auf der Mauer, *Die Schweiz unter Tag*, 22.

→ Figure 3

→ Figure 4+5

special project the Bernese architect Hans Buser was commissioned. He divided the program of 3,000 square meters over two underground floors. To provide comfort for the Federal Councilors, the exposed rock and concrete walls were rendered with vertical wooden planking over insulation boards in the bedrooms and light-beige paneling in the dining rooms. The dining room was even embellished with a trompe l'oeil window into a Segantini painting, whose crisp blue skies compensated for the lack of daylight. The wooden cladding was not a mere aesthetic choice but allegedly added on the explicit wishes of the bunker's other dweller: the Swiss National Bank. The insulation and wood reduced humidity so that the bank could use the room to store their gold bars, coins, and banknotes—assets that, as we now know, included gold looted from Holocaust victims and the federal banks of occupied European countries.[5]

The architectural details described above can be noticed in a series of digitized archival photographs that disclose the bunker's interior. The images originate from a military photo collection in the Swiss Federal Archives, but they are neither indexed nor sufficiently labeled, making them impossible to find with a conventional archival query.[6] Only by uploading the image that featured at the beginning of this chapter to Yandex's reverse image search engine did its algorithm retrieve other photographs from the same bunker. This is an example of how the digitization of archives and its subsequent algorithmic analysis introduces new ways to access archival materials. These sources are normally obscured for historians due to incorrect or insufficient labeling, becoming retrievable through the power of image and text recognition tools.[7]

One of the retrieved archival images depicts an underground corridor with two steel armored doors. Uploading this image into the reverse image search engine again brings up an identical yet aged version of the doors in a photograph taken by a Michele Limina, Bloomberg journalist, during a promotional visit to the company Swiss Data Safe AG.[8] A peephole centered in the middle of the door (evidence 1 in figure 6), two swiveling levers on its edge (evidence 2),

[5] Selected correspondence around the construction of the K8 bunker is available from the fortress construction office in Amsteg. Retrieved from Swiss Federal Archives, E5480A-01#1984/166#24* Stab Geniechef der Armee: Baubüro Amsteg, 1941–1942. For an elaboration on the looted gold acquired by the Swiss National Bank during the Second World War, see Bergier, et al., *Switzerland, National Socialism, and the Second World War*.

[6] Swiss Federal Archives, E5792#1988/204#1302*, 1939–1945.

[7] For a reflection on the access and non-access provided by digitization of archives, see Benhaida, "Entering Archives."

[8] For the photograph by Michele Limina of the same door in 2016, see: https://www.gettyimages.ch/detail/nachrichtenfoto/door-leading-to-a-vault-stands-inside-the-swiss-data-nachrichten foto/611523952?language=de (accessed Dec. 14, 2023).

→ Figure 6

Ludo Groen

a closable recess for pipes (evidence 3), and a concrete filling above it (evidence 4) all resemble the door in the Federal Council bunker. Land ownership records confirm the identity of the facility's current owner, Swiss Data Safe AG.[9] Its website, available in English, German, French, Chinese, and Russian, advertises its services as a duty-free high-security vault for the storage of gold, silver, cash, works of art, data servers, cars, and other valuables.[10] Its founding shareholder, according to the company register known under the name Dolf Wipfli, is an engineer from the neighboring town Schattdorf.[11] A boolean Google Search connecting his name to some of his credentials links to a newspaper article from 2004, when he was awarded a prize for outstanding achievements in the economically struggling canton of Uri. In his acceptance speech, Wipfli thanked "the always very constructive cooperation" of the legislative authorities who introduced a new term to accommodate his business: an "underground commercial zone."[12] The territorial demarcation of such zones is published online in each canton's Cadaster of Public Law Restrictions on Land Ownership. As if subjected to an X-ray of the mountain, the digital platform exposes the bunker's perimeter in a dashed surface labeled as "superimposed special commercial zone." Stretching over 7,000 square meters, the facility indeed has entrances from the previously discussed sides of the mountain (see figure 7).

This is an example of how investigating the contemporary condition of a historical object can help to reconstruct its original design, and how its current use can—sometimes even more so than its intended purpose—reveal the structure's underlying design principles. In the case of the K8 bunker, the Federal Councilors never ended up sleeping a single night inside (although their nine secretaries did, for a teletype exercise, and were disturbed by the noise of the engines), but its secondary use as storage for valuables proved a better match with its architecture.[13]

An open-source website offering tools for company monitoring lists that between 2006 and 2013 Wipfli was also involved in another company: Swiss Gold Safe.[14] Their online sales pitch starts off by

9   The land ownership records are integrated in the cantonal cadaster, accessible via https://oereb.ur.ch/ (accessed Mar. 1, 2023).
10 See the website of Swiss Data Safe: https://www.swissdatasafe.ch/ (accessed Mar. 1, 2023).
11 The commercial register of Canton of Uri is accessible via https://ur.chregister.ch/ (accessed Mar. 1, 2023).
12 "Dätwyler-Stiftung hat Förderpreise verliehen," *Urnerwochenblatt*, Nov. 2, 2004, https://www.urnerwochenblatt.ch/artikel/daetwyler-stiftung-hat-foerder-preise-verliehen (accessed Mar. 1, 2023).
13 Auf der Mauer, *Die Schweiz unter Tag*, 35.
14 The website lixt.ch provides free and paid tools for company monitoring and debt collection, based on data scraped from the public company register. Wipfli is listed between 2006 and 2013 as a "Mitglied" (associate) of Swiss Gold Safe AG.

→ Figure 7

stressing that they offer "bank-independent storage" that is "not regulated by the financial market authorities."[15]

One of the company's six vaults is based in Amsteg as well, and it is certified as an open bonded warehouse, a privately operated duty-free zone that exempts the stored goods from taxation regimes. Different from a duty-free warehouse that is directly operated by the Swiss customs (a *Zollfreilager*, ZFL), in an open bonded warehouse (an *Offene Zolllager*, OZL), the customs entrust a private party to keep a correct administration of all stock movements. An excel sheet on the federal website lists all 665 accredited open bonded warehouses in Switzerland.[16] Swiss Gold Safe is not included in the list, and the only zone in Amsteg is operated by Swiss Data Safe, suggesting that next to data servers also gold and other precious metals are stored in the former Federal Council bunker, just as it was originally planned in 1941.

Certified gold bars and coins in Switzerland are legally exempt from sales taxes, but when investing in white precious metals (such as silver, palladium, and platinum) or, say, works of art, storing them in an open bonded warehouse is particularly lucrative, since no taxes are charged during ownership transactions.[17] If we take a closer look at the dashed plane demarcating the underground commercial zone, it only includes the subterranean part of the facility and not the adjacent building and tunnel that serve as its entrances. This literally means that once the stored goods leave the mountain they become subject to taxation. The zone creates a condition of containment in which the metals stored inside become so precious that they will seldom see the light of day. As such, metals once unearthed through exploitative and extractive forces from mines in the Global South are indefinitely returned to the earth in Switzerland.[18] The only way to still trade the metals without being taxed in Switzerland is by asking an authorized dealer to move them to another duty-free zone or by virtually trading the certificates that transfer beneficiary ownership.[19] While investing in precious metals is advertised as reliable and safe because of

15 The concept of bank-independent storage is advertised on Swiss Gold Safe's website: https://swissgoldsafe.ch/ (accessed Mar. 1, 2023).

16 For the excel sheet, see the website of the Federal Office for Customs and Border Security: https://www.bazg.admin.ch/dam/bazg/de/dokumente/verfahren-betrieb/Aufgaben vollzug/ZVE_1%20KZS/zve_liste.xlsx.download.xlsx/Zentrale %20ZE-ZV-OZL%20Liste.xlsx (accessed Dec. 14, 2023).

17 The concept of the open bonded warehouse and its advantages for customers is explained on the company website of Swiss Data Safe AG: https://www.swissdatasafe.ch/ (accessed Mar. 1, 2023).

18 The colonial entanglements of Swiss gold trade are described in Bandi, Jain, and knowbotiq, "Swiss Psychotropic Gold." See also Denise Bertschi's contribution to the current volume.

19 This business model is based on the fact that guarding and storing gold in bulk is more efficient than in individual safe-deposit boxes at a bank or having to take care of security measures yourself for a lock at home. The concept of a collective storage system and the exemption of taxes on gold are explained on the website of the company Swiss Gold Safe AG: https://swissgoldsafe.ch/ (accessed March 1, 2023).

Ludo Groen

its material backing, the material itself is rarely experienced by their owners as the metals are landlocked in duty-free zones.

Extraterritorial duty-free zones have a long history in the border regions of Switzerland. Despite being a legal, immaterial instrument, they are intrinsically linked to material infrastructures, such as highways and railways. In this capacity, the zones have historically been instrumental in lucratively situating Switzerland as a transit hub between the north and south of Europe—a position it greatly owes to the innovative engineers that found ways to cross its mountainous territory with tunnels, railways, and passes.[20] The web page of the Federal Office of Customs and Border Security emphasizes that these duty-free zones are conceived for goods in transit in border regions, so that they do not have to be cleared by customs and can be exported again afterwards without an abundance of paperwork.[21]

But since the 1970s, these zones have become gradually disconnected from those border regions, reaching "wherever a plane could land or a truck could travel."[22] Notions of time and space have been stretched, as zones no longer only temporarily store goods in border regions but also become permanent storage facilities in the heart of the country. Besides facilitating trade, in some instances these zones can also be considered an inland tax haven, much like the offshore ones in the Caribbean. The zones embody what Keller Easterling describes as "extrastatecraft," an infrastructure with the power to be exempted from the state's legislation for the purposes of economic interest.[23] This space is established either outside of or in partnership with statecraft, as was inadvertently disclosed by Wipfli in his speech when mentioning the cooperation of the canton in introducing new jurisdictions.

Easterling also demonstrates how worldwide these zones are related to tourism "celebrating the vacation from taxes" in places where luxury resorts conveniently converge with offshore finance.[24] Switzerland is traditionally known for excelling in both industries as well. Wipfli's competitor, ironically called Swiss Fort Knox, advertises itself to wealthy international

20 For a historical contextualization of the importance of duty-free zones in Switzerland, see Dommann, "Warenräume und Raumökonomien."
21 Website of the Federal Office for Customs and Border Security: https://www.bazg.admin.ch/bazg/de/home/dokumentation/publikationen/publikationen-zugelassene-empfaenger-und-versender.html (accessed March 1, 2023).
22 A global history of trade zones is given in Easterling, *Extrastatecraft,* here 17–18.
23 Easterling, *Extrastatecraft,* 10.
24 Easterling, *Extrastatecraft,* 19–20.

clients by virtue of its close proximity to a private airstrip and luxury hotels.[25] Its exact location is only disclosed to genuinely interested clients, but a round trip past the most luxurious Alpine resorts soon gets us to Gstaad-Saanen airport, where jetsetters arrive on their way to the eponymous ski resort. Located next to the former military airstrip are a handful of bunkers used until the 1980s to store ammunition and even entire fighter jets. Once again, the cadaster reveals the outline of one of them, which according to the land ownership records is currently owned by BC Business Computers AG.[26] The company is based in Zug, the canton most favored by shell companies, and in 2015 it obtained the exclusive rights to the brand name Swiss Fort Knox. Its trustworthy moniker suggests that the business aims to attract clients from across the Atlantic. This hypothesis can be investigated with open-source intelligence tools as well. The livecam on the website of Gstaad-Saanen airport is pointed towards the mountain that opens into the Swiss Fort Knox facility. A private jet arrives, its passengers descend the swing-open stairs, and are escorted into a black Mercedes that taxies them to the vault. Every time this happens, the plane's tail number can be inserted into an open-source flight tracking service that displays the origin of the flight. Once this action is repeated enough times, the geographical provenance of the capital stored in the mountain vault of Swiss Fort Knox can be mapped out.

    A similar search allows the geological origins of the stored precious metals to be traced. For their purchase, Swiss Gold Safe partners with the authorized dealer Echtgeld AG. Their website lists the various manufacturers of its gold bars, such as the Rand Refinery in South Africa for ¼-ounce Krugerrand coins. Rand Refinery is the world's largest single-site gold refining and smelting complex, situated southeast of Johannesburg, and can be easily geolocated in Google Maps. The refinery is reviewed by various Google users, among them truck drivers rating the logistic handling of all places where they embark and disembark. Some of these rated sites are located close to large gold mines, such as Kusasalethu and Mponeng. In turn, these mines are reviewed by other

[25] For an analysis of the Swiss Fort Knox project, see Berger Ziauddin, "Data Bunker."

[26] The land ownership is listed in the ÖREB-Kataster of Canton Bern. The company register on www.lixt.ch links the business to the brand name.

Ludo Groen

Google users, giving an impression of the lives of local gold miners and their current working and employment conditions. Such subjective and arbitrary observations cannot necessarily be treated as representative for the entire supply chain but become more precise once combined with other pieces of evidence.

Simple exercises like these are only possible because companies make use of infrastructures that are publicly regulated, such as duty-free zones; (formerly) publicly owned, such as military objects; or publicly registered on governmental platforms. A thorn in the side of the discretion preached by the companies involved, the four discussed tools demonstrate the value of keeping public repositories of transport, energy, water, and legal infrastructures. They exemplify how the technologies developed to construct these infrastructures can also be subverted to shed light on company operations.

In this subversion, infrastructural technologies—even if they seek to hide in the shadows—adopt an aesthetic dimension. From the hatches of the special commercial zone to black-and-white aerial surveys, they remind of Walter Benjamin's humbling critique that "a photograph of the Krupp or AEG factory tells us nothing about these institutions." Writing in 1931, Benjamin was referring to artists such as Albert Renger-Patzsch who went out with their novel cameras to "objectively" document the steel architectures of industrialization and the harsh realities concealed behind their facades.[27] A similar way of treating architectural objects as evidential elements can be recognized more recently in the work of forensic architecture. Using 3D-scanning, remote sensing, and satellite imagery, such work adopts a technologized aesthetic of truth finding in which architecture, similarly to Renger-Patzsch, serves as a focal point (rather than subject) of their investigations.[28] "There is much locational and spatial information that can be harvested from within these blurry, shaky and unedited images," its founder Eyal Weizman asserts,

27 Benjamin, "Little History of Photography."
28 See Weizman, *Forensic Architecture*, 9–11.

> A thorn in the side of the discretion preached by the companies involved, the four discussed tools demonstrate the value of keeping public repositories of transport, energy, water, and legal infrastructures.

and "architecture is a good framework to understand the world."[29] That the aesthetics of such territorial investigations are not free of ideologies is also stressed by geographer Philippe Rekacewicz. Rejecting the notion of objectivity, he has argued that the map has nothing to do with reality. Rekacewicz considers the cartographic image as a tool to make the invisible visible, both from the perspective of those in charge, as well the activists intending to unsettle those same power structures. Open-source mapping tools and access to data, according to him, allow "anybody to map anything, however badly or inexactly."[30]

Borrowing from these artists, architects, and geographers, the at times haphazard and incomplete observations presented here do not pretend to uncover any new truths but rather serve to compensate for the lack of historical sources. When researching contested chapters of history, sources found in institutional archives or even oral histories turn out to not always be sufficient. Alternative methodologies, such as open-source intelligence tools, can amplify, unearth, or even substitute the absent evidence. Doing so can contribute to more plural writing of the history of banking in Switzerland—a history that extends from the renowned urban centers of banking to the subterranean Alpine landscape, and ultimately to the infrastructures of gold extraction in the Global South.

[29] Eyal Weizman quoted in Schouten, "Theory Talk #69." See further Bathla, "Complexities and Contradictions."
[30] Rekacewicz, "Radical Cartography," 212.

ACKNOWLEDGMENTS
This chapter presents the methodology followed in the author's doctoral research, conducted jointly between the Institute for the History and Theory of Architecture (gta) and the Institute of Landscape and Urban Studies (LUS) at ETH Zurich, supervised by Laurent Stalder and Milica Topalović in the context of the Swiss National Science Foundation research project "Switzerland: A Technological Pastoral." It is the result of many inspiring conversations with supervisors, guests, editors of this book, and other doctoral researchers at the department.

Ludo Groen

Figure 1+2   Entrance to K8 Federal Council bunker, Amsteg

Subterranean Swiss Banking

Figure 3   Aerial photograph of Gotthardstrasse, Amsteg, 1948, annotated with evidence 1, 2, and 3

Ludo Groen

Figure 4+5   Dining room and bedroom for Federal Councilors in the K8 bunker

Figure 6   Photograph of armored doors inside the K8 bunker, annotated with evidence 1, 2, 3, and 4

Subterranean Swiss Banking

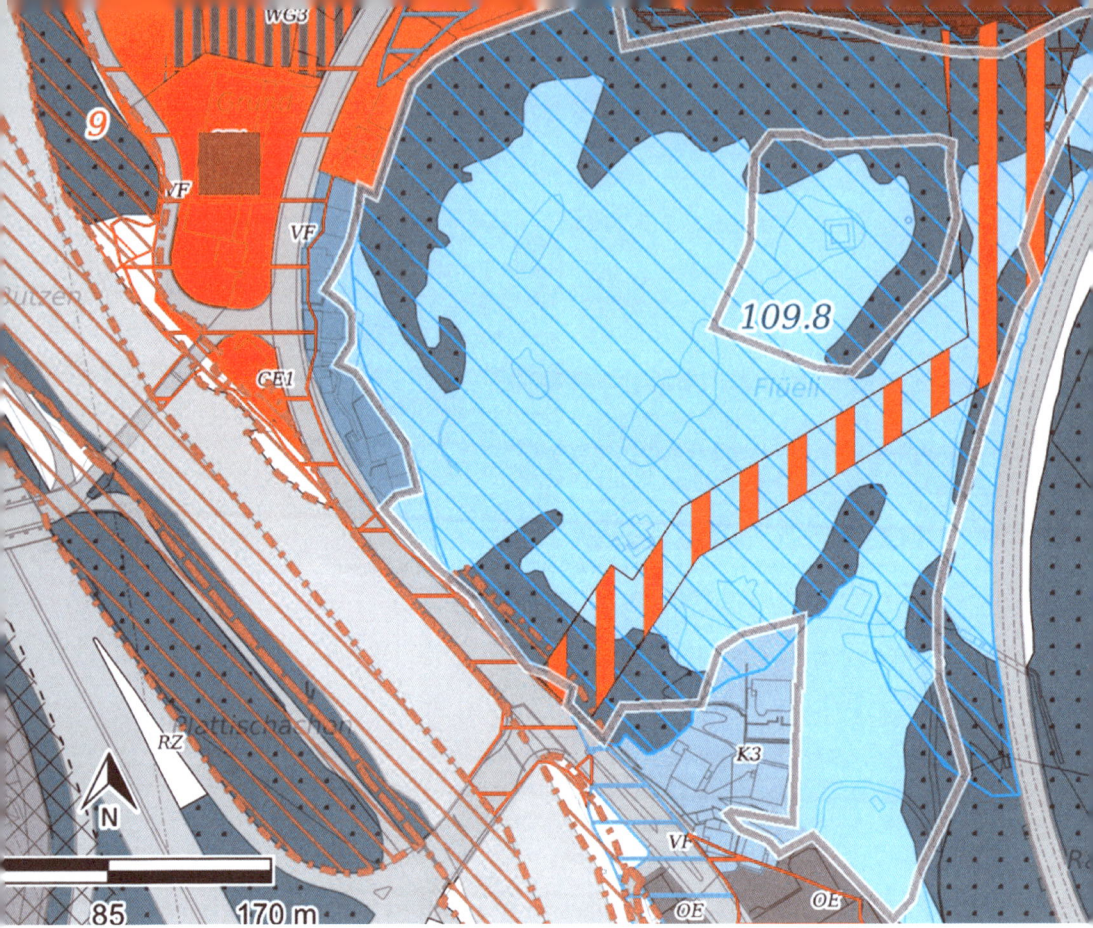

Figure 7   Extract, Cadaster of Public Law Restrictions on Land Ownership (ÖREB), Canton Uri, plot no. 123, Silenen, 2022

Ludo Groen

BIBLIOGRAPHY

A
Auf der Mauer, Jost. *Die Schweiz unter Tag.* Basel: Echtheit Verlag, 2017.

B
Bandi, Nina, Rohit Jain, and knowbotiq. "Swiss Psychotropic Gold—A Critical Fabulation." In *Swiss Psychotropic Gold*, 451–675. Basel: Christoph Merian Verlag, 2020.

Bathla, Nitin. "Complexities and Contradictions in Forensic Architecture." *trans* 36: *Spannung* (2020): 103–108.

Benhaida, Jasmine Sarah. "Entering Archives: Field Notes and Reflections on the Production of Silences." In *Unearthing Traces: Dismantling Imperialist Entanglements of Archives, Landscapes, and the Build Environment*, edited by Denise Bertschi, Julien Lafontaine Carboni, and Nitin Bathla, 61–73. Lausanne: EPFL Press, 2023.

Benjamin, Walter. "Little History of Photography." In *Walter Benjamin: Selected Writings*, vol. 2, edited by M. Jennings, H. Eiland, and G. Smith, 506–30. Cambridge, MA: The Belknap Press, 1999.

Berger Ziauddin, Silvia. "The Data Bunker is Not Just Anywhere." In *Data Centers: Edges of a Wired Nation*, edited by Monika Dommann, Hannes Rickli, and Max Stadler, 290–309. Zurich: Lars Müller Publishers, 2020.

Bergier, Jean-François, et al. *Switzerland, National Socialism, and the Second World War: Final Report.* Zurich: Pendo Verlag, 2002.

D
Dommann, Monika. "Warenräume und Raumökonomien: Kulturtechniken des Lagerns." *Schriften zur Verkehrswissenschaft* 38 (2012): 50–62.

E
Easterling, Keller. *Extrastatecraft: The Power of Infrastructure Space.* New York: Verso Books, 2014.

R
Rekacewicz, Philippe. "Radical Cartography." In *Shifts in Mapping: Maps as a Tool of Knowledge*, edited by Christine Schranz, 210–12. Bielefeld: Transcript Verlag, 2021.

S
Schouten, Peer. "Theory Talk #69: Eyal Weizman on the Architectural-Image Complex, Forensic Archeology and Policing across the Desertification Line." *Theory Talks*, 2015.

T
Toler, Aric. "Guide to Using Reverse Image Search For Investigations." *Bellingcat* (blog), December 26, 2019. https://www.bellingcat.com/resources/how-tos/2019/12/26/guide-to-using-reverse-image-search-for-investigations/ (accessed March 1, 2023).

W
Weizman, Eyal. *Forensic Architecture: Violence at the Threshold of Detectability.* New York: Zone Books, 2017.

IMAGE CREDITS

Figure 1: © Google Street View, 2014
Figure 2: Swiss Federal Archives, E5792#1988/204#1302*, 1939–1945)
Figure 3: swisstopo, LUBIS viewer, 19480090010456, 1948
Figures 4–5: Swiss Federal Archives, E5792#1988/204#1302*, 1939–1945
Figure 6: Swiss Federal Archives, E5792#1988/204#1064*, 1939–1945.
Figure 7: © Cadaster of Public Law Restrictions on Land Ownership, Canton Uri, 2022

Denise Bertschi

Mapping Architectural Traces of the Swiss-South African Gold Trade in Johannesburg: Film as Investigative Spatial Research

Researching Otherwise
Nitin Bathla, ed.

The built urban environment provides traces of evidence on the case of mapping the Swiss–South African gold trade in the 1950s through investigative filmmaking. While critically revisiting Switzerland's role in South Africa's apartheid, this case study presents not only insights into six significant buildings in Johannesburg, where this extractive gold trade was powered from, but offers methodological clues into how such places can be "researched otherwise."

In the first part, the text unpacks five main methodological keys on how to use film as investigative spatial research, useful for landscape and urban researchers engaging in critical investigations. Moving away from literal representation of ecological and economic exploitation, this article contributes to finding "another" aesthetics of ecological and economic horror, still capable of unearthing ongoing injustice. From mapping through walking with the camera to narrating architectural ghost stories through witnessing the materiality of buildings, this article explores the importance of positionality between the camera, the researcher (filmmaker), and the subject, as much as it argues for a transformative power of film in urban research.

The second part introduces the geopolitical and historical context of the presented case study of the Swiss–South African gold trade during apartheid and is dedicated to scrutinizing architectural traces of four of the six relevant buildings in Johannesburg: the Swiss House, the Chamber of Mines of South Africa, the Old Stock Exchange, and the former Precious Metals Development Ltd. The three-screen film *Confidential* offers a multisensory experience not only for the researcher but also for the spectator.[1] The claim is that its images of architectural traces are capable of using the seemingly "innocent" urban space as the archive itself. To witness, visualize, and map "otherwise," the filmic urban scenes reveal ongoing (Swiss) colonial entanglements at the commodity frontier of exploitative wealth accumulation powered by Swiss banks in liaison with the apartheid South African state.

1   *Confidential* is a three-screen film installation conceived by the author in 2018 as the visual outcome of an urban and archival research.

To witness, visualize, and map "otherwise," the filmic urban scenes reveal ongoing (Swiss) colonial entanglements at the commodity frontier of exploitative wealth accumulation powered by Swiss banks in liaison with the apartheid South African state.

→ Video 1
Excerpt from *Confidential*
doi.org/mjh9

Denise Bertschi

Investigative filmmaking in spatial research: methods

Weaving together previously unconnected buildings in Johannesburg's urban tissue, the video *Confidential* proposes to read six buildings, whose multi-layered histories are revisited in this paper. Referring to Tim Ingold's theory of "place making through movement,"[2] it is the walking/moving from one building to the next that combines the symbolic and historical connections of these buildings with each other and conceptually reveal their common denominator, in this case their link to the Swiss–South African gold trade. Through walking with the camera, the researcher physically emplaces themselves in the urban space which they wish to investigate. "As soon as a person walks, he becomes a line,"[3] thus creating a network of relations. While researching by moving between buildings, but also around and within these architectural objects, they become the sites of investigation, where the researchers' primary sensory experiences are made.

The urban researcher engages with all their senses, not only visionary, auditory, tactile, or olfactory but also the less-known vestibular sense, which locates the bodily position in space. This research method stands in stark contrast to armchair theorizing: researching urban structures through walking (with a camera) is a performative act, a gesture of the body based on the thesis that "space matters,"[4] while also seeking spatial justice. Through this performance of walking within a building, its spatial attributes unfold and our knowledge about them increases. Ingold argues that "knowledge is integrated not by *going along* but by *building up*, that is by fitting site-specific fragments into structures of progressively greater inclusiveness."[5] Ways of knowing a place happen as you are going, and fragmental knowledge builds itself up into grasping awareness of the urban space we investigate.

Researching such places otherwise might require mapping otherwise. Mapping otherwise does not refer to classical cartography of metric measurements of spatial relations onto a flattened surface, but by another kind of cartography: through editing the filmic sequences originated from each of the six buildings, the

[2] Ingold, "Against Space," 148.
[3] Ingold, *Lines*, 80.
[4] Soja, *Seeking Spatial Justice*, 2.
[5] Ingold, *Lines*, 50.

film suggests a potential range of new relations between these places, assembled through cutting and rearranging. Additionally, the choice to present the final film as a multi-screen, with three different simultaneous projections, further highlights the interweaving of these places into one net of relations, or what Ingold would call a "meshwork" of paths with varying intensities.[6] Ingold borrows the notion of the meshwork from Henri Levebvre, who wrote of the reticular patterns left by people (and animals) "whose movements weave an environment that is more 'archi-textural' than architectural."[7] The lines of my walks in the city of Johannesburg thereby permitted me to draw such a net-like texture between and within the six architectures, which highlights their essential feel and meaning rather than their design, while also being connected through their common function: housing invisibilized transactions of gold from South Africa to Switzerland in the 1950s.

Aesthetics of the earth in territories of conquest

Despite its importance, I chose not to focus on the materiality of gold itself, whose material attributes of being indestructible and fungible determine why the precious metal became the most stable trading unit. Aiming to avoid the literal, often problematic images of disaster, of disruption, I deliberately chose not to represent the gold mine, exploited mine workers, or destructed landscapes in order not to create even more harm through the act of filming marginal bodies through the camera. What has been called the "moral pause"[8] describes a filmmaker's choice to avoid or exclude some aspects of what they film, in my case people affected by the gold's extractive practices. Neither did I visit the National Archives of South Africa for only a quantitative reconstruction of the complicated economic relations between the two states, Switzerland's gold loans to South Africa having helped the apartheid regime out of serious liquidity problems in critical moments of racial segregation. Rather, I wanted to find other ways of problematizing and make tangible the "morally" risky and umbrageous actions of the Swiss business sector, protected by the Swiss state.

Denise Bertschi

6 Ingold, *Lines*, 80.
7 Lefebvre, *Production of Space*, 117–18.
8 MacDougall, *Looking Machine*, 55.

What is the sight aesthetics of perceiving architectural sites through film? Aiming to find answers, I would like to think about Édouard Glissant's reflection about the "aesthetics of the earth" in territories of conquest. "What is the aesthetics of disruption and intrusion?" he asks.[9] For him, territories (in contrast to "land") continuously need to be expanded, in every dimension: digging deeper (into the mine) and expanding them across space. He uses the term "denaturations" to talk about a process where the "earth" or "nature" is exploited: "Denaturations create imbalance and dry things up."[10]

Hollowing out the gold mines on the territory of Johannesburg denaturates the former geological formation and creates imbalance by extracting and deporting the mineral to the place of accumulation elsewhere. In the spirit of Glissant, I argue that the filmic aesthetics of *Confidential* linked to Swiss gold commerce represent the "aesthetics of the earth as a pitiless panorama of the worldwide commercial market,"[11] even if it does not represent the well-expected images of exploitation. Instead it represents the ruins of the market, the hidden forces of an inescapable logic of powers which act by the mantra: "If there is profit to be made, they will deal with you."[12]

9   Glissant, *Poetics of Relation*, 151.
10 Glissant, *Poetics of Relation*, 151.
11 Glissant, *Poetics of Relation*, 152.
12 Glissant, *Poetics of Relation*, 152.

Mapping through walking in Johannesburg's Mining District

The methodological keys outlined for investigative film research of urban spaces underlie a more classical approach to research, namely archival research. When I spent three months on a research trip to South Africa in 2017 to investigate the role of Switzerland in apartheid South Africa, I began my inquiry at the National Archives of South Africa in Thswane, formerly called Pretoria. Searching the in-house catalog of the archive under the generic term "Switzerland," I discovered two archival boxes with correspondence from the 1950s concerning the gold trade dealings of the Société de banque suisse (SBS) and the Union Bank of Switzerland (which merged with SBS to become UBS in 1998). Going through the innumerable letters contained in the archival boxes, I specifically became interested in the places that these letters were written from. The residence where I was staying during my research stay was in downtown Johannesburg in the Central Business District (CBD), which at the time of the veritable "gold rush" was classified as a "white-only" area in what was known as the "African New York City." Attracted by the physical proximity to where I was staying and guided by the letterheads and their addresses in the Johannesburg CBD, I thereupon chose to visit the sites of these transactions with my film camera. In essence I chose to work with the city, the metropolis, and its urban space as the archive itself.[13] The video installation *Confidential* that emerged out of this work constitutes a cartography of six buildings in Tshwane and Johannesburg's CBD. Thereby, the buildings in which these letters of transaction were written become proxy images to visualize and map differently this exploitative wealth accumulation undertaken by the Swiss banks in liaison with the apartheid state organs as early as the 1950s. I argue that the images of seemingly "innocent" urban spaces, which do not directly feature the aesthetics of ecological and economic horror, still have the capacity to contribute to alternative aesthetics of them.

Material witnessing for architectural ghost stories

This essay argues that through focusing on architectural objects as material evidence, the perception of these buildings through the filmic lens enables this matter to bear witness to its past.[14] If the buildings themselves do not reveal their function in the visible realm and appear as neutral objects embedded within the everyday urban tissue, reconnecting them on a filmic map highlights their common history and complicity in capitalist extractive practices. The investigative research method of mapping through film reveals their true function in a spatial order, witnessing invisibilized extractions and trade of gold, the life vein of the city of Johannesburg.

When looking at close-ups of architectural details—the debris of derelict modern buildings where once the Swiss-South African gold transactions were powered—the images of *Confidential* are haunted by

[13] Mbembe and Nuttall, "Introduction," 12.
[14] See Schuppli, *Material Witness*.

Denise Bertschi

what lies *beyond* the lens, outside of its frame. The almost banal or even cryptic images may well deceive, and we sense the striking absence of a history carefully buried behind the official version of the past. They take the pulse of these places and material traces to fly in the face of willful oblivion and turn the wishful innocence or seeming neutrality of architecture inside out.

How can these architectural material traces be read as alternative imaginaries, as added to the visual repertoire of planetary destruction and even if the immediate image does not show it? To answer these questions, I call upon Avery Gordon's *Ghostly Matters* to introduce the figure of the ghost as a mediator between the visible and the invisible spheres: "The ghostly haunt gives notice that something is missing—that what appears to be invisible is announcing itself."[15] Gordon defines the figure of the "ghost or the apparition as a form by which something lost, or barely visible, or seemingly not there to our supposedly well-trained eyes, makes itself known."[16] The images of the deserted Old Stock Exchange, covered in dust, ask us to look deeper, through the sediments of history, to unearth the "real" intentionality of the existence of these spaces as capitalist places of power. "Power can be invisible … a routine."[17]

The routine of walking following the architectural signs of capitalist powerhouses (such as banks, chambers of commerce, and other strongholds of capitalism) often leaves us numb towards their significance and destructive nature. *Confidential* is a contribution to (re-)direct our gaze towards such places and to make the invisibility that dwells in them visible. It is an attempt to make apparent visual evidence of absence—the eminent absence of the exploited lands and peoples. The ghostly uses the image as a liminal space to hopefully affect the viewer to sense architecture and urban spaces in a transformative way.

Representing such places in their muteness highlights the places' gathered experiences and histories. I draw upon Doreen Massey's definition of place as "woven together out of ongoing stories, as a moment within power-geometries, as a particular constellation within the wider topographies of space, and as a

[15] Gordon, *Ghostly Matters*, 15.
[16] Gordon, *Ghostly Matters*, 8.
[17] Gordon, *Ghostly Matters*, 3.

process, as unfinished business."[18] The moving images presented through film might appear almost banal or even cryptic, but they may well deceive: one only feels the current pulse of these buildings, yet they still represent a space of "simultaneity of stories-so-far."[19] Thereby, these various places are woven together to amalgamate not only their present condition but all the histories they lived through in a coexistence of time and space, thereby holding a place of memory for Swiss involvement in the colonial extraction of gold during the apartheid rule.

Investigating with the camera: positionality between filmmaker, camera, and subject

All images in *Confidential* are filmed with a fixed position, with the camera on a tripod. Each chosen perspective is filmed for about 15 to 30 seconds and thereby produces a photographic moving image. As architectural objects themselves do not move much, subtle movements such as the breeze of air-conditioning moving office-curtains, elevators going up and down, or people swiftly passing by a hallway are often the only movements one can see. Yet these slow images still sense an altered notion of time, a time-space relation that is meant to evoke in the spectator a ghostly awareness of what might lurk behind the images.

Adjacent to the aesthetic choice to use long shots without many movements, I, as the holder of the camera and the lens, am the embodied witness of how much access I was able to receive to these buildings. It was my deliberate choice to work with a fixed rather than a zoom lens. This method ensured that the produced image is never "closer" to the studied architectural object than the researcher had access to, thereby securing the filmmaker's occurrence of the moment-by-moment inscription while engaging with the filmic subject, the building.[20] Degrees of access mean that some buildings in *Confidential* can only be seen from the outside. Other buildings are more closely investigated, with their inner life depicted from basements to rooftops.

18 Massey, *For Space*, 132.
19 Massey, *For Space*, 9.
20 MacDougall, *The Looking Machine*, 32.

Denise Bertschi

Transformation through multi-sensory experience: from researcher to spectator

As a case study, *Confidential* shows that lens-based works can represent more general commonalities of spatial experience, ones that cannot be represented through written descriptions.[21] Thus, watching these filmic inquiries might be able to create affinities defying spatial distances between the viewer and the represented place. The implication for the audio-visual medium is that it has some agency to evoke embodied sensory experience in watching and listening to the footage, while the viewer engages with its content open for critical thought. How to then read these urban "archi-textural" meshworks as presented visually? The proposed methodology engages the viewer with the transformative possibility of multi-sensory experiences (as triggered through multi-screen film projections), thereby offering the viewers of such films "a space for disruption and transformation."[22] Working with multiple screen projections further emphasizes overlapping multisensory experiences of places, while different shots and angles (from close-up to wide shots, from high-angle to long-angle) are shown simultaneously. The filmmaker can thereby guide the narrative towards highlighting specific details that seem important to the overall storyline or provide certain evidence of how the chosen architectural object functions as a witness of the entanglement with the main storyline, namely Swiss involvement in an extractive economy and economic support of apartheid South Africa. I thereby suggest that while we tend to value architecture as a neutral player,[23] investigative film practice offers a new reading of urban tissues and a look behind the walls and closed doors.

Buildings

The selection of the six buildings is based on the archival findings among the consulted collection of correspondence on the Swiss gold trade, conceptually drawing an imaginative map. I will now focus on four of the six buildings portrayed in *Confidential* alongside offering some methodological reflections.

21 See Pink, *Future of Visual Anthropology*.
22 Grimshaw, *Ethnographers' Eye*, 120.
23 Kiesewetter, "Normalisierung von Rechts."

Mapping Architectural Traces

The Central Business District (CBD): an urban tissue of gold

The turbulent history of Johannesburg's CBD urban space was marked by many social and economic transitions over the past century. From a prosperous mining town, where gold was first discovered in 1890, to the installation of racial segregation, Johannesburg came back full circle to the reappropriation of the built environment by its racialized majority. "It is a city with an underneath, a city built on the extraction of gold."[24]

In the late 1980s, towards the end of apartheid, businesses left the area (as part of "white flight") to the so-called more secure northern suburbs, such as Santon, as more Black people inhabited the buildings, sometimes in ruins, in the CBD. By the end of 1990s, the CBD was often called a ghost town, a term bearing a violence of erasure in itself, as it defines the new occupation of the city center by Black people as "ghostly." "During apartheid, the right to live in the city was constantly threatened. They (the Black majority) were to work in the city but not to live in it," as Achille Mbembe recalls; "This explains perhaps the force and power of attempts to conquer the right to be urban in the present."[25] Through the initiative of the Johannesburg City Government, the neighborhood is slowly becoming gentrified (with trends including the widespread use of CCTV surveillance cameras for instance), and businesses, banks, and the mining industry have settled there again.

As a Swiss artistic researcher in Johannesburg, I situated myself by deliberately putting into focus the role of Switzerland and the Swiss banks here, which were highly influential in boosting the global export trade of South African gold into the global market, with its peak occurring when the global Gold Pool was moved from London to Zurich in 1968.[26] The Swiss Gold Pool was arranged between the South African government and the three main Swiss banks: the Union Bank of Switzerland, the Swiss Bank Cooperation (which merged with the Union Bank of Switzerland to form UBS in 1998), and Credit Suisse (merged with UBS in 2023). The pool, especially powered by UBS to assure a Swiss monopoly on South African

[24] Mbembe und Nuttall, "Afropolis," 282.
[25] Mbembe und Nuttall, "Afropolis," 282.
[26] Kreis, *Switzerland and South Africa*, 323.

Denise Bertschi

gold,[27] immediately became the biggest financial partner of the apartheid regime in South Africa for its gold suppliers, a shift that represented a vital lifeline to apartheid South Africa for both economic and political reasons. "While other nation states imposed economic sanctions on the apartheid regime of South Africa, Swiss authorities long adhered to the position that South Africa is a state like any other. Swiss big business corporations saw an attractive trade partner in South Africa; in part, they also profited from the boycotts of others."[28] Officially, Switzerland hid behind its status of "diplomatic neutrality" in order to not have to make the "sacrifices" that protesting racial segregation happening in South Africa might entail.[29]

The money flow of such major transactions is obviously a very material one. The letters I found in the South African National Archives were traces of what powered this extractive economy. People sat in offices and wrote letters on their typewriters that shifted semi-transformed gold to bank accounts in the European metropoles of financial accumulation. Around 1950, South Africa was the world's biggest gold producer, and by the early 1970s three-quarters of this South African gold was imported to Swiss banks.[30] Until this day, most of the gold traded in the world, often of doubtful provenance, passes through Switzerland, where it gets refined.[31]

27 Bott, "South African Gold," 128.
28 Kreis, *Switzerland and South Africa*.
29 Kreis, *Switzerland and South Africa*, 327.
30 Kreis, *Switzerland and South Africa*, 318.
31 Franciolli, "Shady Origins of Gold Refined in Switzerland."

The Swiss House on Main Street: an infrastructure of ideological proximity in the Mining District

Confidential is characterized by walking with the camera as a research method. While I walked through the Mining District of Johannesburg to investigate one of my chosen buildings, the Chamber of Mines of South Africa, I discovered another building by chance that became significant for my research: the Swiss House. Its entrance is decorated with seven cast-bronze motifs, most of them of animals, face masks, and flower motifs in a quite standardized "African" style. Just one of the casts depicts another flower, a gentian, one of the most emblematic flowers of the Alps, with notable connotations as a Swiss national symbol.

→ Figure 1

Mapping Architectural Traces

To find these images juxtaposed next to each other above a door bearing the letters SWISS HOUSE on the main mining street of Johannesburg and located just one building away from the Chamber of Mines was surprising, yet it clearly indicated a cohesion, which further confirmed my thesis about the importance of Switzerland in the South African (gold) extraction economy. My walking practice thereby further condensed the dots on mapping Swiss gold business in South Africa.

Upon further archival research, I found that the Swiss House was indeed a center for the main infrastructural agents to enable such trading connections. The building was erected in 1969 and in 1972 housed the Swiss Reinsurance company SwissRe, by 1979 the Swiss Bank Corporation, by 1985 the Swiss General Consulate in South Africa on the second floor, and by 1986 Swissair.[32] This meant that infrastructure linked to politics, travel, banking, and insurance were the main tenants of the Swiss House from its construction until the late phase of apartheid, when South African cities were subject to deep racial segregation policies. These agents—political, economic, and infrastructural—were all notable players in enabling and backing this important gold trade relationship. Them all being neighbors to the Chamber of Mines, the most important South African agent for gold mining, makes not only geographic proximities but also ideological proximities within a racial capitalist order apparent.[33] Mapping through filming architectural objects in the urban environment linked to the Swiss gold trade in Johannesburg made these adjacencies evident, and more so, visible.

From the roof top of the Swiss House, the camera's eye[34] moves to the surrounding skyscrapers and fixes on a neighboring building that was formerly called the Chamber of Mines. This institution dates to 1889, a year after gold was first discovered on the geological plateau of the Witswatersrand-rock formation. Since its founding, the Chamber of Mines's mission has included regulating the mining

[32] Institutions and dates emerged in an email exchange between the author and the Johannesburg Heritage Association in 2017.
[33] For a discussion of the term "racial capitalism," see Robinson, *Black Marxism*.
[34] Berger, *Ways of Seeing*, 21.

Mapping through filming architectural objects in the urban environment linked to the Swiss gold trade in Johannesburg made these adjacencies evident, and more so, visible.

Denise Bertschi

sector and representing it vis-à-vis multiple stakeholders. To reach the top of the Swiss House, the concierge of the building, who permitted me access to its hidden corners, accompanied me to the 1960s elevator built by the Swiss company Schindler, which was not a surprise but offered another material trace of the Swiss economic presence there. Today, instead of assisting gold flows, the tenant of the Swiss House is the city government's Water Johannesburg department, charged with regulating flows of water to the city's inhabitants.

Chamber of Mines of South Africa at 5 Hollard Street: an architectural signifier for extraction

The Chamber of Mines building is not publicly accessible, and I was not granted permission to enter it. The visual exploration by my camera was thereby limited to the building's facade and its adjoining streets and plazas. The first Chamber of Mines building was erected here in 1889 followed by a renovation in 1921 and a successive one in 1951, giving it its appearance today. The contemporary building is a great example of Johannesburg's early development from a mining town into an industrial metropolis tied to the world market, emulating Manhattan paradigms and giving it its common moniker "Little New York."[35]

Scanning the facade of the Chamber of Mines without being able to dig deeper into the visual indexes of this powerful mining institution, the camera stops at some aluminum art carvings relating to different aspects of mining activities that "decorate" all four sites of the building. The next shot focuses on the fountain located close to the entrance, which represents the Witwatersrand basin, including a map of the goldmines in its own basin. The form of the fountain references the largest gold nugget (of 9 kilograms) ever mined in South Africa. The video representation of the fountain sculpture hopefully provokes reflections on the extractive capitalist activities on Witswatersrand geological formation. How does "geology become an operator for power?" asks Kathryn Yusoff.[36] She argues that geology is a "signifier for extraction, where a trans-mutation of matter occurs, that

35 Chipkin, *Johannesburg Style*.
36 Yusoff, *A Billion Black Anthropocenes or None*, 8.

→ Figure 2

renders matter as property: The cut into the geological strata is a cut of property that enacts the removal of matter from its constitutive relations." Geology, to follow Yussof, "creates an *a*temporal materiality dislocated from place and time."[37] This is especially true in the racialized capitalism in the mines in South Africa, with the seemingly peaceful flow of water from the fountain in front of the Chamber of Mines thereby becoming a placeholder for this violent geological intrusion.

In the 1950s the Chamber of Mines was where the Swiss Bank Cooperation (SBC) offices sent their bids for monthly gold tenders. "As you know, we have been buying all along very substantial quantities of gold in South Africa," Mr. Nussbaumer, the director of SBC stated in a letter to the Secretary for Finance of the Union of South Africa dated March 1953.[38] The letter further reveals that the Chamber of Mines had requested a permanent bank representative to be on the spot in Johannesburg to make firm bids regarding the gold-trading price. This caused a problem for the Swiss bank, as at this point they were not yet physically located in South Africa and were hesitant to appoint such a representative, "primarily because of the highly confidential nature of the gold bids, but also because another bank would probably charge a rather stiff commission for this delicate service." In a subsequent letter, Nussbaumer asked for personal advice on whether the Secretary of South African's Finance had any suggestions about a special agent with "moral qualities and with the right background."[39] Finally, an appropriate person was found in the form of Mr. R.S. Mennie, located at the former Johannesburg Stock Exchange in Newtown, 17 Diagonal Street, which is the next location on the filmic map.

[37] Yusoff, *A Billion Black Anthropocenes or None*, 16.
[38] National Archives of South Africa, Tshwane, Treasury: F9/2255/4/12 and F9/2255/4/12.
[39] National Archives of South Africa, Tshwane, Treasury: F9/2255/4/12 and F9/2255/4/12.

Old Johannesburg Stock Exchange at 17 Diagonal Street: a frozen scene of the invisibilized global market

How can the Old Johannesburg Stock Exchange building at 17 Diagonal Street be read in this ongoing cartography of Swiss involvement of trading gold from South Africa? Today the building is partly deserted and partly in use by smaller businesses unrelated to its

→ Figure 3

Denise Bertschi

former use (like a security company called Scorpion or a funeral service). Accessing the building required a lot of correspondence. Finally, the caretaker of the building immediately brought me down to the basement of the building. He opened a barred door, mentioning this was the most emblematic space in the whole building, a space abandoned since the end of the 1990s. The now automated stock exchange moved to Santon, a newly developed part of Johannesburg, which became the city's new financial center following the abolition of apartheid.[40]

The camera approaches this main space using different shots, such as close-ups and wide-angle shots, in order to grasp the spirit of the place. The camera focuses on the layers of dust on the former trading tables, where one can still see scribbles or stickers of the brokers who once worked there. The voluminous room, with its sacral appearance, is marked by six tessellated "windows" in colored glass, each backed with light and dedicated to a major South African business sector, such as agriculture, mining, or transport. The ghostly atmosphere of the space is emblematic. As the lens focuses on close-ups of its dusty footprints, one can literally feel a sense of abandonment in the frozen scene.

The visuality of this building would presumably not be taken into consideration by economic historians working on the Swiss gold trade, but personally I would argue that precisely these images, transcending the atmospheric patina of this space, establish evidence of it. The filmic approach offers the viewer an opportunity to examine the properties of the space (textural, sonorous, vestibular, or proprioceptional), informed in turn by the sensory experiences of the filmmaker, transmitting them through the film camera. The result of this practice has been called "a sensory cinema," based on "the ability of films to stimulate a broad range of the senses, not least the sense of touch."[41] Such research by image production obviously does not focus on the precise analytical numbers of this trade, neither does it deliver quantitative results. Rather, these images are another way of making perceptible urban spaces of a highly invisibilized global market, often sealed behind heavy doors.

40 The Johannesburg Stock Exchange, Africa's biggest bourse, goes back to 1897, founded in the immediate aftermaths of the Wits' goldrush.
41 MacDougall, *Looking Machine*, 165.

Mapping Architectural Traces

Emerging again from these hidden secrets of the Old Johannesburg Stock Exchange's basement, the camera takes a ride in the windowed elevator towards the glass-fronted entry hall, an architectural treasure of the building. While moving towards the top, one crosses the strata of history inscribed in these built environments.

Precious Metals Development Ltd. at 36 Staib Street: the fear of gentrification and the camera

A short anecdote from the production process of *Confidential* illustrates the ongoing territorial struggles in the city after apartheid. Here the next step in a spatial production of inequality is marked by a new segregating mechanism: gentrification. The film makes this phase explicit, including the fear it arouses among certain social groups, at the same time critically reflecting on the power of the camera in this process.

→ Figure 4

One example can be seen at the location of the former Precious Metals Development Ltd at Staib Street 36 in New Doornfontein, a suburb of Johannesburg. The company was specialized in manufacturing precious metal products for the global market. It still exists today but is no longer located in the same modernist brickstone building (erected in 1949) at the corner of Staib Street, having in the meantime relocated close to the international Airport OR Tambo, a tellingly advantageous location for such a business. From there, refined gold is shipped around the world through the bullion markets located in London and Zurich.

The 1949 building has a high aesthetic architectural value and appears on the index of the Johannesburg Heritage Foundation. Nevertheless, visiting the site in 2018 I found it abandoned and was exposed to the social conditions of the people who currently inhabit it. The building has been squatted and Google images from 2022 reveal that its condition has degraded even further. Nonetheless, and despite quite precarious living conditions, what was important there while filming was that the building is actually home to people.

Denise Bertschi

When I first visited the place to take some shots for my video work, I was advised to take a security person to accompany me while I filmed with my small camera on a tripod. Even if my film equipment was far from impressive, I was told that it would be "safer" to have someone keeping an eye on me while my own eyes were busy looking into the camera. I took the advice and worked together with a security guard, a local of Johannesburg who joined me in my walks. Regarding the social situation we found on site, I decided to keep a distance in portraying the building: first to not offend people living there in quite poor conditions; and second, to not be naive in my positionality as a white woman with a camera entering a social space which could be read as affronting. Despite our efforts to act politely, some women approached us and spoke to us in Zulu about their fear the felt about the presence of the camera and me taking "pictures." Fortunately, the security person was able to speak with them in Zulu, and he translated to me that these ladies were worried about me taking pictures out of fear that the building might be in the process of being sold, which would mean their forceful expulsion. This experience taught me about the importance of a collaborative approach to image-making with locally embedded people, people who know the social context and how to respectfully act in it. We tried to calm the women and reassure them that the images had another purpose that would hopefully not threaten them. Nevertheless, the encounter reminded me about the power of an image-making device, especially in postcolonial contexts. Ariella Aïsha Azoulay states that "Photography is an apparatus of power."[42] She notes that this apparatus of power is tightly composed of its components: the camera, the photographer, the photographed environment (in this case the social space of Staibstreet 36), and the photographed subject or object. But in Azoulay's concept of the "civic contract of photography," the spectator of the produced images is equally part of this contract. The experience in Staibstreet 36 highlights these different participants in the contract of photography and the need to pay attention to all of them while producing images, especially in such conflicting

[42] Azoulay, *The Civil Contract of Photography*, 81.

places. Correspondingly, *Confidential* is conceptually based on the decision to focus on "architectural traces" as a way to avoid focusing on people, often people tangibly affected by the issues that the film tries to address in the first place. It is thereby a strategy to move away from classical ethnographic filmmaking "about" exploited people, for example, and instead to focus on spaces which produced the exploitation in the first place. Nevertheless, when one films in public spaces of the city, the camera and the photographer (or filmmaker) is always embedded in social power dynamics where the camera can easily symbolize threat.

43 Mbembe and Nuttall, "Introduction," 17.

Conclusion

This article proposes different methodological clues to reading the multi-layered strata of history in urban environments, as well as the present, including a "presentness of the past,"[43] through investigative practices in filmmaking. As a case study, the video *Confidential* investigates how architectural spaces that underwent different rhythms of segregation and multiple uses in apartheid South Africa still comprise the spirit of these different strata of history. The camera in *Confidential* seeks to access these micro-localities, connect them to each other, and create a group of places that become, united in the film, a meta-network of architectural objects that once served the same goal: to host white men who facilitated and boosted the beginnings of an accumulative extraction business, much to the profit of the Swiss banks and, indirectly, Switzerland as a nation. The spatiality of a global economy (such as the gold trade) thereby collides with a racially segregated organization of space. As such, several times coexist simultaneously in one place and one globalized extractivist trade network, often occurring behind closed doors and on confidential letters, which then becomes apparent through the material traces of these architectural structures. I argue that the investigative filmmaking practice applied in *Confidential* tries to do more than just map these places linked to the Swiss gold trade in South Africa. Instead, it also senses the strata of social change through the spatial injustice produced

Denise Bertschi

by apartheid ideology. In the process, the film-lens becomes a mediator between these interconnected nodes of capitalist accumulation and rewires a lost connectivity of time-space relations. This urban material can encompass both the contemporary use of buildings after the tremendous changes following the abolition of apartheid and their former extractivist use. The geographer Jacques Lévy states that while "the experience of the space is initially (multi)sensorial, the sight plays a fundamental role."[44] In this sense, a fixed camera sensing only some seconds of a years-long process of urban transformation remains a powerful tool to bring (back) to *sight*, and thereby to consciousness, the spatiality of this redistribution of wealth and the spatial injustice it produces.

The applied investigative filmic method does not seek to portray a documentary style image, but rather attempts to capture the ghostly atmosphere of these spatial entities as a palimpsest of diverse use and social constructs. Selected through archival findings of the correspondence on the gold trade between apartheid South Africa and UBS Switzerland, they conceptually form a map that lets these places of trade speak for themselves. In the process, the images of these selected buildings do not stay neutral; rather, they become ambassadors for a global extractive economy. This is not a direct depiction; instead it offers the viewer a fresh way to read the city and familiar places or buildings. This way, slow film sequences of heavy closed doors or dusty desks of the former Johannesburg Stock Exchange become a sign for the complicated images one would associate with the bodily and territorial exploitation of the labor of mining—and exploitation of the miner's body as well as the rocks to extract the shining gold and liberate it to join the material flows of the markets. The function of this building was to host a powerful actor in the beneficiation process to mine, refine, and expel the precious stones of the geological formation of the Witwatersrand plateau to the global capitalist's centers, such as London and Zurich. The relocation of this immense value (in the commodity of gold) away from South African land helped produce the inequality which still exists between these geographies.

[44] Lévy and Lussault, *Dictionnaire de la Géographie*, 904.

Mapping Architectural Traces

To finish, I would like to think along the lines of Walter Rodney, who described "how Europe underdeveloped Africa," and who argues in reverse that "Africa developed Europe."[45] Given the fact that the monthly value of gold sold to Switzerland as early as in the 1950s quadrupled in the following years,[46] one can safely apply Rodney's telling concept to the architectural structures mapped otherwise through *Confidential*. While the gold accumulated in secret high-security gold depots somewhere in Switzerland and Europe, the social injustice these transactions produced are potentially visible in the social living conditions at Staib Street 36 in Johannesburg, as an example. Such places, put into focus in *Confidential*, bring back the *longue-durée* effects of such social transformations of space under capitalist extraction. Even if the current spatiality of Staib Street 36 seems unconnected to the gold depots in Switzerland, the production of these very places is highly interlinked.

For urban researchers and spatial practitioners seeking to find critical yet sensory methods of analysis, *Confidential* is an exemplification of researching otherwise: it maps an early but important phase of economic expansion of Swiss banks to South Africa in the 1950s, laying the basis of what later becomes a highly powerful economic support structure to maintain the racist apartheid system. It is a visual approach in spatializing where such business happened. The images in *Confidential* are thereby visual evidence and a counter-archive, contrasting to the correspondence found in the two folders marked "Sale of semi-processed Gold to the Swiss Bank Cooperation/Union Bank of Switzerland" from 1953 when these banks had already bought substantial amounts of gold from the South African mines but were not yet physically present in South Africa. This work is a visual witness for what later became a highly profitable relation for Switzerland, as well as a moral failure: The Swiss state circumnavigated and bypassed international mandatory sanctions against the white-only apartheid government of South Africa in a moment

45 Rodney, *How Europe Underdeveloped Africa*.
46 Kreis, *Switzerland and South Africa*, 323.

> Such places, put into focus in *Confidential*, bring back the *longue-durée* effects of such social transformations of space under capitalist extraction.

Denise Bertschi

when the regime became increasingly isolated internationally. This moral failure had bloody consequences for a racially segregated society, with Switzerland as an active part of what Hennie van Vuuren calls a "global covert network of corporations, banks, governments and intelligence agencies across the world, who helped illegally supply guns and move cash in one of history's biggest money laundering schemes."[47]

Nevertheless, and even if interpreted as ruins of capitalism in a city whose "sole reason for its creation was the pursuit of material wealth,"[48] this doesn't mean that the architecture in *Confidential* can't be the birthplace of something new—a destruction followed by reconstruction of forms that makes way for the "new." In the view of Achille Mbembe, the metropolitan nature of Johannesburg is more than "its ceaseless metamorphosis" where the tension is literally built into "its morphology and geological structure between the life below the surface, what is above, and the edges."[49] Following this argument, *Confidential* does more than just document these (partly ruined) buildings linked to the Swiss–South African gold trade from the last midcentury. Instead, it equally witnesses a present moment in a long metamorphosis of Johannesburg as a repository of possibilities.

47 van Vuuren, *Apartheid, Guns and Money*, 174.
48 Mbembe and Nuttall, "Introduction," 18.
49 Mbembe and Nuttall, "Introduction," 18.

ACKNOWLEDGMENTS
The research for the film *Confidential*, on which this article is based, was conceived and produced during an artistic studio residency of the Swiss Arts Council Pro Helvetia in Southern Africa, in Johannesburg in 2017/18. Special thanks for introducing me to the social, cultural, and architectural context of Johannesburg goes to Nolan Oswald Dennis, Joseph Gaylard, Abri de Swardt, Bettina Malcomess, Uriel Orlow, Niren Tolsi, and the generous team of the National Archives of South Africa, as well as the Architecture Heritage Foundation of Johannesburg.

Figure 1 Swiss House, Johannesburg, film still from *Confidential* by Denise Bertschi, 2018

Figure 2 Chamber of Mines of South Africa, Johannesburg, film still from *Confidential* by Denise Bertschi, 2018

Denise Bertschi

Figure 3 Old Johannesburg Stock Exchange: film still from *Confidential* by Denise Bertschi, 2018

Figure 4 Precious Metals Development Ltd, Johannesburg: film still from *Confidential* by Denise Bertschi, 2018

Mapping Architectural Traces

BIBLIOGRAPHY

A

Azoulay, Ariella Aïsha. *The Civil Contract of Photography*. New York: Zone Books, 2012.

B

Berger, John. *Ways of Seeing*. London: Penguin, 1972.

Bott, Sandra. "South African Gold at the Heart of the Competition between the Zurich and London Gold Markets 1945–68." In *The Global Gold Market and the International Monetary System from the Late 19th Century to the Present—Actors, Networks, Power*, edited by Sandra Bott. London: Palgrave Macmillan, 2013, 109–38.

C

Chipkin, Clive M. *Johannesburg Style: Architecture & Society, 1880s–1960s*. Cape Town: D. Philip Publishers, 1993.

F

Franciolli, Riccardo. "The Shady Origins of Gold Refined in Switzerland." SWI Swissinfo.ch. January 8, 2019. https://www.swissinfo.ch/eng/business/multinationals_the-shady-origins-of-gold-refined-in-switzerland/44621040.

G

Glissant, Édouard. *Poetics of Relation*, translated by Betsy Wing. Ann Arbor: University of Michigan Press, 1997.

Gordon, Avery F. *Ghostly Matters: Haunting and the Sociological Imagination*. Minneapolis: University of Minnesota Press, 2008.

Grimshaw, Anna. *The Ethnographer's Eye: Ways of Seeing in Anthropology*. Cambridge: Cambridge University Press, 2001.

I

Ingold, Tim. "Against Space: Place, Movement, Knowledge." In *Being Alive: Essays on Movement, Knowledge and Description*. Abingdon: Routledge, 2022: 145–155.

Ingold, Tim. *Lines: A Brief History*. New York: Routledge, 2007.

K

Kiesewetter, R. "Normalisierung von Rechts." *ARCH+ 235: Rechte Räume: Eine Europareise* (May 2019): 122–29.

Kreis, Georg. *Switzerland and South Africa 1948–1994: Final Report of the NFP 42+Commissioned by the Swiss Federal Council*. Bern: Peter Lang, 2007.

L

Lefebvre, Henri. *The Production of Space*, translated by Donald Nicholson-Smith. Cambridge, MA: Blackwell, 1991.

Lévy, Jacques, and Michel Lussault. *Dictionnaire de la Géographie*. Berlin: Editions Belin, 2003.

M

MacDougall, David. *The Looking Machine: Essays on Cinema, Anthropology and Documentary Filmmaking*. Manchester: Manchester University Press, 2019.

Massey, Doreen. *For Space*. London, Thousand Oaks, CA, and New Delhi: SAGE Publications, 2005.

Mbembe, Achille, and Sarah Nuttall. "Afropolis: From Johannesburg." *PMLA / Publications of the Modern Language Association of America* 122, no. 1: *Cities* (January 2007): 281–88.

Mbembe, Achille, and Sarah Nuttall. "Introduction: Afropolis." In *Johannesburg. The Elusive Metropolis*, edited by Sarah Nuttall and Achille Mbembe. Durham, NC, and London: Duke University Press, 2008: 1–36.

P

Pink, Sarah. *The Future of Visual Anthropology: Engaging the Senses*. New York: Routledge, 2006.

R

Robinson, Cedric J. *Black Marxism: The Making of the Black Radical Tradition*. Chapel Hill and London: University of North Carolina Press, 2000.

Rodney, Walter. *How Europe Underdeveloped Africa*. New York: Verso Books, 2018.

S

Schuppli, Susan. *Material Witness. Media, Forensic, Evidence*. Cambridge, MA: MIT Press, 2020.

Soja, Edward W. *Seeking Spatial Justice*. Minneapolis: University of Minnesota Press, 2010.

V

van Vuuren, Hennie. *Apartheid, Guns and Money: A Tale of Profit*. London: Hurst Publishers, 2018.

Y

Yusoff, Kathryn. *A Billion Black Anthropocenes or None*. Minneapolis: University of Minnesota Press, 2019.

IMAGE CREDITS

Figures 1–4: Denise Bertschi

Denise Bertschi

Bertschi, Denise. "Mapping Architectural Traces of the Swiss–South African Gold Trade in Johannesburg: Film as Investigative Spatial Research." In Nitin Bathla, ed., *Researching Otherwise: Pluriversal Methodologies for Landscape and Urban Studies.* Zurich: gta Verlag, 2024, 215–239. https://doi.org/10.54872/gta/4692-8.

Mapping Architectural Traces

Johanna Just

Multispecies Walking: Ways of Knowing and Researching Landscapes with Experts

Researching Otherwise
Nitin Bathla, ed.

Lorch am Rhein, November 15, 2021. It is cold and misty. For hours we wade through the river, passing the town, the car park of the industrial area, meadows, and autumn-colored forest, slowly making our way upstream. The water depth varies between 30 and 100 centimeters. It is difficult to move. As we walk, several fish float by. He identifies sea trout, an escaped rainbow trout, many smolts and chubs, and even a rare schneider. The water is clear, oxygen-rich, and thriving with life. The ground is sandy, sometimes gravelly, sometimes made from pavers, covered in decaying leaves. He helps me read the topography, notice holding pools and spawning pits.[1] The gravel beds form ideal breeding grounds for female salmon; the loose substrate can protect the eggs and shelter the young offspring from predators. All conditions seem right; all our senses are aimed at finding her.[2]

[1] A holding pool is an area in a river where the water flow is calmer, so it becomes a resting place for fish. Jörg Schneider, personal communication, Nov. 15, 2021.
[2] I am following a group of biologists, anglers, and regional authority representatives under the guidance of freshwater ecologist Jörg Schneider, through the river Wisper. We are searching for returning female salmon. Historically mid-November marks the date of their return for spawning. Jörg Schneider, personal communication, Nov. 15, 2021; see also Just, "Repopulating a River."
[3] See Just, "Cultivating More-than-Human Care."

→ Figure 1

Introduction

How can we understand spaces as formed by more-than-human relations? How can we foreground the underlying structures of inhabitation, maintenance, and care that shape the land? In my research, I explore disturbed landscapes along the Upper Rhine through the lens of three animals that are intertwined with the region. During my fieldwork, I took a series of guided walks with experts that helped me get closer to, perceive, and understand the spatial context with other-than-human inhabitants in mind.[3] I accompanied ecologists, biologists, and birders, among others, through floodplains, rivers, fields, and neighborhoods to learn how we cohabit and share spaces with fish, birds, and insects.

 Building on this experience, I suggest possible starting points for a multispecies approach towards researching and knowing landscapes through *multispecies walking*. As an ethnographic practice, this

Johanna Just

form of guided walking helps to challenge the human dimension as an absolute reference point for spatial research: "Since a thing cannot be known directly or totally, one can only attune to it, with greater or lesser degrees of intimacy. ... Attunement is a living, dynamic relation with another being—it doesn't stop."[4]

Through this quote, Timothy Morton highlights the impossibility of directly knowing how other beings perceive the world—only by attuning to them can we get a sense of it. As spatial researchers and practitioners wanting to challenge the anthropocentric gaze, we rely on experts who have built the dynamic relations with other beings that Morton describes. As we walk with them, they can teach us attentiveness, help us tune into other worlds and contemplate more-than-human spatial relations.

This chapter begins with discussing ethnographic walking practices and the work of scholars from multispecies studies and animal geography. I elaborate on how multispecies walking is informed by these fields and how it might contribute to them in turn, offering a mode to sense more-than-human relations through following a nonhuman under the mediation of an expert. I then give an overview of the research method, referring to an example of my fieldwork on the Upper Rhine. Here I explore the floodplains as a vital milieu, guided by a mosquito expert. Finally, I draw on mnemotechnics and the notion of *fields of memory* to show how gaining expertise through multispecies walking can be understood as walking-as-knowing.

Sensing vital milieus

The walking method described in this essay draws on work from multispecies anthropology, animal geography, and the ethnographic practice of walking as a spatial research strategy. The latter has been extensively discussed by urban anthropologists and architects, such as Christina Moretti[5] and Francesco Careri.[6] Moretti for instance primarily focuses on walking alone in urban environments, and reminds us that "walking with others can help us appreciate people's senses of place while urging us to reflect on the social relations that shape them."[7] She describes the performative qualities of walking and suggests

4   Morton, *Being Ecological*, 89.
5   Moretti, "Walking."
6   Careri, *Walkscapes*.
7   Moretti, "Walking," 95.

that following local guides or going on organized walking tours can help gain new insights and perspectives on the context.[8] Her words resonate with the work of Nazlı Tümerdem and the writings of Maggie O'Neill and Brian Roberts. While Tümerdem reflects on walking as collective practice,[9] the latter argue that "walking is an excellent method for entering into the biographical routes, mobilities, and experiences of others in a deeply engaged and 'attuned' way."[10] O'Neill and Roberts introduce the Walking Interview as a Biographical Method (WIBM), a technique where a researcher accompanies an interviewee on a routine activity or chosen route. While the authors discuss different modes of conducting an interview on the move, they claim that interviewing while walking helps the researcher to understand social and material circumstances as they collectively pass through locations familiar to the interviewee. Alexandra Horowitz, on the other hand, focuses on walking with experts. Taking eleven walks, each accompanied by a different expert—a geologist, a sound designer, and a dog, among others—she explains how our experiences and the expertise of those around us shape our perception. She shows how guides can help us overcome the limitations of our own perspective: they do a "selective-enhancing for us, highlighting the parts of the world that they see but which we have either learned to ignore or do not even know we *can* see."[11]

When discussing the relevance of walking for ethnography, Jo Lee Vergunst and Tim Ingold also point towards walking as a way to research more-than-human social relations, suggesting that "we can see not only that walking is a social activity, but also that the social relations of walking crosscut the divide between humans and animals, and between the pacing of two feet and of four."[12] Scholars from the field of multispecies anthropology, like Heather Swanson or Anna Tsing, have further developed research methods that help them understand how more-than-human relations shape worlds and places, whereby they attune to trees, fish, or fungi to counteract anthropocentric perspectives—often with the help of local guides or experts from the natural sciences.[13] While Swanson gets to know Pacific salmon

[8] Moretti, "Wandering Ethnographer."
[9] For an example of her work, see Tümerdem, "'A New Way of Being on Earth.'"
[10] O'Neill and Roberts, *Walking Methods*, 15.
[11] Horowitz, *On Looking*, 14.
[12] Vergunst and Ingold, *Ways of Walking*, 12.
[13] Tsing, *In the Realm of the Diamond Queen*; Tsing, "Arts of Inclusion"; Swanson, "Methods for Multispecies Anthropology." The necessity of forming alliances with experts who are familiar with other species and their environments for multispecies studies has also been described by van Dooren, Kirksey, and Münster, "Multispecies Studies."

Johanna Just

through the lens of a science lab manager,[14] Tsing uses guided walking to explore the Indonesian rainforest with the help of a Meratus leader: "It was with Ma Salam that I first learned how to walk through Meratus social space. Where I at first saw only the forest's natural beauty, he showed me how to read the forest socially. [...] He pointed to the remains of old cultivation and inhabitancy that I might otherwise never have noticed."[15]

The field of animal geography opens up new ways of looking at more-than-human spaces and spatial relations by introducing notions like animals' mobilities, geographies, and dwellings or by looking at the interrelations between nonhuman life and infrastructure.[16] While Timothy Hodgetts and Jamie Lorimer discuss modes of understanding animals' spaces,[17] Maan Barua shows how more-than-human geographies overlay our shared environments. He researches the spatial relations of human–elephant cohabitation in India following the trails of an elephant herd under the guidance of conservation researchers.[18]

Building on the work of these scholars, multispecies walking combines aspects from ethnographic walking practices, multispecies studies, and animal geography. Rather than attuning to the "biographical routes"[19] of the human interviewee or guide, the opportunities emerge from walking with a nonhuman through the mediation of an expert who has experience with another species and has gotten to know their way of life, their mobilities, and geographies.

As an expert becomes more and more attuned to a species, they get to know the land as their milieu —as a space of becoming, where things are active through their interrelations with others.[20] Accompanying an expert guide is therefore not primarily about the expert but about their *expertise*: As the person who senses the milieu, the expert acts as a mediator between researcher, species, and environment. Walking with them, we can gain an augmented perspective on the land; following them as a situated body —not as a shadow, such as commonly conceived in ethnographic practice[21]—and trying to understand their rhythms, practices, and ways of sensing, they can help us tune into milieus and make us notice spatial

14 Swanson, "Methods for Multispecies Anthropology."
15 Tsing, *In the Realm of the Diamond Queen*, 66.
16 See Hodgetts and Lorimer, "Animals' Mobilities'"; Hodgetts and Lorimer, "Methodologies for Animals' Geographies"; Barua, "Bio-Geo-Graphy"; Barua, "Infrastructure and Non-Human Life."
17 Hodgetts and Lorimer, "Methodologies for Animals' Geographies."
18 Barua, "Bio-Geo-Graphy."
19 O'Neill and Roberts, *Walking Methods*, 15.
20 See Berque, *Poetics of the Earth*.
21 Shadowing in ethnography describes the practice of following a person over a defined time span as they carry out their job to gain insights into their behavior or the behavior of a representative societal group. Hereby the researcher keeps their interactions minimal and focuses primarily on the observed participant. See Bartkowiak-Theron and Sappey, "Methodological Identity of Shadowing." During a multispecies walk, the researcher takes a more active and situated role.

interrelations beyond ordinary anthropocentric biases. Through multispecies walking, we get to know seasonal rhythms or patterns of inhabitation, maintenance, and care, finally generating new ways of seeing, smelling, and hearing urban and non-urban contexts as shared vital milieus.

Guided walks along the Upper Rhine

To introduce multispecies walking as a method for spatial research, I turn to my own fieldwork undertaken in the Upper Rhine Valley. I explored disturbed and highly modified sites along the river—flooded gravel pits, engineered floodplains, the channelized Rhine—by looking at three different animals that are historically entangled with the area: the sand martin, floodwater mosquitoes, and the Atlantic salmon. My aim was to find out what rhythms define the sites; what practices of maintenance, care, or disruption overlay them; and what role they might play in the web of more-than-human relations.

Hoping to answer these questions, I followed a group of experts on the species. I accompanied them mostly in their weekly, monthly, or yearly routines, alongside which we had semi-structured or informal conversations. This resulted in a set of very particular, sometimes very long, and unusual guided walks. For example, to trace returning female salmon in the Rhine system I joined an electrofishing survey walk through the river Wisper,[22] I accompanied several birders on their yearly journey of counting nesting sand martins, and I followed different members of an anti-mosquito association on control walks through boggy forests, meadows, and residential and industrial areas. Throughout these experiences, the multispecies walking method developed, allowing me to challenge my anthropocentric perspective on the area I was researching. Following experts allowed me to follow a fish, a bird, an insect: they directed my gaze, ears, and senses, helping me become attentive toward the animals' milieus. I got to know seasonal rhythms, understand different layers of inhabitation and maintenance of the sites, and appreciate how different species, including humans, cohabit and interact, opening a

[22] See introduction to this chapter; see also Just, "Repopulating a River."

Johanna Just

new perspective on the entanglement of landscapes in more-than-human relations.

Multispecies walks are immersive and captivating, but there is also an element of uncertainty and dependency. The researcher has to prepare for these uncontrollable aspects [23] and document the endeavor in the best way possible. During my fieldwork, I primarily used three methods of documentation: I recorded the walks with a simple voice recorder, I took smartphone pictures as we went along,[24] and I wrote illustrated notes upon my return. While walking, I asked: What connects my guide to this site? What do they know about the land and water, about how it is inhabited and used? How does their relation to a certain species influence their actions?

The following is an excerpt of walking with an expert when researching the interrelation between humans, floodwater mosquitoes, and the Upper Rhine's floodplains during my fieldwork in spring 2022.

Walking with a mosquito expert

Au am Rhein, March 15, 2022.[25]

9 a.m. It is drizzling; I am waiting in front of the church. I just walked for 50 minutes from the train station at Durmersheim because I missed the bus. As he arrives in the car, I recognize him; I had googled him before.

Artur Jöst, an experienced KABS biologist, is the district leader of this Rhine section.[26] Together with his colleagues, he regularly registers the mosquito population and decides whether microbial insecticide needs to be applied to reduce their numbers. Mid-March marks the beginning of the mosquito season, and today we meet to control the larvae density in the flooded areas that border the communities of Au and Mörsch. I join him in the car, and our first stop is the KABS storage at Au. We collect waders, and before we start he shows me the area on a set of maps. KABS members have

→ Figure 2

23 Best practice includes researching the contact person, the planned activity and location, and sharing the information with a trusted person before meeting, as well as considering appropriate outdoor clothing.
24 When recording and taking pictures, I ensured to have written consent by the experts beforehand.
25 If not specified otherwise, the information in the section is derived from the walk with Artur Jöst on March 15, 2022, and based on observations and personal communication.
26 KABS, short for Kommunale Aktionsgemeinschaft zur Bekämpfung der Stechmückenplage (communal action group to control the mosquito pest), is an association that controls the mosquito population along the Upper Rhine. See more at their webiste, https://www.kabsev.de (accessed Dec. 7, 2023).

created highly detailed topographical surveys of the region to monitor and control the mosquito population along the Upper Rhine. The color-coded maps indicate the terrain height and help identify which area will collect water in case of flooding or when the groundwater level rises. Our first site is a shrubby and marshy place bordering the residential area north of Mörsch. On the map, it appears as a blue patch, indicating its wet existence.

Dressed in waders and raincoats, and equipped with a ladle with a long handle, we make our way through the bushes. When approaching a larger area of stagnant water, Artur stops to show me how to use the ladle for 'dipping.' With a skillful move, he quickly probes the water, trying not to disturb what is living beneath the surface. Together we glance at the sample: it is thriving with microfauna, and he knows all their names. We count at least thirty mosquito larvae of the *Aedes* type[27] among other little creatures. The number lies above the threshold and needs to be registered. Although Artur likes to carry physical maps with him, every detail is stored in a GIS-powered smartphone application, which is his main working tool. He notes the larvae number in his app, and we repeat the sampling multiple times along the water's edge, always recording the numbers. This way, he maps out the area that will be treated with Bti[28] by helicopter in the coming days.

We continue the process, moving from one site to the next, from flooded forests to flooded meadows. Sometimes we find many larvae, sometimes none. As we walk, Artur tells me how he knows the landscape, which former

27 Mosquitoes of the genus *Aedes* are floodwater mosquitoes that occur in masses along Upper Rhine. See KABS, "Wiesen- und Auwaldstechmücken."

28 Bti, short for *Bacillus thuringiensis israelensis*, is a bacterium used by KABS as biological microbial insecticide in liquid or granular form to kill mosquito larvae along the Upper Rhine. See KABS, "B.t.i."

→ Figure 3

→ Figure 4

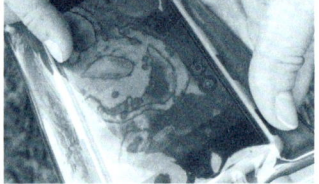

Johanna Just

meander we are walking in, and which plants indicate wetness and can be used as a guide to show potential flooding in areas that cannot be accessed because of dense vegetation. And importantly, he tells me how he knows mosquitoes: the Upper Rhine Plain hosts about thirty-five different species with various dwelling preferences—Artur recognizes them from the larvae shape and movement. He explains how mosquitoes sense the elements: as embryos in tiny eggs, they feel the oxygen level in the water and only hatch when the level is low enough, indicating that potential predators have already died. They also sense where water meets land and distinguish precise locations for laying their eggs into the earth right at the threshold. As flying insects, they sense the smell and heat of humans, which the females bite for a protein-rich meal that nourishes their growing eggs. Artur also knows the humans that live adjacent to the mosquito territory. As we bypass the residential area, he tells me of their fear of mosquitoes and their anxiety about the wetness that is historically rooted in the region and keeps them from appreciating the beauty of the bordering floodplains. Artur believes that his work reducing mosquito numbers also helps to improve the relationship between the residents and what lies beyond their backyard. After six hours of walking and wading through wet undergrowth in a light drizzle, I am freezing and exhausted and it is time for me to leave.

→ Figure 5–8

Walking-as-knowing

In her book *The Art of Memory*, Frances Yates describes the practice of mnemotechnics developed by the ancient Greeks as a spatialized memory system where information is tied to imagined places by placing images as visual clues.[29] Referring to the Roman rhetorician Quintillian, Yates describes how one moves "in imagination through [a] memory building …, drawing from the memorised places the images … placed on them" to recall information.[30] However, the writings of St. Augustine, a key historical figure trained in the mnemonic technique, suggest that not only fictional buildings—palaces of memory—but also imagined landscapes—fields of memory—can serve as a holder for information: "And I come to the fields and spacious palaces of my memory, where are the treasures of innumerable images, brought into it from things of all sorts perceived by the senses."[31] While Yates primarily speaks about architectural memory *palaces*,[32] the *fields* go mostly unnoticed. Multispecies walking as a spatial research method in the field draws new attention to the concept, revealing parallels between the mnemonic technique and the spatialized knowledge of an expert.

Etymologically derived from the Latin *expertus*, "expert" primarily refers to someone with experience.[33] Looking at the words that make up the term— *ex* ("out") and *per-* ("through") and *eō* ("I go")[34]—invites imagining an alternate reading of the word that suggests a connection to the fields of memory. Experts like Artur can be seen as people for whom walking is a way of knowing; they gain experience and acquire knowledge by going through fields, both physical and mental. In this process, the land, which they got to know as milieu, manifests in their memory as a "mental map":[35] all its features are "incorporated into their own embodied capacities of movement, awareness, and response."[36] Similar to the memory places in classic mnemotechnics, this map holds images or objects and is connected in nodes and links rather than indicating spatial distances like a geographical map. When walking with Artur, he describes these images as topological features, indicator plants, or insects. They become visual clues for the expert, containing information about the species and its way of life.

An example posed by Tim Ingold supports this argument. He describes the hunter as an expert revealing insights to an accompanying non-expert:

29 Yates, *The Art of Memory*, 23.
30 Yates, *The Art of Memory*, 3.
31 Saint Augustine, *Confessions of Saint Augustine*, Book X.
32 Yates, *Art of Memory*.
33 "Expert." *Etymonline*, 2020. https://www.etymonline.com/word/expert (accessed Oct. 16, 2022).
34 "Experience" is composed of *ex* ("out") and *peritus* (from the verb *perire*, "experience"). Although *perire* is commonly translated as "to perish," looking at the components that make up the word—*per* ("through") plus *eō* ("I go")—*perire* invites highlighting its spatial character. See *Wiktionary* entries "Expert" at https://en.wiktionary.org/w/index.php?title=experience&oldid=69421007 (accessed Oct. 16, 2022) and "Perire," https://en.wiktionary.org/w/index.php?title=perire&oldid=67346915#Latin (accessed Oct. 16, 2022).
35 Lynch, *Image of the City*, 88.
36 Ingold, *Being Alive*, 47.

Johanna Just

"Thus the experienced hunter is the knowledgeable hunter .... He can tell things from subtle indications that you or I, unskilled in the hunter's art, might not even notice." For Ingold, an expert is a person who can explicate knowledge by picking up clues in the environment: "A person who can 'tell' is one who is perceptually attuned to picking up information in the environment that others, less skilled in the tasks of perception, might miss, and the teller, in rendering his knowledge explicit, conducts the attention of his audience along the same paths as his own."[37] Gilles Deleuze would go even further: the expert-hunter, for instance when reading animal tracks, becomes animal; leaving behind their familiar anthropocentric framing and tuning into the animal's way of life, they develop "an animal relationship with an animal."[38]

Hence walking with the expert allows the researcher not only to participate in the expert's knowledge but also approximate the animal's milieu: collectively walking, the land unfolds like a field of memory —retaining and releasing the expert's knowledge about the place and its entanglements in more-than-human relations. Encouraged by the researcher, their company and curiosity, the expert picks up these visual clues, shares information, and recalls memories, often using the land as both a reference point and to visualize their explanations. Experiencing this process, multispecies walking, in turn, helps the researcher to build a new spatialized way of relating: as they learn about underlying complexities, inhabiting species, and practices that shape the land, they gain their own sense of milieu.

Conclusion

As researchers and spatial practitioners working in times of environmental crisis, we have to expand our repertoire, look beyond existing methods, and identify ways of building bridges with other disciplines that can help us challenge anthropocentric perspectives and develop sensitivity and attentiveness towards more-than-human relations. In this essay, I have shown how guided walking with experts can form a starting point for a multispecies approach towards researching and knowing landscapes. I have

[37] Ingold, *Perception of the Environment*, 190.
[38] *L'Abecedaire de Gilles Deleuze*, 5.

elaborated on how multispecies walking as a research method is derived from ethnographic walking practices and influenced by the work of scholars from multispecies studies and animal geography. In the example of my fieldwork on the Upper Rhine, where I have undertaken several guided walks with fish, bird, and insect experts, I have shown how multispecies walking expands limited human perception towards other-than-human realities, allowing us to notice patterns of inhabitation, maintenance, and care.

Following experts in their routine practices through the field and along their mental maps, multispecies walking helps gain a new, augmented perspective on the land: unlike walking alone or guided walking in urban ethnography, the method builds on the experience of an expert with a certain species. This knowledge allows the expert to see and sense the land as milieu, and it allows the researcher to tap into it. Referring to the classic art of memory, I have further shown how gaining expertise can be understood as a spatialized way of relating or walking-as-knowing, suggesting parallels to the little-noticed notion of fields of memory.

While there are currently limited examples illustrating how insights derived from multispecies walking can be integrated into spatial practice, the work by landscape architect Thomas Hauck and biologist Wolfgang Weisser on animal-aided design can serve as a guidepost.[39] Multispecies walking promises a better understanding of complex, more-than-human spatial relations and suggests less anthropocentric and more sensitive approaches towards engaging with urban and non-urban contexts. Therefore, the value and urgency of further research into translating insights gained from the method becomes apparent.

39 With their practice of animal-aided design (AAD), Hauck and Weisser specialized on how to integrate the needs of animals into urban and landscape planning. See Hauck and Weisser, *AAD*. In the context of *Co-Habitation*, an exhibition by Arch+ in 2021 that focused on human–animal relationships in urban spaces, a guided walk was offered to teach participants about non-human species inhabiting the city. See the post on "Organism Democracy: Regulatory Regimes" at https://archplus.net/en/cohabitation/#article-29099 (accessed Dec. 7, 2023).

ACKNOWLEDGMENTS

I would like to thank Jörg Schneider and Artur Jöst—who provided me with many stories and insights—for their generous time, Agostino Nickl for his editorial advice, Nazlı Tümerdem for her literature suggestions on walking, and Andrej Radman and Stavros Kousoulas for the enriching discussions in the context of the Spring Semester 2023 seminar "Ecologies of Architecture" at TU Delft, which have been inspiring for this chapter. Thanks to my PhD dissertation supervisors Teresa Galí-Izard and Philip Ursprung, as well as to my colleagues at the Chair of Being Alive and the Institute of Landscape and Urban Studies at ETH Zurich, for their continuous support. I am grateful to the editor of this publication, Nitin Bathla, and to Jan Silberberger and Thomas Skelton-Robinson for their insightful and constructive comments.

Johanna Just

Figure 1   Walking with Jörg Schneider and his team through the river Wisper, Lorch am Rhein, November 15, 2021

Multispecies Walking

Johanna Just

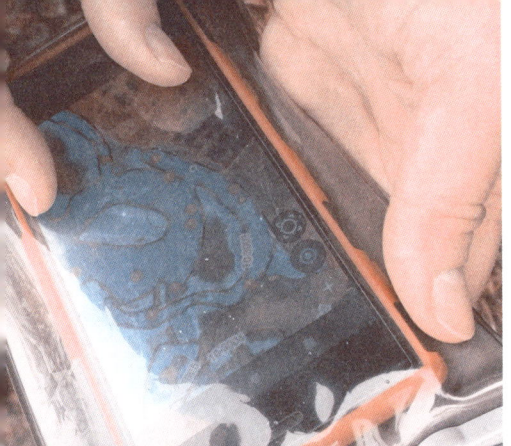

Figure 2–5 Walking with Artur Jöst during a mosquito control walk, Au am Rhein/Rheinstetten Mörsch, March 15, 2022

Multispecies Walking

Johanna Just

Figure 6–8   Walking with Artur Jöst during a mosquito control walk,
              Au am Rhein/Rheinstetten Mörsch, March 15, 2022

Multispecies Walking

BIBLIOGRAPHY

B

Baldner, Leonhard. *Das Vogel- Fisch- und Thierbuch des Strassburger Fischers Leonhard Baldner aus dem Jahre 1666*, edited by Robert Lauterborn. Ludwigshafen: Lauterborn, 1666.

Bartkowiak-Theron, Isabelle, and Jennifer Robyn Sappey. "The Methodological Identity of Shadowing in Social Science Research." *Qualitative Research Journal* 12, no. 1 (April 2012): 7–16. https://doi.org/10.1108/14439881211222697.

Barua, Maan. "Bio-Geo-Graphy: Landscape, Dwelling, and the Political Ecology of Human-Elephant Relations." *Environment and Planning D: Society and Space* 32, no. 5 (October 2014): 915–34. https://doi.org/10.1068/d4213.

Barua, Maan. "Infrastructure and Non-Human Life: A Wider Ontology." *Progress in Human Geography* 45, no. 6 (December 2021): 1467–89. https://doi.org/10.1177/0309132521991220.

Berque, Augustin. *Poetics of the Earth: Natural History and Human History*, translated by Anne-Marie Feenberg-Dibon. New York: Routledge, 2019.

C

Careri, Francesco. *Walkscapes: Walking as an Aesthetic Practice*. Barcelona: Gili, 2002.

H

Hauck, Thomas E., and Wolfgang W. Weisser. *AAD— Animal Aided Design*. Munich: Technische Universität München, 2015.

Hodgetts, Timothy, and Jamie Lorimer. "Animals' Mobilities." *Progress in Human Geography* 44, no. 1 (2020): 4–26. https://doi.org/10.1177/0309132518817829.

Hodgetts, Timothy, and Jamie Lorimer. "Methodologies for Animals' Geographies: Cultures, Communication and Genomics." *Cultural Geographies* 22, no. 2 (2015): 285–95. https://doi.org/10.1177/1474474014525114.

Horowitz, Alexandra. *On Looking: About Everything There Is to See*. New York: Scribner, 2014.

I

Ingold, Tim. *Being Alive: Essays on Movement, Knowledge and Description*. London and New York: Routledge, 2011.

Ingold, Tim. *The Perception of the Environment: Essays on Livelihood, Dwelling and Skill*. Taylor & Francis e-Library / Routledge, 2002. https://doi.org/10.4324/9780203466025.

J

Just, Johanna. "Cultivating More-than-Human Care: Exploring Bird Watching as a Landscaping Practice on the Example of Sand Martins and Flooded Gravel Pits." *Frontiers of Architectural Research* 11, no. 1 (2022): 1205–13. https://doi.org/10.1016/j.foar.2022.04.007.

Just, Johanna. "Repopulating a River: Reflections on the Return of the Rhine Salmon." *Algae Review*, no. 1 (2023): 26–33.

K

KABS (Kommunale Aktionsgemeinschaft zur Bekämpfung der Schnakenplage e.V– Biologische Stechmückenbekämpfung am Oberrhein). "B.t.i." https://www.kabsev.de/1/1_3/1_3_2/1_3_2_2/index.php (accessed December 7, 2023).

KABS (Kommunale Aktionsgemeinschaft zur Bekämpfung der Schnakenplage e.V– Biologische Stechmückenbekämpfung am Oberrhein). "Wiesen- und Auwaldstechmücken." https://www.kabsev.de/1/1_4/1_4_2/1_4_2_1/index.php (accessed December 7, 2023).

L

L'Abecedaire de Gilles Deleuze, avec Claire Parnet. TV movie interview by Claire Parnet, directed by Pierre-André Boutang and Michel Pamart. Transcript translated by Charles J. Stivale. 1996.

Lynch, Kevin. *The Image of the City*. Cambridge, MA: MIT Press, 2008.

M

Moretti, Christina. "The Wandering Ethnographer: Researching and Representing the City through Everyday Encounters." *Anthropologica* 53, no. 2 (2011): 245–55.

Moretti, Christina. "Walking." In *A Different Kind of Ethnography: Imaginative Practices and Creative Methodologies*, edited by Dara Culhane and Denielle Elliott, 91–111. North York, Ontario: University of Toronto Press, 2017.

Morton, Timothy. *Being Ecological*. Cambridge, MA: MIT Press, 2018.

O

O'Neill, Maggie, and Brian Roberts. *Walking Methods: Research on the Move*. New York: Routledge, 2019.

S

Saint Augustine. *The Confessions of Saint Augustine*, translated by Edward B. Pusey. Project Gutenberg, 2002. https://www.gutenberg.org/files/3296/3296-h/3296-h.htm (accessed October 16, 2023).

Swanson, Heather Anne. "Methods for Multispecies Anthropology: Thinking with Salmon Otoliths and Scales." *Social Analysis* 61, no. 2 (Summer 2017): 81–99. https://doi.org/10.3167/sa.2017.610206.

T

Tsing, Anna Lowenhaupt. "Arts of Inclusion, or, How to Love a Mushroom." *Australian Humanities Review* 5, no. 50 (2011): 5–22.

Tsing, Anna Lowenhaupt. *In the Realm of the Diamond Queen: Marginality in an Out-of-the-way Place*. Princeton: Princeton University Press, 1993.

Tümerdem, Nazlı. "'A New Way of Being on Earth'." *Landscape Architecture Europe* 6 (2022): *Second Glance*, 312–23.

V

van Dooren, Thom, Eben Kirksey, and Ursula Münster. "Multispecies Studies: Cultivating Arts of Attentiveness." *Environmental Humanities* 8, no. 1 (May 2016): 1–23. https://doi.org/10.1215/22011919-3527695.

Vergunst, Jo Lee, and Tim Ingold, eds. *Ways of Walking: Ethnography and Practice on Foot*. London and New York: Routledge, 2016.

Y

Yates, Frances A. *The Art of Memory*. Vol. 3 of *Frances Yates: Selected Works*. London and New York: Routledge, 1999.

IMAGE CREDITS

Figures 1–10: Johanna Just

Just, Johanna. "Multispecies Walking: Ways of Knowing and Researching Landscapes with Experts." In Nitin Bathla, ed., *Researching Otherwise: Pluriversal Methodologies for Landscape and Urban Studies*. Zurich: gta Verlag, 2024, 241–259. https://doi.org/10.54872/gta/4692-9.

Afterword

At the conclusion of this whirlwind journey traversing a pluriverse of epistemologies and methodologies, we hope this book has offered its readers some hints and orientations that can be assimilated into their own ways of knowing and researching the world. Readers will note that the chapters assembled in this book provide reflections from practitioners of sensory, collaborative, and restitutive methods, rather than from researchers merely analyzing methods. The readers should thus exercise caution, and instead of treating these methods as some sort of formulaic principles, they should pay attention to the difference and specificities of the lifeworlds they are engaging. Positioning and grounding methods in material lifeworlds is a crucial first step towards researching otherwise. Rather than take them as a given, readers are correspondingly encouraged to experiment with the methods presented here and to revise and adapt them to their research interests.

The tools presented in this book—such as drawing, photography, sounding, filmmaking, and cartography—might at first seem like hard-to-penetrate specialized domains, but, as highlighted by the authors, they can be acquired and trained to cross the borders of disciplinary silos. The chapters in this book illuminate ways through which researchers can use these tools to enhance their sensoriums, allowing for a focus on marginal and more-than-human worlds. This can be especially helpful for academics and practitioners from future-oriented professions, such as planning, architecture, and urban and landscape design, who not only seek to unmask and unearth systems of power and domination but also dream possible other worlds.

Another important consideration for the readers of this book while crafting their own methodologies is to identify the ways in which they can research alongside communities and their other-than-human companions, rather than treating them as passive subjects. In addition to building collectives and spaces of solidarity, this can help researchers to immerse themselves into pluriverses hidden just below the surface. Such immersion in everyday lifeworlds can help undo the refraction of colonial modernity that seeks to silo and border worlds and ways of knowing, offering openings towards worlds otherwise. Thus it is hoped that this book will provide inspiration for breaking through the disembodiment of research and provide pathways towards developing rigorous epistemologies and methodologies.

Nitin Bathla

ACKNOWLEDGMENTS

Several people have worked tirelessly behind the scenes to help the loose thoughts and deliberations that I had on starting out with this project take the material form of this book. Of the people that I would like to thank and acknowledge foremost are Moritz Gleich and Jennifer Bartmess at the gta Verlag, who have offered kind, continuous, and generous handholding and constant support for this publication, from the start until the end. I would also like to thank Jan Silberberger, the external peer reviewer for the volume, for his comments that helped improve the content of this book.

Thanks also to the participants of my doctoral methodology seminars at the Institute for Landscape and Urban Studies (LUS) at ETH Zurich since spring semester 2023, who served as crucial interlocutors for this book, especially Santiago del Hierro, Stefan Laxness, Emma Kaufmann LaDuc, Shriya Chaudhry, Qianer Zhu, Ina Valkanova, Jacopo Zani, and Sarem Sunderland, along with others who also feature as contributors in this volume. Crucially, I would like to thank professors Freek Persyn, Teresa Galí-Izard, Hubert Klumpner, Milica Topalovic, Christian Schmid, Tom Avermaete, and Maria Conen, who have opened a hopeful and experimental space for landscape and urban thought.

A part of this research was conducted in the "New Urban Agendas under Planetary Urbanisation" module at the Future Cities Lab Global at ETH Zurich. Future Cities Lab Global is supported and funded by the National Research Foundation, Prime Minister's Office, Singapore under its Campus for Research Excellence and Technological Enterprise (CREATE) program and ETH Zurich, with additional contributions from the National University of Singapore, Nanyang Technological University, and the Singapore University of Technology and Design.

Acknowledgments

The research and publication of this project were
supported by the Institute of Landscape and Urban
Studies (LUS) and Netzwerk Stadt und Landschaft
(NSL) at ETH Zurich and by the institutions mentioned
in the acknowledgments.

The prepress of this publication was supported by
the Swiss National Science Foundation (SNSF).

This publication has been peer reviewed according
to SNSF standards.

Project management and proofreading
    Jennifer Bartmess
Copyediting
    Thomas Skelton-Robinson
Concept, layout, and typesetting
    Offshore: Isabel Seiffert and Christoph Miler
Printing
    Longo, Italy
Typefaces
    Malte Bentzen Serif B (Malte Bentzen)
    Prophet (Dinamo)
Paper
    Lessebo White rough, 90g/sqm

© 2024
gta Verlag, ETH Zurich
Institute for the History and Theory of Architecture
Department of Architecture
8093 Zurich, Switzerland
www.verlag.gta.arch.ethz.ch
© Texts: by the authors
© Illustrations: by the image authors and their legal
successors; for copyrights, see image credits

Every reasonable attempt has been made by the authors
and the publisher to identify owners of copyrights.
Should any errors or omissions have occurred, please
notify us.

The entire contents of this work, insofar as they do not
affect the rights of third parties, are protected by copyright. All rights are reserved. No part of this publication may be reproduced, stored in a retrieval system, or
transmitted, in any form or by any means, electronic,
mechanical, photocopying, recording, or otherwise, without the written permission of the publisher.

Creative Commons License CC BY-NC-ND

ISBN (print) 978-3-85676-467-8
ISBN (PDF) 978-3-85676-469-2
https://doi.org/10.54872/gta/4692